AMERICAN PRONUNCIATION

AMERICAN PRONUNCIATION

JOHN SAMUEL KENYON, Ph.D.

Professor of the English Language, Emeritus, in Hiram College

Tenth Edition

"A teacher of speech untrained in phonetics is as useless
as a doctor untrained in anatomy."
—George Sampson, M.A.

GEORGE WAHR PUBLISHING COMPANY

ANN ARBOR, MICHIGAN

1950

COMPOSED, PRINTED AND BOUND BY
The Collegiate Press
GEORGE BANTA PUBLISHING COMPANY
MENASHA, WIS.

PREFACE TO THE FIRST EDITION

This book is designed primarily for a textbook on pronunciation. Its material is presented from the point of view of a teacher of college students who for some years has laid it before them with varying success, but at least with increasing hope and growing confidence in the value of the effort. Though in form it is adapted to pedagogical ends, in content it is believed to be scientifically trustworthy. If the scholar finds in it an annoying fulness of statement with somewhat of repetition, he is asked to remember that this is due to its aim.

The author has found the excellent books on phonetics that are based on British pronunciation unsuccessful in teaching American pronunciation, and believes that more American works on the subject are needed. College teachers of English are increasingly realizing that the teaching of pronunciation is inadequately provided for by the comparatively slight contact and scattered criticisms of speech in the classroom. The student needs some introduction to the whole subject as a science with its own set of principles that will guide him independently of the instructor. Accordingly the teaching of phonetics to undergraduates is on the increase, and it is hoped that this book will assist in that direction.

The book should also be useful to public-school teachers who desire to fit themselves more fully to guide their pupils in their use of speech. Not that they will wish to present the material in this form to their pupils, but that they can find here systematically treated virtually all the problems of pronunciation they are daily encountering, many of which are insoluble without a scientific approach to them. Textbooks of grammar and composition contain only scattered comments on pronunciation, and a good deal of their information is false or misleading.

The field of English as a subject for teaching has been revolutionized in the past twenty-five or more years by the great specialists in the different parts of the field in European and American universities. Yet the very names of these scholars are often unfamiliar to the great body of American schoolteachers and the intelligent public. It is one purpose of this book to make a little of this material more generally accessible.

The author has tried to avoid dogmatism with regard to preferable pronunciations. No attempt is made to set up or even to imply a standard of correctness based on the usage of any part of America. He believes that the state of cultivated pronunciation in America does not warrant the more prescriptive method used by Professor Daniel Jones and Mr. Walter Ripman with reference to standard pronunciation in England. Whether there is ever to be a single standard in America or not, the time is not yet ripe for it. This book is therefore primarily a science of pronunciation; and though the author believes that the art of good pronunciation can be best attained through the scientific approach, the art as such is here little emphasized. The main purpose of the work is to help the student to study the facts of pronunciation till he is somewhat conversant with phonetic principles. He will then be in a better position to consider questions of correctness. The author is aware that an attitude of great confidence as to correctness is likely to gain a quicker audience; but he prefers the slower way of helping to disseminate sound knowledge, with faith in the greater soundness of the culture that will result from it.

With this principle in mind, the author has based his observations on the cultivated pronunciation of his own locality—the Western Reserve of Ohio. It is his belief, however, that this is fairly representative of what will here be called the speech of the North, which is virtually uniform in its most noticeable features from New York State west, in the region north of a line

drawn west from Philadelphia. There is no intention of implying any preference for this speech over that of the East or the
South. The main differences in the pronunciation of these different regions are pointed out, with the aim of making the book
useful in different parts of the country.

The author is deeply indebted to the British phoneticians
Sweet, Ripman, Jones, and Grant, to the Danish scholar Jespersen, and to the Americans Emerson, Krapp, and Grandgent
(see Bibliography). It would be impossible to indicate all that
he has learned from them which appears in this book; yet he
has tried to take nothing, without acknowledgment, not common to students of phonetics, or that he has not thoroughly
tested by his own observation. The personal debt is especially
great to Professors O. F. Emerson of Western Reserve University and Charles H. Grandgent of Harvard University for
guidance and encouragement, and to my colleague, Professor
Lee Edwin Cannon, for assistance in reading proof and for
valuable suggestions.

Hiram, Ohio, January 1, 1924.

PREFACE TO THE FOURTH EDITION

The gratifying reception of *American Pronunciation* indicates the rapidly increasing interest in the history and phonetics
of American English, and a desire to put aside the still abundant
quackery based on eighteenth century knowledge and twentieth
century ignorance about matters of standards and correctness.

That Professor Krapp's term, General American, is abun-
dantly warranted for the type of pronunciation chiefly described
in this book is shown by even the most conservative estimates
of the number speaking it in the United States and Canada (see
section 5 below). Certain criticisms, however, make it necessary
to affirm again that the author does not advocate this or any

one type as the sole standard for America. To help students escape from such a point of view was one of the objects of this book. The author admits no rivalry in his admiration of that clear, intelligent pronunciation of the best types of Southern and Northern British, of Scottish standard English, of Eastern, Southern, and General American, which is the best index of personality, that most interesting of all facts. But apparently this does not satisfy such critics. One must not even describe or speak respectfully of the traditional speech of ninety million people. Some of the astonishing specimens of neither fish nor flesh nor good red herring that greet the radio listener appear to be prophetic of what we may expect from a continued fostering of the naïve assumption that only one form of speech can be correct.

It is impossible to add the names of all those scholars to whom the author has become indebted for valuable criticisms and help since the publication of the first edition; but he cannot refrain from mentioning with gratitude Professors Samuel Moore, Hans Kurath, and Miles L. Hanley in America, and Professor Daniel Jones, Mr. A. Lloyd James, and Mr. Stephen Jones in England.

Hiram, Ohio, August 22, 1930.

PREFACE TO THE SIXTH EDITION

The present edition has been entirely rewritten. My experience in teaching both undergraduates and graduates has made it increasingly evident that even those students who have studied foreign language have little idea of the principles and processes of language. I have introduced considerable in the way of question and suggestion intended to awaken the interest of students in their mother tongue, its behavior and laws of development, particularly as these have a bearing on an intelligent attitude toward what constitutes good English speech.

The arrangement of material is somewhat shifted. The teacher is free to change the order of presentation or to omit what does not suit his purpose.

It is impossible to name all those scholars who have made this book possible. In addition to those named in former prefaces, I wish to express special obligations to Dr. Bernard Bloch, of the Linguistic Atlas of the United States and Canada, and to Professor William Cabell Greet of Barnard College, Columbia University, and editor of *American Speech* for valuable suggestions; to Mr. Martin Joos of the University of Wisconsin, for valuable suggestions and for making the Index; to Professor Miles L. Hanley of the University of Wisconsin for valuable suggestions and for reading proof; to my colleague, Dr. Ralph H. Goodale, for the uniform-scale photographs in figure 8; and to my daughter, Martha E. Kenyon, of the James Ford Rhodes High School, Cleveland, for making the drawings (except Figs. 8 and 9). I also desire to thank the G. and C. Merriam Co., publishers of *Webster's New International Dictionary*, for their kind permission to use certain material contributed to the *Second Edition* (1934).

Hiram College, April 9, 1935.

PREFACE TO THE TENTH EDITION

Although the main substance of the book remains the same as in the sixth and subsequent editions, innumerable changes in detail have been made in the tenth. In particular the use of the phonetic symbols **r** and ɚ has been simplified and brought into conformity with that in the *Pronouncing Dictionary of American English*. The sections on the phoneme have been rewritten in the interest of greater clearness for the elementary student, and have been shifted to a later position in the book in order to give the beginning student the benefit of more phonetic knowledge before taking up the study of the phoneme and its bearing on phonetic facts.

The Index has been greatly expanded by the addition of many more words of phonetic interest and by references to many aspects of American speech, so that it may serve not only for current guidance in progress through the book, but also for a convenient means of reviewing the whole work.

Finally, I wish to bear witness to my sense of gratitude to the late George Wahr and my admiration for his scholarly spirit that led him in 1923 to undertake the publication of this book when such works gave little promise of being self-supporting, and when this one had been refused by several publishing houses.

J. S. K.

Hiram College, October 27, 1949

TABLE OF CONTENTS

BIBLIOGRAPHICAL NOTE

Among the works on pronunciation that have been found useful, the following may be mentioned here for the convenience of those who wish to pursue the subject further.

American Speech, A Quarterly Journal of Linguistic Usage, William Cabell Greet, Editor, New York, 1925–.

LILIAS E. ARMSTRONG, *The Phonetics of French*, London, 1932.

ERNEST A. BAKER, *French-English and English-French Dictionary*, London, 1931 (referred to as Baker).

BERNARD BLOCH and GEORGE L. TRAGER, *Outline of Linguistic Analysis*, Baltimore, 1942.

ALBERT C. BAUGH, *A History of the English Language*, New York, 1935.

LEONARD BLOOMFIELD, *Language*, New York, 1933.

OLIVER F. EMERSON, "The Ithaca Dialect" in *Dialect Notes*, I, 3, 4, pp. 85 ff. (1891). Pub. by the American Dialect Society, Cambridge, Mass.

JÖRGEN FORCHHAMMER, *Die Grundlage der Phonetik*, Heidelberg, 1924.
   Sprachlautlehre, Heidelberg, 1928.

G. E. FUHRKEN, *Standard English Speech*, Cambridge, 1932.

CHARLES H. GRANDGENT, *German and English Sounds*, Ginn, Boston, 1892.
   "From Franklin to Lowell, A Century of New England Pronunciation," in *Pub. of the Mod. Lang. Assoc. of America*, XIV, 2, 207 ff. (1899).
   "English in America," in *Die Neueren Sprachen*, II, 443 ff. (1895).
   Articles on American pronunciation in *Mod. Lang. Notes*, V, 461 ff. (1890), VI, 82 ff. and 458 ff. (1891), VII, 96 ff. (1892), VIII, 273 ff. (1893).
   "Fashion and the Broad A" and "New England Pronunciation" in *Old and New*, Harvard Univ. Press, 1920. (The first also in the *Nation*, Jan. 7, 1915.)

WILLIAM GRANT, *The Pronunciation of English in Scotland*, Cambridge University Press, 1913.

JEREMIAH J. HOGAN, *The English Language in Ireland*, Dublin, 1927.

A. LLOYD JAMES, *Historical Introduction to French Phonetics*, London, 1929.

OTTO JESPERSEN, *A Modern English Grammar on Historical Principles*, Part I, Heidelberg, 1909.
   Lehrbuch der Phonetik, Vierte Auflage, Leipzig and Berlin, 1926.
   Phonetische Grundfragen, Leipzig and Berlin, 1904.

DANIEL JONES, *The Pronunciation of English*, Cambridge, 1914.
   Phonetic Transcriptions of English Prose, Oxford, 1914.
   An English Pronouncing Dictionary on Strictly Phonetic Principles, London and New York, Ninth edition, 1948.
   An Outline of English Phonetics, Third ed., New York, 1932.

JOHN S. KENYON and THOMAS A. KNOTT, *A Pronouncing Dictionary of American English (PDAE)*, G. and C. Merriam Co., Springfield, Mass., Revised, with *Addenda*, 1949.

GEORGE PHILIP KRAPP, *The Pronunciation of Standard English in America*, Oxford University Press, New York, 1919.
The English Language in America, New York, 1925.

E. KRUISINGA, *A Handbook of Present-Day English, Part I, English Sounds*, Fourth ed., Utrecht, 1925.

MARK H. LIDDELL, *The Laws of English Rhythm*, Lafayette, Indiana, 1914.

R. J. LLOYD, *Northern English*, Leipzig and Berlin, 1908.

THOMAS R. LOUNSBURY, *The Standard of Pronunciation*, New York, 1904.

KARL LUICK, *Historische Grammatik der Englischen Sprache*, pp. 1–1149, 1921–40.

SAMUEL MOORE, *Historical Outlines of English Phonology and Morphology*, Second ed., Ann Arbor, 1929.

A New English Dictionary on Historical Principles, Oxford, 1888–1933 (referred to briefly as the *Oxford*).

HAROLD E. PALMER, J. VICTOR MARTIN, and F. G. BLANDFORD, *A Dictionary of English Pronunciation with American Variants*, Cambridge, 1926.

HAROLD E. PALMER, *A Grammar of Spoken English on a Strictly Phonetic Basis*, Cambridge, 1924.

ROBERT MORRIS PIERCE, *International French-English and English-French Dictionary*, New York, 1904. Consulting editors, Paul Passy and George Hempl.

PAUL PASSY and DANIEL JONES, *Le Maître Phonétique*, Organ of the International Phonetic Association, Aube and London, Quarterly.

EDUARD PROKOSCH, *Sounds and History of the German Language*, New York, 1916.

WILLIAM A. READ, "Some Phases of American Pronunciation," *Jour. Eng. and Germanic Philol.*, Urbana, Ill., April, 1923, pp. 217–244.

R. H. STETSON, *Motor Phonetics*, in *Archives Néerlandaises de Phonétique Expérimentale*, La Haye, 1928.

HENRY SWEET, *A Primer of Phonetics*, Third ed., Oxford, 1906.
The Sounds of English, Second ed., Oxford, 1910.

CHARLES KENNETH THOMAS, *An Introduction to the Phonetics of American English*, New York, 1947.

M. V. TROFIMOV and DANIEL JONES, *The Pronunciation of Russian*, Cambridge, 1923.

IDA C. WARD, *The Phonetics of English*, Cambridge, 1931. Third ed., 1939.

Webster's New International Dictionary, Second Edition, Springfield, Mass., 1934.

JOSEPH and ELIZABETH MARY WRIGHT, *An Elementary Middle English Grammar*, Second ed., Oxford, 1928
An Elementary Historical New English Grammar, Oxford, 1924.

INTRODUCTION

There are few subjects on which educated Americans are so ready to pass judgment and give advice on the basis of so little sound knowledge as the pronunciation of the English we use. Influenced by certain types of teaching in the schools, by the undiscriminating use of textbooks on grammar and rhetoric, by unintelligent use of the dictionary, by manuals of "correct English," each with its favorite (and different) shibboleth, and, it would seem, by anybody or anything that has an air of cocksureness about it, we accept rules of pronunciation as authoritative without inquiry into either the validity of the rules or the fitness of their authors to promulgate them.

Some of the rules are well founded, no doubt; but many of them are quite without foundation in the usage of past or present. Some of them are purely traditional, formulated a century or two ago on theoretical grounds by teachers and writers who had no adequate knowledge of the history or phonetics of English; and they have been reverently copied and taught by later writers and teachers without a knowledge of either their ultimate origin or their validity. Yet we not only accept many of these rules ourselves, but seek to impose them on others by criticizing their pronunciation when it differs from what we suppose correct.

A remarkable aspect of our readiness to criticize pronunciation is the fact, which becomes overwhelmingly obvious to even the beginner in phonetics, that we do not know what sounds we ourselves actually pronounce, until we have attained some elementary knowledge of phonetics. To the teacher of even mature students in phonetics certain deficiencies appear at the beginning. Students have no definite notion of the position of the accent in words; they cannot distinguish between spelling and sound; often they cannot isolate a sound from the rest of a word; often they cannot distinguish between voiced and voiceless consonants, even after knowing the meaning of the terms; between such different sounds as the vowel of *father* and that of *all* or that of *poor* and that of *purr;* between a simple vowel as in *let* and a diphthong as in *ice*.

A serious aspect of this general lack of knowledge of the simplest phonetic facts of our own language, is that many schoolteachers have wrong habits of speech, usually artificially acquired, and they unintentionally mislead their pupils in pronunciation. This is to be deplored, not as a matter of blame to the teachers, but as a serious defect in an educational system which fails to provide and require the necessary preparation of the teacher. Realizing this defect, the Board of Education in England several years ago made phonetics a requirement in the preparation of elementary-school teachers.

To cite only a single instance of the present situation in our schools, the writer has repeatedly heard schoolteachers insist on the full pronunciation of the vowels in the unaccented syllables of words—a rule which neither they nor their pupils can follow in natural, unconscious speech. One city teacher of high standing drilled her pupils carefully to pronounce the noun *subject* with the full sound of the *e* as in *let*, and in the same recitation, after passing to another topic, herself repeatedly pronounced the same word naturally, with obscure *e* (1), as is usual in standard English. The author has observed scores of similar instances of false teaching in the pronunciation of teachers otherwise well prepared and devoted to their work.

A valuable result of an elementary knowledge of phonetics is the interest it creates in the pronunciation of English in different regions of America and England. Probably no intelligent person actually expects cultivated people in the South, the East, and the West to pronounce alike. Yet much criticism, or politely silent contempt, of the pronunciations of cultivated people in other localities than our own is common. A student of phonetics soon learns not only to refrain from criticizing pronunciations that differ from his own, but to expect them and listen for them with respectful, intelligent interest. He is able to refer the pronunciations he hears to natural and regular laws of linguistic development and behavior. He is apt to learn that certain tendencies he has been tempted to criticize are just as natural and reasonable as many that he follows himself. As his observation becomes more accurate, he will cease to help perpetuate such popular fallacies, as, e.g., that the Bostonian drops all his *r's*, or that every Englishman drops his *h's*. He will learn that he has been observing the speech of others only in the most superficial and fragmentary way; and, in turn, his attention will be sharpened to the peculiarities of the speech of his own region.

Some knowledge of phonetics will not only broaden one's mind in his attitude toward the speech of other localities, but will put him in a more rational position with reference to the questions of authority and standards of usage. No standard of speech can be slavishly followed with safety. There can be no standard of speech that dispenses with a large element of individual choice requiring the decisions of the judgment in applying it. The student of phonetics substitutes an enlightened judgment in matters of pronunciation for every other kind of authority. Not that he becomes independent of standards, but that he learns to evaluate those standards as well as to render intelligent to himself his own attitude toward them.

Illustration of the statements in the last two paragraphs is found in the questions and discussion that frequently arise over the pronunciation of *u* in *rule, lute, blue, new, tutor*, of *tu* in words like *nature, fortune*, of *du* in *education, verdure*, of *a* in *ask, class, half, laugh, aunt*, of *o* in *coarse, door, core*, of *a* or *e* in *care, there*, and in many similar questions. The oft repeated question,

"Which is correct?" and the too oft repeated dogmatic answer
are both quite inapplicable to the cases. For an intelligent
answer something more is needed than a firm conviction of one's
own way of pronouncing them and a readiness to criticize those
who differ. There is necessary some knowledge of the phonetic
nature of these sounds, and of their historical development and
distribution, together with the judicial state of mind that results
from such knowledge.

Among the practical uses of phonetics is to be mentioned its
effect in stimulating good articulation. Familiar knowledge and
daily observation of the manner in which the sounds of speech
are made with the speech organs develops an habitual consciousness of the operation of those organs in daily speech that results
in improved articulation. The habit of good articulation—which
in its purely muscular aspects can be taught by a good elocution-
ist—by the study of phonetics is at the same time combined with
some scientific knowledge of the phonetic structure of English,
so that the result is not artificial but natural. And the need in
present American speech of clear and deliberate enunciation,
which at the same time shall not be artificially "elocutionary,"
is very great, not only in respect to the communicative and expressive function of spoken English, but also in respect to its
function in the interpretation of literature—especially poetry.

Great as is the practical value of phonetics, and the need of
such study in America for the improvement of our speech, the
author wishes to emphasize his firm conviction, not much shaken
by the numerous onslaughts of recent educational theory, of the
supreme importance of the study of speech as a part of the
larger field of English considered as a branch of science. Whatever of practical value phonetics, or any study of English, may
have, its place in an educational program is determined by its
value as a branch of knowledge.

Phonetics has exceptional qualities as a branch of science

adapted to educational ends. Its large field of basic facts—its raw material—lies all about us and is immediately available to every student—the facts of pronunciation always within reach of our personal observation. Moreover, they are facts of constantly vital and social interest. They are elemental facts of mental behavior in one aspect of experience; and the observation of these facts constitutes as real an approach, so far as it goes, to the understanding of mental phenomena as the study of psychology.

The handling of these facts by the student involves the same mental processes of accurate observation, comparison, logical deduction, and generalized concepts, that have been rightly the chief argument for the disciplinary value of the study of Latin and Greek. No argument has been adduced for the disciplinary value of Latin and Greek that does not equally apply to the study of English language if undertaken with equal thoroughness. The author would heartily approve more study of Latin and Greek, but we should open our eyes to the wealth of material, fresh and unstaled, which we have mostly neglected, in our native language, admirably suited as a basis of a sound culture in a program of liberal arts, and implying as well a far more certain attainment of the practical ends already theoretically claimed for the study of English.

HISTORICAL SUGGESTIONS

In order to understand many aspects of our modern English it is essential to be able to form some idea of the way in which various features of our language have come to be what they are. It is therefore necessary for the student of phonetics to have some background of the history of the English language. The following facts should be mastered by the student.

1. English is a descendant of the Germanic branch of the Indo-European family of languages. Latin and Greek are sister branches to the Germanic. Since English is descended from the Germanic branch, and French and Spanish from the sister Latin branch, English may be said to be a cousin of French and Spanish. Since modern German and English are both descendants from the Germanic branch, they are sister languages, more recently related than Latin and Germanic.

The speakers of the English descendant of the Germanic branch migrated from northwestern Europe to England in the fifth century A.D. There the language went on developing. The earliest written records of English we have are from the seventh century. The language from that time till about 1150 is called Anglo-Saxon or **Old English (OE)**. King Alfred, who wrote several important works, may conveniently be taken as the chief representative of the Old English period. From the reign of Henry II (about 1150) to that of Henry VIII (about 1500) the language is called **Middle English (ME).** Chaucer (1340–1400), in the reign of Richard II, may be taken as the chief representative of Middle English. From about 1500 to the present is **Modern English (MnE),** that from 1500 to 1700 being **Early Modern (EM),** and from 1700 to 1950+, **Late Modern (LM).**

The student should avoid the mistake of applying the term "Old English" to any stage of early English later than 1150. The term is often wrongly applied to Chaucer's English, or even

8

to Shakespeare's. Chaucer's language is Middle English, and Shakespeare's Early Modern. Some try to avoid ambiguity by calling English before 1150 "Anglo-Saxon," a term misleading in other respects. The name was never applied to their language by the Anglo-Saxons themselves, and it unfortunately helps to foster the too prevalent notion that King Alfred's English was a foreign tongue that did not become English till it was united with French. King Alfred and his contemporaries called their language "English," and neither its name nor its essential character was changed by the later assimilation of French and Latin words to its vocabulary. The student should learn these periods carefully, as frequent reference is made to them.

2. Until the **Scandinavian Conquests** and extensive fusion with the English people (8th–11th cc.), and the **Norman Conquest** (1066), the words in English were mostly native; i.e., words that had descended from parents to children through the West Germanic branch from the original word-stock of Indo-European. But from their Norwegian and Danish neighbors in England the English borrowed several hundred words, as *fellow, loose, raise*, etc. Likewise a great number of place-names in England are of Scandinavian origin, from which many family names are derived.

When the **Norman French** settlers came to England in 1066, they of course brought with them their own language—a northern dialect of French. This was spoken in England until about 1350 in a form gradually changed from its continental original and now called **Anglo-French.** Because the government and the church in England were then under the control of the Normans, French was the language of the higher classes and of literature, while English continued to be spoken by the native lower classes. About 1350 English again became the language of the ruling class, and French became a possession of only the educated. In the meantime the Central, or Parisian, French had exerted such influence on Anglo-French that Parisian French was now the preferred form in England, and the great body of **French loan-words** taken into English from about 1250 to 1400 are chiefly of the **Central French** form. However, a few Anglo-French speech sounds came into English from the French spoken in England and developed into Modern English along with other English sounds.[1]

After about 1250—nearly two hundred years after the conquest—Parisian French words flowed into England in great numbers for nearly two hundred years,[2] and were learned and used as English words alongside the native words. In the main they were pronounced—except for the inflectional endings—as French was at that time pronounced, which was very different from modern French. The accent was at first that of the French, usually near the final syllable, but this soon shifted in many words to a place near the beginning, where most native words were accented, though often in the longer words a secondary accent remained where the main French accent had been. In the following centuries many **Latin words,** too, were introduced through literature and scholarship, and became assimilated into the English word-stock.

3. Important as are these two great additions—the French and the Latin—to the English vocabulary, they did not otherwise much affect the language. They did not essentially modify the pronunciation of native words, or the grammar and syntax of English. The **essential structure** of English is today what it was in King Alfred's day, before the Norman Conquest.

Important changes, however, were already going on before

[1] See §§30 and 35 of *A Brief History of the English Language*, pp. lxxxiv–v of *Webster's New International Dictionary, Second Edition.*

[2] The influx, in somewhat lesser numbers, has continued to the present day. See Jespersen, *Growth and Structure of the English Language*, Leipzig, 1905, §95, and A. C. Baugh, in *Mod. Lang. Notes*, February, 1935, pp. 90–93, and his *History of the English Language*, N. Y., 1935, §123, esp. p. 207.

the influx of the new borrowed words. They are chiefly of five kinds: (1) Changes in the **meanings** of words—not of great importance in the study of phonetics. (2) Changes in **syntax,** or construction—also of minor importance to phonetics. (3) Changes in **inflectional endings** for number, case, tense, etc. These are of considerable importance to phonetics, for change and loss of inflectional endings have brought about many changes in pronunciation. (4) Changes in **stress.** These have also caused considerable changes in pronunciation—especially in the shifting of the accent in borrowed words. (5) Changes in **consonant and vowel sounds.** These are of central importance to phonetics. Many of the foregoing changes are still going on. They will be referred to as occasion requires.

4. Changes in pronunciation arise from two principal sources —**phonetic change** and **change by analogy. Phonetic change** is the gradual, progressive, unconscious change in the sounds of words that results in part, at any rate, from our inability to imitate and reproduce perfectly what we hear. Thus the word *stone*, which in King Alfred's time was pronounced "stahn" with *a* as in *father*, changed so gradually that few, if any, realized that any change was going on till it reached its present pronunciation. And so with other phonetic changes. **Analogical change** is quite different in its operation. It can best be exemplified. When a child says *goed* for *went*, he does so not because he has heard *goed*, but because he has frequently heard *showed, snowed, tried, rained, burned,* and many others—all indicating past time by means of a **d** sound at the end. Hence by imitating, not the whole word, but the method of adding endings, he adds the same ending to *go* before he has fully learned the form *went*. Though *goed* is often heard in children's speech, the form has never got into general use. But in the past, children and adults have created many such new forms, many of which have become general and have crowded out older forms. For instance, the proper past tense of the verb *step* was formerly *stōp*. But some one at some time first said *stept* instead of *stōp*, in imitation of many verbs that formed their past tense by adding a **t** sound, such as *lost, stopt, walkt*, etc. Many other speakers did the same thing, till finally everybody gradually abandoned the old form *stōp* and adopted the new form *stept*.²ª

In the same manner a large number of verbs have been changed by analogy from the "strong" to the "weak" conjugation. OE had the same two classes of verbs as MnE—the "irregular" or "strong" verbs like *drive, drove, driven; sing, sang, sung; fall, fell, fallen;* and the "regular" or "weak" verbs like *fill, filled, filled; deem, deemed, deemed; keep, kept, kept*. But from the earliest historical period of the English language the strong verbs have been constantly changing to the form of the weak. The following verbs were originally strong, but by analogy have become weak: *bake, bow, carve, chew, creep, delve, flee, help, laugh, melt, milk, mourn, seethe, shave, shove, spurn, step, swell, wash, yell, yelp, yield;* and about sixty others.

Another example of change by analogy is the plural *-s* of nouns. Formerly only one group of nouns formed their plural by the addition of *-s*. Some made the plural by adding *-en*, as three nouns still do—*oxen, children, brethren;* others by adding *-e*, of which no trace remains; others had the plural identical with the singular, as a few still do—*deer, sheep, swine*. But finally, by analogy of the group that added *-s*, all regular nouns have now come to form their plural in *-s*.

5. Though a **standard literary English** arose in Chaucer's day, it was in the 16th c. that the speech of London, Oxford, and Cambridge gained a place as the **spoken standard** to which the educated in various parts of England tended to conform. But their adherence to this type of speech was never complete, and

²ª Strictly, these are not directly changes in pronunciation, but substitution of different grammatical forms. Changes in speech sounds by analogy are rarer; as the British pronunciation of *lather* as lɑðɔ by analogy of *father, rather;* or the ĕ of *friend* from *friendship*, or the ĭ of *wind* from *windmill*. See also *Webster, Pronunciation,* §1.

even today speakers in south England vary considerably in their pronunciation of present-day "Standard English."

Some of the features of standard English in the 17th c., when America was settled, were the following: (1) r was sounded wherever it was spelt. (2) The vowel of *half, last, path, dance* was like that today in *hat, man.* (3) The vowel in *stop, rob* sounded like the short of the one in *father.* (4) The vowels of *hate, spade,* and of *note, rode* were simple vowels, not diphthongs as in present British. (5) The vowel in *due, true* was ɪu, not a *yoo* and *oo* sound as in present British. (6) The vowel in *borne* was ō, distinct from the *aw* sound in *born.* (7) The vowel of *talk, draw* was nearer the *ah* sound than today. (8) The h in *what, when* was sounded. (9) Words like *dictionary, cemetery, dormitory* had a secondary accent on the third syllable.

By 1800 the speech of London had so changed from the standard form that was still used away from the metropolis that it became the basis of a **new standard form,** while the older one continued to be spoken in the more remote districts, especially the North and America, to which it had been taken in the 17th c. By 1900 the new British type had the following features among others: (1) r was sounded only before a vowel. (2) The vowel in *half,* etc., had become that in *father.* (3) The vowel in *stop, rob* had moved toward that in *talk.* (4) The vowels of *hate, spade,* and of *note, rode* had become diphthongs. (5) The diphthong in *due, true* had become *yoo* and *oo* sounds. (6) The vowel of *borne* had become like that in *born.* (7) The vowel in *talk* had gone nearer to ō. (8) The h sound had gone from *what, when.* (9) *Dictionary,* etc., had lost the secondary accent.

As shown long ago by W. D. Whitney and E. S. Sheldon,[3] and recently by Dr. Orbeck,[4] American English came, not chiefly from British local dialects, but from standard British of the 17th c. The striking resemblance of General American to Northern British in certain features has been cited to show that

---

[3] See *Dialect Notes,* Vol. I, p. 292.

[4] Anders Orbeck, *Early New England Pronunciation,* Ann Arbor, 1927.

GA came from northern England. But these features belonged to 17th c. Southern British. The same is true of resemblances to GA found in other British local dialects: they have disappeared from standard British but remained in GA.

Exactly how the three chief types of American English— **Eastern, Southern,** and **General American**—are derived from British is not yet determined. But there is much evidence that the chief colonial centers, Boston, New York, Richmond, and Charleston, continuing in closer cultural contact with London than did the rest of the rapidly increasing colonial population, shared more of the advancing changes of Southern British. Hence Eastern and Southern American today are more like present Southern British than is GA, which preserves more features of the 17th c. standard British.

A rough computation based on recent census estimates indicates that approximately eleven million Americans and Canadians now speak the Eastern type of American English, twenty-six million the Southern, and ninety million the General American type.[5]

A careful distinction must be made between *standard* English and *uniform* English. The following statements should be thoughtfully pondered:

I am not one of those who believe in the desirability or the feasibility of setting up any one form of pronunciation as a standard for the English speaking world.—Daniel Jones, M.A., Professor of Phonetics, University College, London, in *An English Pronouncing Dictionary*, 1924, p. ix.

The so-called standard language is not a fixed and infallible standard, but is itself constantly changing with the course of time, and is different in the different places where it is spoken.—Edward S. Sheldon, late Professor of Romance Languages, Harvard University, in *Dialect Notes*, I, p. 287.

[5] This represents a revision in the light of later population figures of an estimate published in *Le Maître Phonétique* for Jan.–Mars, 1927. See also comments by C. K. Thomas, *Quarterly Journal of Speech*, Nov., 1927.

A sufficient definition of the term standard will perhaps be found in the statement that speech is standard when it passes current in actual use among persons who must be accounted as among the conservers and representatives of the approved social traditions of a community.—George P. Krapp, Ph.D., late Professor of English, Columbia University, in *The English Language in America*, I, p. 7.

The listener who writes to ask the "correct way" of pronouncing a word quite evidently assumes that there *is* a "correct way." In all these queries and criticisms there is implied the idea of a standard pronunciation. We have a standard yard, a standard pound weight, a standard sovereign, and a standard pint. The yard does not vary from Aberdeen to Plymouth, and the pint pot contains as much in Mayfair as in Bethnal Green. Unfortunately, speech is not capable of rigid measurement, and there is no absolute standard of pronunciation. Pronunciation varies from district to district, from class to class, from character to character, in proportion to the local, social, or personal difference that separates them. . . . It is quite evident that we are not entitled to conclude that there is *one* standard pronunciation, *one* and *only one* right way of speaking English. There are varieties that are acceptable throughout the country, and others that are not.—A. Lloyd James, M.A., Professor of Phonetics, University of London, and Honorary Secretary, Advisory Committee on Spoken English of the British Broadcasting Corporation, in *Broadcast English*, I, 3d ed., 1935, pp. 9 f.

When we consider all the varieties of English spoken by those who are admitted to speak "good English" in the different British colonies and in the different parts of the United States, we must recognise that there is still no Standard Spoken English in any strict sense of the term. In every part of the English-speaking world some type of spoken English, that which is used by the educated and superior class within the community, is considered "good English," as contrasted with the "Vulgar English" and local dialects spoken by other classes of the community. If we use the term Standard Spoken English at all, we must recognise that it is merely a convenient way of speaking of the various kinds of "good English" that are current in various parts of the English-speaking world.—Samuel Moore, Ph.D., late Professor of English, University of Michigan, and Editor of the *Middle English Dictionary*, in *Historical Outlines of English Phonology and Morphology*, 2d ed., 1929, p. 114.

The question, "What pronunciation is correct?" is too often raised without first considering the most important of all conditions for answering it; namely, "Correct for what occasion and under what circumstances?" Good spoken English, even in the same dialect, is not all alike. Omitting consideration of natural local dialect of the uneducated, which is "good" in its place, there is, first, the kind of speech appropriate to the most informal and personal occasions, the most informal colloquial style.[a] Then there is that colloquial style which has been aptly called "the speech of well-bred ease."[b] Both styles use such familiar contractions as *I'm*, *he's*, *it's*, *doesn't*, *don't*, *can't*, *shan't*, *won't*, etc., the chief difference between the first and the second being in vocabulary and speed of utterance. Next there is a more formal colloquial speech, which cannot be sharply distinguished from the more familiar colloquial, differing somewhat in the vocabulary called forth by more formal circumstances and less familiar acquaintance, but also making considerable use of the contractions mentioned. More formal still is the public-speaking style. In this the need of being understood by large audiences calls forth more careful sentence structure and more deliberate and clearer enunciation, especially of the consonant sounds and the accented vowel sounds. Most formal of all is the public-reading style, used in declamation, literary reading, and church services. For practical purposes we may then designate four principal styles of good spoken English as (1) **familiar colloquial,** (2) **formal colloquial,** (3) **public-speaking style,** and (4) **public-reading style.**

The difference between these styles has often been exaggerated, and the effort to use a supposed formal style has led to artificial elocutionary delivery and distorted pronunciation of words that have had the effect of removing such utterances from the actual interests of life and giving them an air of unreality. The

---

[a] Look up the definition of *colloquial* in *Webster*. The term is often misused. See *English Journal*, Jan. 1948, p. 25.

[b] Also called "Easy English" by Mr. Wallace Rice in the *English Journal, College Edition*, June, 1934.

present tendency among the most cultivated and effective public speakers is toward a more or less formal colloquial style for public address,[c] the difference from familiar colloquial being more in subject matter and vocabulary than in pronunciation.

The most important of all styles is the **familiar cultivated colloquial,** both because it is most used by the most important people, and because it forms the basis of all more formal styles both spoken and written. Professor Henry Cecil Wyld, of Oxford University, writes: "This style of literary prose is alive and expressive, chiefly in so far as it is rooted in that of colloquial utterance. The general atmosphere of both is the same in any age. . . . The style of Literature is rooted in the life and conversation of the age. From these sources alone can prose renew its life from generation to generation. When Literary prose style loses touch with the spoken language it becomes lifeless and unexpressive, powerless to 'strike the ear, the heart, or the fancy,' remote alike from human feeling and from the speech of man because it has never known real life and movement."[d]

A thoughtless mistake made by many teachers and writers on English is to assume that the most formal style is the only one to be considered correct, to whom the word *colloquial* is synonymous with *bad*. On this, too, Professor Wyld makes the observation that there is very little actual difference between the best formal and the best colloquial style: "As a matter of fact, the platform or pulpit pronunciation of the best public speakers hardly differs from that of the home circle. Of what use is it to insist that the pronunciation of the schoolroom shall be grander and more elaborate than that heard in Westminster Abbey, or in the High Court of Parliament?"[e]

---

[c] Cf. the article "The King's English," in *American Speech*, June, 1931, p. 368.

[d] *History of Modern Colloquial English*, London, 1925, pp. 157, 188.

[e] *The Teaching of Reading*, London, 1924, p. 19.

THE REPRESENTATION OF SPEECH SOUNDS

6. Language is primarily speech; primarily, both in origin and in respect to importance. The first parent speech of our language originated, gradually developed, split up, in the course of group migrations, into many sister languages, underwent numberless changes in word-stock, word meanings, grammar and syntax, and pronunciation, centuries before any one succeeded in making language visible to the eye in writing. Written English in our present alphabet is hardly fifteen hundred years old. In present importance, also, spoken English is far in advance of written. Even people engaged chiefly in intellectual affairs speak a hundred words where they write one; with the average man the ratio of spoken to written is far greater. But the measure of the relative importance of speech and of written or printed language is not quantitative; a personal interview is far better than a letter to accomplish a practical end. Speech is a living activity inseparable from personality; written or printed language is only an imperfect picture of it.

In the study of language we are constantly tempted to forget that speech is primary, and writing and reading secondary, because speech is wholly unconscious in its beginning with the individual, and virtually so throughout life. But our conscious efforts with language—our first laborious reading, spelling, and writing, the later study of grammar and composition, and of literature, and our study of the printed page in other subjects—all these deal with the written or printed representation of speech to the eye; and so in our conscious intellectual life the written language assumes a prominence all out of proportion to its actual daily importance. Particularly in phonetics is it necessary to remind ourselves at every turn that **the real language is**

18

speech—spoken groups of words—and not the written or printed signs representing it to the eye.

7. Though the English people who migrated to the British Isles in the fifth century possessed an alphabet, called runes, when they came, the great body of their literature was not written down, but was composed and spoken orally, and transmitted by memory. In the sixth century the missionaries from Rome who had settled in Ireland began to Christianize England in Northumbria, and thus introduced the **Roman alphabet** into England for the writing of the native language.

A few changes in the use of the letters have been made since the Roman alphabet began to be used to represent English sounds. The OE scribes used for the first sound in *we* the runic character ρ called *wĕn*. In the thirteenth century this was abandoned and *uu* or *vv* ("double *u*"), and then *w*, was used in its place. A rune ρ, called *thorn*, was used for the two *th* sounds now heard in *thin* and *this*. The use of this character for the *th* sound persisted in occasional use till the seventeenth century, though after printing began, the letter *y* was often used when type fonts lacked ρ. This is sometimes seen now in imitation of old style, though most people are now unaware that it stands for the *th* sound, and wrongly pronounce it as *y* in *you*. Cf. §187.

8. Until the seventeenth century *u* and *v* were not used as now—*u* for the vowel and *v* for the consonant—but were regarded as merely different forms of the same letter, each of which represented either a vowel or a consonant sound. The usual rule was to use *v* at the beginning of a word for consonant or vowel, and *u* in the middle or at the end as consonant or vowel. Thus in the Authorized Version of the Bible in 1611 we find, "When thou tillest the ground, it shall not henceforth yeeld vnto thee her strength: A fugitiue and a vagabond shalt thou be in the earth" (Gen. 4: 12); and this is the usage throughout the Bible and books of the sixteenth century and before. Milton in 1645 followed the present method of using *u* for the vowel and *v* for the consonant, regardless of position in the word. But not till the nineteenth century did dictionaries separate words with initial *u* from those with initial *v*.

9. Likewise *i* and *j* were formerly merely different forms of the same letter, which had the value either of the vowels in *it* and *ice* or of the first consonant in *jug*. At first ɪ alone was used, without the dot. When initial, this was often prolonged above the line to keep it distinct from the following letter. This form finally appeared, after printing began, as I. The dot was added to ɪ, also to avoid confusion with adjacent letters, as today. In medieval European writing, at the end of words i was often prolonged below the line, giving the form j. This was used by English scribes in numerals, as *j*, *ij*, *iij*, *vj*, *xij*, etc., and at the end of Latin words such as *filij*. (In English words final *i* was replaced by *y*.) These different forms were used as vowel or consonant. Thus we find in the Bible of 1611, "I am iealous for Ierusalem, and for Zion, with a great iealousie" (Zech. 1: 14). Again Milton was among the first to adopt the present practice of using *i* for vowel and *j* for consonant, but dictionaries did not separate words with initial *i* and *j* till the nineteenth century, and *u* and *v*, *i* and *j* were not separated in the British Museum catalog till about 1930.

10. When English began to be written in Roman letters, the spelling was as nearly phonetic as possible; i.e., each scribe represented his own English sounds by the letter that stood for the Latin sound nearest to his own. But even at first there were some discrepancies. For example, the letter *f* was used both for the sound in *fat* and for that in *over* (then spelt *ofer*); *s* stood for the sound in *fast* and in *rise;* þ stood for the sound of *th* in *thin* and in *writhe*, and ð stood for the same also; *g* stood for the sound in *get* and in *yet*. As time went on, there was a constantly increasing discrepancy between sound and spelling. An alphabet remains comparatively fixed, and habits of spelling tend to remain, rather than to change—especially since the use of printing—for they are based on visible and conscious imitation. Speech, on the other hand, is based on unconscious and somewhat imperfect imitation, and so changes by imperceptible and continuous variation. Thus the word *man* is still spelt as it was in King Alfred's time, but has changed in pronunciation from "mŏn" to its present pronunciation. *Hope* in Chaucer's day was pronounced "haw-puh"; but though it has changed to its present sound, it is still spelt *hope* as it was in Chaucer's day. So after English sounds began to be represented in Roman letters, the sounds tended to depart farther and farther from what the letters had at first suggested. It is obvious that if this divergence between sound and spelling continued, the sounds would after a while become entirely different from what the letters had at first suggested. Then either the spelling must fail to serve its purpose, and new letters must be used, or the letters must gradually come to suggest different sounds from those at first associated with them. In fact, the latter is what happened, but not with all the letters at the same time. From the fifteenth to the seventeenth centuries the sounds of English had so changed that it is now true with most vowel sounds and some consonant sounds that the letters do not ordinarily stand for the sounds which had been associated with the Roman letters in English down to the fifteenth century, and in other European languages down to the present time. The change in vowel sounds that occurred from the time of Chaucer to the present is called **The Great Vowel Shift,** and consisted, for the long vowels, in the raising of the tongue for each vowel except the two already highest (iː and uː), which became diphthongs. See §244.

11. The attempt in English to keep up with the changing sounds by using the same letters with changed values was not entirely successful. Hence we find in present English that the single letter *a*, for example, represents the different vowel sounds in such words as *name, bare, man, father, all, village, lunar, sofa;* the letter *e* spells the different sounds in *be, here, there, bed, alert, England, moment, added,* and very often no sound at all, as in *life, make;* and so with other vowel letters. The consonants are more consistent with their spelling: *b, h, j, k, l, m, q, v, z* nearly always denote one sound each, though most of them can be silent. But *c* denotes the sounds in *city, sacrifice,* v. (*z*), *cat, vicious; d* those in *day, walked; f* those in *life, of; g* those in *get, age,* or none, as in *caught; n* those in *fin, finger,* or none, as in *solemn; s* those in *say, rise, sure, measure,* or none, as in *island.* On the other hand, the same sound is often represented by more than one letter; thus the vowel sound in *mate* is represented by *a;* the same sound in *they* by *ey,* in *vein* by *ei,* in *hail* by *ai,* in *break* by *ea,* in *gauge* by *au.* The sound represented by *e* in *be* is represented by *ee* in *see, ea* in *heap, ie* in *believe, ey* in *key, ei* in *seize, i* in *machine, eo* in *people.* The obscure sound at the end of *sofa* may be represented by any vowel letter and by many combinations, as by *a* in *sofa, e* in *fallen, i* in *possible, o* in *gallop, u* in *suppose, ai* in *villain, ou* in *famous, eou* in *outrageous,* etc.

12. It is obvious from these illustrations that we could not form a definite idea how present-day English is pronounced if we were dependent solely on the current spelling and had not already learned to speak before learning to spell. Much more is it true then, that we cannot *study* pronunciation successfully with only the ordinary spelling to guide us and to represent it with. In order to consider pronunciation scientifically, and to record and communicate the results of our study, we must make

use of some system of symbols that shall unmistakably represent the sounds of speech.

In the main, such a phonetic alphabet must meet two requirements: (1) each symbol shall represent only one speech sound; (2) each speech sound shall have a symbol to represent it. Several such phonetic alphabets are in use by phoneticians and lexicographers. The one now most widely used is that of the **International Phonetic Association** (IPA) and is used in this book. The official publication of the IPA is *Le Maître Phonétique* (Quarterly), and contains articles and specimens in various modern languages, printed in this alphabet.

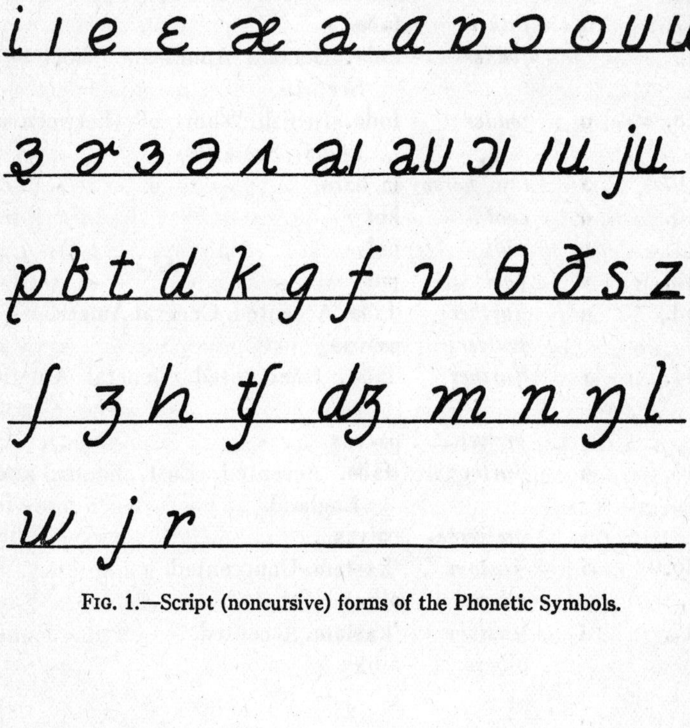

Fig. 1.—Script (noncursive) forms of the Phonetic Symbols.

PHONETIC SYMBOLS

VOWELS

No.	SYMBOL	KEY WORD	PRONUNCIATION
1.	i	*beet*	**bit**
2.	ɪ	*bit, easy*	**bɪt, izɪ**
3.	e	*bait*	**bet**
4.	ɛ	*bet*	**bɛt**
5.	æ	*bat*	**bæt**
6.	a	Sc. *cat*	**kat.** Between æ and ɑ; see §18.
7.	ɑ	*father*	**fɑðɚ**
		fodder	**fɑdɚ.** General American "short *o*"; See §19.
8.	ɒ	*fodder*	**fɒdə.** British "short *o*" (between ɑ and ɔ); See §19.
9.	ɔ	*law, horse*	**lɔ, hɔrs**
10.	o	*coat*	**kot**
11.	ʊ	*pull*	**pʊl**
12.	u	*pool*	**pul**
13.	ɜ	ˈ*further*	ˈ**fɜðɚ.** Accented. General American.
		*per*ˈ*verse*	**pɚ**ˈ**vɜs**
14.	ɚ	ˈ*further*	ˈ**fɜðɚ.** Unaccented. General American.
		*per*ˈ*verse*	**pɚ**ˈ**vɜs**
15.	ɜ	ˈ*further*	ˈ**fɜðə.** Accented. East, South, and England.
		*per*ˈ*verse*	**pə**ˈ**vɜs**
16.	ə	ˈ*custom*	ˈ**kʌstəm.** Unaccented.
		*a*ˈ*bove*	**ə**ˈ**bʌv**
17.	ʌ	ˈ*custom*	ˈ**kʌstəm.** Accented.
		*a*ˈ*bove*	**ə**ˈ**bʌv**

Diphthongs

No.	Symbol	Key Word	Pronunciation
18.	aɪ	*ice*	aɪs
19.	aʊ	*house*	haʊs
20.	ɔɪ	*boy*	bɔɪ
21.	ɪu	*abuse*	əbɪuz
22.	ju	*use*	juz

For other diphthongs, see §§352 ff.

Consonants

Symbols not numbered have their usual names

No.	Symbol	Key Word	Pronunciation	No.	Symbol	Key Word	Pronunciation
		Stops		26.	ʒ	*vision*	vɪʒən
	p	*peep*	pip		h	*hail*	hel
	b	*bib*	bɪb			Affricates	
	t	*toot*	tut	27.	tʃ	*church*	tʃɜtʃ
	d	*did*	dɪd	28.	dʒ	*judge*	dʒʌdʒ
	k	*cook*	kʊk			Sonorants	
	g	*gag*	gæg		m	*maim*	mem
		Fricatives			n	*noon*	nun
	f	*fife*	faɪf	29.	ŋ	*sing*	sɪŋ
	v	*valve*	vælv		l	*lull*	lʌl
23.	θ	*ether*	iθɚ			Glides	
24.	ð	*either*	iðɚ		w	*wail*	wel
	s	*cease*	sis		hw	*whale*	hwel
	z	*zones*	zonz		j	*young*	jʌŋ
25.	ʃ	*mission*	mɪʃən		r	*road*	rod

Note: A phonograph record of the author's speech sounds may be got from National Council of Teachers of English, 211 W. 68th St., Chicago.

13. Accent is indicated by the mark (ˈ) for **primary accent** and (ˌ) for **secondary,** each placed **before** the accented syllable, as in ˈshoeˌmaker ˈʃuˌme kɚ, ˈdrawing ˌroom ˈdrɔ ɪŋ ˌrum. Wholly unaccented syllables are not marked, as in ˈnation ˈne ʃən, beˈfore bɪˈfor. When it is desired to indicate a subordinate accent weaker than secondary, this may be indicated by a dot, thus .: ˌmisˌunderˈstanding ˌmɪs.ʌn dɚˈstæn dɪŋ, in which four degrees of accent are perceptible by comparison of adjacent syllables— **primary, secondary, light,** and **no accent.** It is usually sufficient to recognize three degrees only—primary, secondary, and no accent. Syllables with a considerable degree of accent are often left unmarked when adjacent to the syllable that has primary accent, as in ˈaccent ˈæk sɛnt, ˈcontract ˈkɑn trækt. See §§104 ff. The primary accent mark is generally omitted from words accented only on the first syllable.

14. The sign ː after a vowel symbol indicates that the vowel is relatively **long in duration.** The sign · may be used to indicate **intermediate** length. When length signs are systematically used, short vowels are unmarked. In American transcription it is seldom important to indicate length.

15. The plus sign (+) placed after a symbol (usually a vowel symbol), indicates a pronunciation of it with more advanced tongue position (§§65 ff.); thus ɑ+ means "advanced ɑ." Similarly the minus sign (−) means "with retracted tongue," as æ−, "retracted æ." The sign ⊥ means "with raised tongue," as ʊ⊥, "raised ʊ," and the sign ⊤ means "with lowered tongue," as ɛ⊤, "lowered ɛ." The signs may be combined; as ɪ⊤−, "lowered and retracted ɪ."

In this book spellings are printed in *italics* and sounds in **boldface.** In works where **boldface** is not so used, and in written work, it is customary to place phonetic symbols in square brackets [ ] to distinguish them from ordinary spelling.

16. In this book the same symbol ɪ is used for both the

accented and the unaccented vowel, though they often differ slightly. For the final vowel in words like *easy* many speakers pronounce **i**, fewer in the South and Eastern New England. The author pronounces **ɪ** in such words.[f]

17. The vowel in words like *air, care, there* sounds between **ɛ** in *very* **vɛrɪ** and **æ** in *bat* **bæt**, *carry* **kærɪ**. Two varieties are in standard use, one nearer to **ɛ** and the other nearer to **æ**. It may be written as in **kɛr, ðɛr** or **kær, ðær**, according as it most resembles **ɛ** or **æ** (see §§358 ff.).

18. The sound **a** (No. 6) as heard in *cat, man*, etc., in the pronunciation of standard English in Scotland and northern England,[6] is a sound acoustically between **æ** in *sand* and **ɑ** in *father*. It occurs in General American only in the diphthongs **aɪ** and **aʊ**, and as an occasional unconscious variant of **æ**. It is used by some speakers in New England and New York City in words like *ask*. See §§273–85. In transcription it must not be substituted for **ɑ**.

19. The vowel **ɒ**, which sounds between **ɑ** and **ɔ** as it is regularly pronounced in England and locally in America in words with "short *o*" like *not, top, watch, what*, is not often heard in General American, being usually replaced by **ɑ**. See §§286 ff.

20. The symbols **ɜ** and **ɚ** each represent simple *r*-colored **vowels**, expressed in current spelling by a vowel letter and *r*, as in *further* **fɜðɚ**. The vowel **ɜ** occurs only in **syllables of perceptible accent**, as in **ˈ***person* **ˈpɜsn̩**, **ˈ***per*ˌ*vert* (n.) **ˈpɜˌvɜt**, and is always **syllabic** (is the main vowel of the syllable).[6a] The unaccented **ɚ** is likewise always syllabic, but shorter; as in *better* **ˈbɛtɚ**, *maker* **ˈmekɚ**.

The syllabic *r* sound is sometimes transcribed with the

---

[f] See §§253 f. and C. K. Thomas, *Phonetics*, p. 48.

[6] See Grant, §§8, 143; Lloyd, *Preface* and §90.

[6a] Many transcribers use the form **ɝ** with hook at the top as in **ɚ**. **ɜ** and **ɝ** are to be regarded as equivalent, **ɜ** being easier to write (Fig. 1).

phonetic symbol ŗ (*stirring* stɹ̩ɪŋ, *better* bɛtŗ) or with r (bɛtr). But there is the same reason to use a different symbol for a syllabic *r* sound (bɛtɚ) than for a nonsyllabic *r* sound (*rate* ret, *far* fɑr, *farm* fɑrm) as there is to use a different symbol for a syllabic **u** sound (*duel* **du-əl**) than for the corresponding non-syllabic **u** sound (*dwell* **dwɛl**), or a different symbol for a syllabic **i** sound (*Bostonian* bɔsˈtoniən) than for the corresponding non-syllabic **i** sound (*onion* ʌnjən). For the relation of consonant **r** to the *r*-colored vowel ɝ or ɚ is the same as that of consonant **w** to vowel **u** or ʊ, and of consonant **j** to vowel **i** or ɪ; the consonants **w**, **j**, **r** being glide consonants, often called semivowels. See §§29, 35, 63.

In some former editions of this book the symbol ɚ was used both for a syllabic vowel (*better* bɛtɚ, *perceive* pɚˈsiv) and for a nonsyllabic vowel forming the latter part of a diphthong (fɑɚ, fɑɚm); but experience with elementary classes has convinced the author that, in spite of slight theoretical inconsistency, the practice adopted in *PDAE* (see §26 of that book) is more practical, in which ɚ stands solely for the *r*-colored vowel that forms a syllable either alone (bɛt-ɚ) or with a consonant (pɚˈsiv), and in which **r** stands both for the consonant (ret, traɪ) and for the nonsyllabic vowel forming a diphthong with the preceding vowel (fɑr, fɑrm). When *r* comes between vowels (*very*), there is even better reason to use the symbol **r,** for the sound may be either a consonant (vɛ-rɪ) or a nonsyllabic vowel (vɛr-ɪ). Both pronunciations occur and are not easy to distinguish in current speech. Cf. §236.

The distinction between consonant **r** and nonsyllabic vowel **r** is easily made by remembering that consonant **r** always occurs just before a vowel in the same syllable (**ret, tri, bɪˈriv, fæk-tə-rɪ, fæk-trɪ**), while vowel **r** always immediately follows a syllabic vowel in the same syllable, making an **r** diphthong (**dɪr, fɑr, fɑrm, fɑr-ðɪŋ**); but ɚ always represents a simple monophthongal syllabic *r*-colored vowel.

21. Observe that the symbol ə (No. 16), when it is the only vowel of the syllable, is to be written only in wholly unaccented syllables, as in *above* ə'bʌv, *custom* ˈkʌs-təm, *sofa* ˈso-fə; or in unstressed monosyllables, as *two of the men* ˈtu əv ðə ˈmɛn. In the speech of those who "drop their *r*'s" ə may also be part of an accented syllable, but only the unaccented part, as in *merely* ˈmɪə-lɪ. Hence ə occurs only in unstressed positions. Likewise the symbol ɚ is to be written only in unstressed positions, either an unaccented syllable of a word (ˈbɛt-ɚ, pɚˈsiv) or an unstressed monosyllable (*two or three* ˈtu ɚ ˈθri).

On the other hand, the symbols ɜ and ʌ are not to be written in wholly unaccented syllables or unstressed monosyllables. Note the following examples of the correct use of these symbols: *survey* (vb.) sɚˈve, *survey* (n.) ˈsɜˌve; *pervert* (vb.) pɚˈvɜt, *pervert* (n.) ˈpɜˌvɜt; *London* ˈlʌndən; *unless* ənˈlɛs, *unlace* ʌnˈles; *undone and done up* ʌnˈdʌn ən ˈdʌnˈʌp; *misunderstand* ˌmɪsʌndɚˈstænd; (Note that in the last three examples ʌn- has a minor unmarked accent. See §13, next-to-last sentence.) *upon* əˈpʌn, *up and down* ˈʌp ən ˈdaʊn; *he heard her* hi ˈhɜd ɚ; *her mother, not her* hɚ ˈmʌðɚ, nɑt ˈhɜ.

It should be noted that ə is not only an unaccented substitute for accented ʌ, but for all other accented vowels as well; as in ˈkɑntrækt—kənˈtrækt; kwaɪˈitəs—kwaɪət; moˈmɛntəm—ˈmo-mənt; ˈmænlɪ—ˈpostmən; ɪmˈpoz—ˌɪmpəˈzɪʃən, etc. Likewise ɚ is the unaccented substitute not only for ɜ, but for the various combinations of accented vowels with a following **r**. Compare ˈpɑrtɪ—pɚˈtɪkjələ; ˌsɪməˈlærətɪ—ˈsɪmələ; rɪˈkɔrd—ˈrɛkɚd; ˈbordɚ—ˈkʌbɚd. See *Gradation*, §§130 ff.

22. In transcribing words like *abuse, cure, few*, etc., the student must observe whether he pronounces ɪu or ju, both of which are current. ɪu is never used initially. For ɪu see §344.

23. For convenience, the letter **g** is printed for the symbol **g**, but in written transcription **g** should always be used.

24. The symbols m̩, n̩, l̩, called "syllabic *m, n, l*," indicate

m, n, and **l** sounds that form syllables without any vowel whatever, either alone, as in *stop 'em* stɑp m̩, *listen* lɪs-n̩, *battle* bæt-l̩,
or with one or more other consonants, as in **o-pm̩,** a frequent pronunciation of *open, listened* lɪs-n̩d, *handled* hæn-dl̩d. The sound
ŋ can also be syllabic, as frequently heard in *I can go* aɪ kŋ go,
where the syllabic marker is omitted for typographical reasons.
For fuller treatment of syllabic consonants, see §§88–92.

   25. Caution: Do not use at all the symbols **c, q, x, y.** Use only
the symbols as given in the tables, which are sufficient to
transcribe all the sounds of English. Moreover, these four letters
are IPA symbols for certain sounds of other languages (e.g., **x**
is the sound of *ch* in Scottish *loch* lɒx and German *ach* ɑx, and
y is the sound of French *u* in *lune* lyn and German *ü* in *fühlen*
fyːlən).

   Remember that the symbol **g** stands *only* for the sound in
gag gæg, and **j** only for the first sound in *young* jʌŋ. Do not use
either **g** or **j** for the sound in *gem* dʒɛm or *judge* dʒʌdʒ.

   26. The following passage, transcribed in a colloquial style
in the author's pronunciation, contains all the regular sounds of
General American. Bear in mind that it is not presented as a
model of pronunciation, but simply as an example of natural
speech in a certain style.

rɪp væn ˈwɪŋkl̩

ðə gret ˈɛrɚ ɪn rɪps ˌkʌmpəˈzɪʃən wəz ən ɪnˈsɪupərəbl̩ əˈvɝʒən
tu ɔl kaɪndz əv ˈprɑfɪtəbl̩ ˈlebɚ. ɪt ˈkudn̩t bi frəm ðə wɑnt əv
ˌæsəˈdɪuəti ɚ ˌpɝsəˈvɪrəns, fɚ i wəd sɪt ɑn ə wɛt rɑk, wɪð ə rɑd əz
lɒŋ ən ˈhɛvɪ əz ə ˈtɑrtɚz læns, ən fɪʃ ɔl de wɪðˈaut ə ˈmɝmɚ, ˈivən
ðo i ˈʃudn̩t bi ɪnˈkɝɪdʒd baɪ ə ˈsɪŋgl̩ ˈnɪbl̩. hid ˈkærɪ ə ˈfaulɪŋˌpis
ən ɪz ˈʃoldɚ fɚ aurz təˈgɛðɚ, ˈtrʌdʒɪŋ θru wudz n̩ swɔmps, ənd ʌp
hɪl ən daun del, tə ʃut ə fɪu skwɝlz ɚ waɪld ˈpɪdʒɪnz. hi wəd
ˈnɛvɚ rɪˈfɪuz tu əˈsɪst ə ˈnebɚ, ˈivən ɪn ðə ˈrʌfɪst tɔɪl, ənd wəz ə
ˈforˌmost mæn ət ɔl ˈkʌntrɪ ˈfrɑlɪks fɚ ˈhʌskɪŋ ˈɪndɪən kɔrnɚ

ˈbɪldɪŋ ston ˈfɛnsɪz; ðə ˈwɪmɪn əv ðə ˈvɪlɪdʒ, tu, jus tu ɪmˈplɔɪ
ɪm tə rʌn ðɛr ˈɛrəndz, ən tə du sʌtʃ ˈlɪtl̩ ad dʒʌbz əz ðɛr lɛs
əˈblaɪdʒɪŋ ˈhʌzbəndz ˈwudn̩t du fɔr ðəm. ɪn ə wɜd, rɪp wəz ˈrɛdɪ
tu əˈtɛnd tu ˈɛnɪˌbadɪz ˈbɪznɪs bət ɪz on; bət əz tə ˈdurɪŋ ˈfæmlɪ
ˌdɪutɪ, ən ˈkɪpɪŋ ɪz farm ɪn ˈɔrdɚ, hi faʊnd ɪt ɪmˈpasəbl̩.

ɪn fækt, hi dɪˈklærd ɪt wəz əv no jus tə wɜk ʌn ɪz farm; ɪt wəz
ðə most ˈpɛstlənt ˈlɪtl̩ pis əv graʊnd ɪn ðə hol ˈkʌntrɪ; ˈɛvrɪˌθɪŋ
əˈbaʊt ɪt wɛnt rɔŋ, ənd ˈwud go rɔŋ, ɪn spaɪt əv ɪm. hɪz ˈfɛnsɪz
wɚ kənˈtɪnjuəlɪ ˈfɔlɪŋ tə ˈpisɪz; hɪz kaʊz wəd ˈiðɚ go əˈstre, ɚ gɛt
əˈmʌŋ ðə ˈkæbɪdʒɪz: hi ˈkudn̩t ˈkipm̩ ət hom; wɪdz wɚ ʃur tə gro
ˈkwɪkɚ ɪn ˈhɪz fildz ðən ˈɛnɪ ˌhwær ɛls; ðə ren ˈɔlwɪz med ə
pɔɪnt əv ˈsɛtɪŋ ɪn dʒʌst əz i hæd səm ˈaʊt-əv-ˌdor wɜk tə du;
so ðət ðo ɪz ˌpætrəˈmonɪəl əˈstet əd ˈdwɪndl̩d əˈwe ʌndɚ ɪz
ˈmænɪdʒmənt, ˈekɚ baɪ ˈekɚ, ənˈtɪl ðɚ wəz ˈlɪtl̩ mor lɛft ðən ə
mɪr pætʃ əv ˈɪndɪən kɔrn ən pəˈtetuz, jɛt ɪt wəz ðə ˈwɜst-kən-
ˈdɪʃənd farm ɪn ðə ˈnebɚˌhud.

27. Isolating sounds from words. A difficulty for the beginner is to learn to isolate the separate speech sounds from the
combinations in which they occur in speech. The current spelling
is deceptive because a single sound may be spelt with more than
one letter, as f in *phonetics* foˈnɛtɪks, p in *happy* hæpɪ, θ or ŋ
in *thing* θɪŋ, ʒ or ɪ in *journeyed* dʒɜnɪd; or two sounds spelt with
one letter, as ks in *tax* tæks; or a sound with no letter, as p in
warm()th wɔrmpθ, k in *leng()th* lɛŋkθ, and t in *eigh()th* etθ.
Some single sounds are always spelt with two letters, as θ or ð
with *th*, and others usually so, as ʃ with *sh*, tʃ with *ch* (or *tch*).
Hence it is necessary to consider the *sounds* and guard against
deceptive spelling. It is best to sound the word without looking
at the spelling and listen while repeating it. After the sound is
perceived and pronounced separately, select the symbol which
expresses it. Remember that the tables contain *all* the separate
sounds; avoid confusing one sound with two, as ŋ with ɪŋ.

Isolate and write the symbols for each sound in the following words, marking the accent of the plurisyllables: *speak, stopped, rabbit, cupboard, doubt, castle, talked, wished, robbed, dodged, healed, showed, snail, sinner, quick, school, liquor, extinct, accent, ached, except, singer, finger, running, thirsty, practice, Carlisle, exhibit, champagne, church, blackbird, shoemaker, dialect, dining-hall, knighthood, exhaust, quart, anguish, somewhat, buckwheat, everywhere, designate, fatality, ascertain, circumvent, momentum, landlord, losing, balloon, wardrobe, migrate, mouthful, township.*

THE ORGANS OF SPEECH

28. The sounds of speech are produced by breath forced from the lungs and modified by the vocal organs. These are:

(1) The **Larynx,** or voice-box. This is an enlargement of the upper end of the windpipe that appears on the outside as the "Adam's apple." It contains the **vocal cords,** so called. They are not cords, but a pair of folds in the mucous membrane containing ligament and muscle fiber and extending inward from the right and left walls of the larynx somewhat like ledges, with their inner, free edges running from front to back. A more descriptive name is **vocal lips.** They are also attached in front to the front wall of the larynx, and at the back to two swinging, gate-like cartilages called the **arytenoids** (ˌærɪˈtinɔɪdz). The opening between the vocal lips is called the **glottis,** the part from the arytenoids to the front being the longer and called the **cord glottis,** or glottis proper, and the shorter part between the cartilages, the **cartilage glottis,** or **whisper glottis.**

Each glottis can be opened and closed independently. When the cord glottis is wide open, the air passes freely through as in ordinary breathing. When the cord glottis is lightly closed, breath forced out sets the edges of the cords into musical vibration, or **voice.** This is heard in all the vowel sounds and in the voiced consonants, such as **v, z, d.** When the cord glottis is firmly closed and the cartilage glottis is slightly open, breath forced out produces by friction the **whispering voice.** This is heard by whispering any of the vowels or voiced consonants, and is different from the fricative sound heard in the voiceless consonants **f, s.** When both cord glottis and cartilage glottis are firmly closed the breath is prevented from passing out. When they are closed at the end of a sound, or just before the beginning of one, there is produced what is called the **glottal stop.**

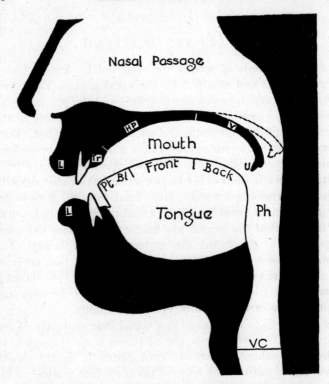

FIG. 2.—Conventionalized Diagram of the Speech Organs.
LL=Lips. Pt=Tongue Point. Bl=Tongue Blade.
Tr=Teethridge. HP=Hard Palate. V=Velum (soft palate): black:
lowered, or open; dotted: raised, or closed.
U=Uvula. Ph=Pharynx. VC=Vocal Cords.

This is a regular speech sound of some languages, but not in standard English. For its occasional occurrence in English, see §48.

(2) The **Tongue.** This very flexible muscle is attached to the lower jaw so that its whole body moves up and down with the jaw. The parts of the tongue referred to are: (a) the **point,** or

tip; (b) the **blade,** including the point and a little back of the point; (c) the **front,** from the blade back to about the middle; and (d) the **back,** the remaining part back of the middle.

(3) The **Teeth**—upper and lower.

(4) The **Teethridge,** or **Alveoli** (æl'viə₁laɪ). The upper teethridge is more important in speech than the lower.

(5) The **Lips.**

(6) The **Hard Palate**—the roof of the mouth from the teethridge back to about the middle.

(7) The **Soft Palate,** or **Velum** ('viləm), from the middle to the back end of the roof of the mouth. The velum can be raised to the back wall of the throat where it enters the nasal cavity, so as to shut off the passage of air into the nasal cavity.

(8) The **Uvula.** This is a soft appendage hanging down from the back end of the velum. It is of little use in standard English but is used in some other languages.

(9) The **Nasal Cavity.** This rises from the back of the throat over the velum, is divided from front to back in the nose by the septum, and terminates in the nostrils.

The Organic Formation of the Consonants

29. In the following brief description of the organic formation of the consonants, the four movable speech organs are mentioned in order from front to back: (1) **Lips,** (2) **Tongue,** (3) **Velum,** (4) **Vocal Cords.** The four possible contacts or approaches of the tongue are to the (1) **Teeth,** (2) **Teethridge,** (3) **Hard Palate,** (4) **Velum.** Outward breath-pressure is assumed in all cases. When not mentioned, the lips (open) and tongue are in neutral resting position.

The Stops

p Lips closed, velum closed, vocal cords apart (silent). **Voiceless lip stop.**

b   Lips closed, velum closed, vocal cords vibrating (sounding). **Voiced lip stop.**

t   Tongue point on teethridge with sides touching, velum closed, vocal cords apart. **Voiceless tongue-point stop.**

d   Tongue point on teethridge with sides touching, velum closed, vocal cords vibrating. **Voiced tongue-point stop.**

k   Tongue back on velum with sides touching, velum closed, vocal cords apart. **Voiceless tongue-back stop.**

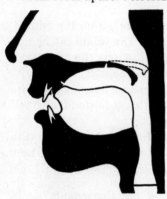 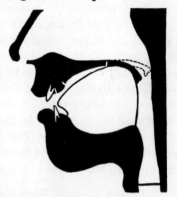

FIG. 3.—Positions for **t, d, l, n.**
Dotted velum = **t, d, l.**
Black velum = **n.**

FIG. 4.—Positions for **k, g, ŋ.**
Dotted velum = **k, g.**
Black velum = **ŋ.**

g   Tongue back on velum with sides touching, velum closed, vocal cords vibrating. **Voiced tongue-back stop.**

ʔ   Glottis firmly closed. **Glottal stop.**

The Fricatives (ˈfrɪkətɪvz)

f   Lower lip on upper teeth, velum closed, breath fricative between teeth and lip, vocal cords apart. **Voiceless lip-teeth fricative.**

v   Lower lip on upper teeth, velum closed, breath fricative between teeth and lip, vocal cords vibrating. **Voiced lip-teeth fricative.**

θ   Tongue blade on points of upper teeth, velum closed, breath fricative between tongue and teeth, vocal cords apart. **Voiceless tongue-blade-teeth fricative.**

ð   Tongue blade on points of upper teeth, velum closed, breath fricative between tongue and teeth, vocal cords vibrating. **Voiced tongue-blade-teeth fricative.**

s   Tongue blade near teethridge with narrow chink over the point, velum closed, breath fricative in narrow jet through

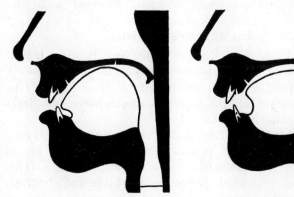

Fig. 5.—Position for **j**.   Fig. 6.—Position for **ʃ**.

the chink and against the upper and lower teeth, vocal cords apart. **Voiceless tongue-blade alveolar fricative.**

z   Tongue blade near teethridge with narrow chink over the point, velum closed, breath fricative in narrow jet through the chink and against the upper and lower teeth, vocal cords vibrating. **Voiced tongue-blade alveolar fricative.**

ʃ   Tongue blade farther from teethridge than for **s** and more spread laterally, tongue front raised nearer to hard palate, velum closed, breath fricative in a broad stream over blade and front, vocal cords apart. (Lips sometimes protruded.) **Voiceless tongue-blade and -front alveolopalatal (ælˈvi-əloˈpælətl̩) fricative.**

ʒ   Tongue blade farther from teethridge than for **z** and more spread laterally, tongue front raised nearer to hard palate, velum closed, breath fricative in a broad stream over blade and front, vocal cords vibrating. (Lips sometimes protruded.) **Voiced tongue-blade and -front alveolopalatal fricative.**

h   Mouth shaped for following sound, velum closed, vocal cords closing to position for voice with simultaneous breath pulse, breath slightly fricative on vocal cords. **Stressed glottal fricative.**

The Affricates (ˈæfrɪkɪts)

tʃ   Tongue blade on teethridge farther back than for **t,** then withdrawing through position for ʃ, velum closed, breath first stopped and then fricative, vocal cords apart. (Lips sometimes protruded.) **Voiceless tongue-blade and -front alveolopalatal affricate.**

dʒ   Tongue blade on teethridge farther back than for **d,** then withdrawing through position for ʒ, velum closed, breath first stopped and then fricative, vocal cords vibrating. (Lips sometimes protruded.) **Voiced tongue-blade and -front alveolopalatal affricate.**

The Sonorants (səˈnorənts)

m   Lips closed, velum open, vocal cords vibrating. **Voiced lip nasal.**

n   Tongue point on teethridge with sides touching, velum open, vocal cords vibrating. **Voiced tongue-point alveolar nasal.**

ŋ   Tongue back on velum with sides touching, velum open, vocal cords vibrating. **Voiced tongue-back velar nasal.**

l   Tongue point on teethridge with sides free, velum closed, vocal cords vibrating. **Voiced tongue-point alveolar lateral.**

The Glide Consonants

w   Lips closely rounded, tongue back raised toward velum (position for **u**), lips and tongue gliding to position for the following vowel, velum closed, vocal cords vibrating. **Voiced labiovelar** (ˈlebɪoˈvilɚ) **semivowel.**

j   Tongue front near hard palate (position for **i**), gliding to position for the following vowel, velum closed, vocal cords vibrating. **Voiced tongue-front palatal semivowel.**

r   Tongue sides against molars, point raised toward hard palate, body contracted laterally (position for the vowel ɜ),

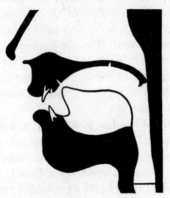

FIG. 7.—Position for **r**.

gliding to following vowel, velum closed, vocal cords vibrating. **Retroflex[7] tongue-point and -blade semivowel.**

30. Consonants Grouped by Places of Articulation. The dash is between approaching or touching organs.

1. Lips		**p, b, m**
2. Lips, and tongue back—velum		**w, (h)w**
3. Lip—teeth		**f, v**
4. Tongue blade—teeth		**θ, ð**
5. Tongue point—teethridge		**t, d, n, l**
6. Tongue blade—teethridge		**s, z**

[7] The term *retroflex* is here used loosely of varying degrees of tongue-point elevation.

7. Tongue blade and front—teethridge and palate   ʃ, ʒ, tʃ, dʒ
8. Tongue point—palate   r
9. Tongue front—palate   j
10. Tongue back—velum   k, g, ŋ
11. Glottis   h, h(w)

31. Stops, Fricatives, Affricates, Sonorants, and Glides. From the foregoing descriptions of the manner of forming the consonants, the groupings according to the similarity of organic formations become evident. The six consonants **p, b, t, d, k, g** are the **stops**—consonants formed by complete stoppage of the breath stream by means of the velum and the lips or the tongue. The glottal stop, not a regular English consonant, is formed by stoppage at the glottis.

32. The nine **fricatives f, v, θ, ð, s, z, ʃ, ʒ, h** are characterized by audible and essential friction of the breath upon the speech organs, which are narrowed toward each other sufficiently to make the impact of breath upon them heard.

33. The two **affricates tʃ** and **dʒ** combine the features of the stops and the fricatives, beginning with a complete stoppage of the breath and ending with a fricative sound. The essential characteristic of an affricate is a stop followed by a homorganic fricative; i.e., a fricative formed by a relatively slow opening of the speech organs from the position taken by them to stop the breath. Other similarly formed sounds, as **tθ** (etθ), **tr** (traɪ), **ts** (gɛts) are not true affricates in English; that is, though organically similar, they are not *used* in English as independent speech sounds. See further under **tʃ, dʒ** in *Consonants in Detail*.

34. The sonorants **m, n, ŋ, l** in English depend for audibility upon voice, which is the only actual physical sound heard in them. If they are made voiceless, they become inaudible unless they are turned into fricatives by increased force of breath. They are not normally completely voiceless in English. See §41.

The acoustic identification of the sonorants depends, like that of the other consonants, upon the place of articulation.

35. The glides **w, j, r** are formed by rapid movement of lips or tongue away from the position of one of the vowels **u** (or near it), **i** (or near it), or **ɜ** (or near it). Their audibility depends upon voice, and their acoustic identification upon the effect of the movement on the sound of the voice. See §§63, 224 ff.

36. Voiceless and Voiced Consonants. Since all English consonants except **h** are articulated in the mouth, they may be formed either with or without the vocal cords vibrating.[8] In some cases the sound of the voice is mingled with other noises of the consonant, so that at first it may be difficult to hear whether a consonant is accompanied by voice or not. One test is to stop the ears while sounding alternately such pairs as *fife* and *five*, prolonging the last sound. Another test is to rest the finger on the outside of the larynx, where the vibration of the vocal cords can be felt. In holding the sound of **f** by itself observe that the only thing heard is a fricative rustling of the breath past the lip and teeth. In sounding **v** the same friction is heard with the sound of the voice added, the vibration of the vocal cords.

37. In the list of consonant symbols test all the consonants to see whether they are voiceless or voiced, and then arrange in pairs those consonants that are made with the same speech organs except the vocal cords; i.e., pairs of corresponding voiceless and voiced consonants.

What sounds in the list have no corresponding voiceless

---

[8] Voiceless consonants are also called *breathed* (**brɛθt**), an adjective formed by Sweet from the noun *breath* (**brɛθ**) just as *voiced* is formed from the noun *voice*. Kruisinga (*Le Maître Phonétique*, Avril–Juin, 1934, p. 48) points out that it is a blunder to confuse the word and its application with the past participle *breathed* (**briðd**) of the verb *to breathe*. On the whole, *voiceless* seems a better term than *breathed* (**brɛθt**). The term *unvoiced* is bad because it also means "devoiced."

ones? What voiceless one has no corresponding voiced? Test the vowels for voice, and then find the etymology of the words *vowel*, *vocal*, and *voice*.

38. Find pairs of words, such as *peg—beg*, for every pair of voiceless and voiced consonants, in which one word of the pair differs from the other only by corresponding voiceless and voiced sounds; i.e., in which the voiceless and voiced sounds are mutually distinctive. Write the pairs in phonetic symbols.

The sounds **hw** and **w** are not strictly such a pair of voiceless and voiced consonants, though they are used in much the same way to distinguish words, as *where—wear*. As usually pronounced in America **hw** is **h** followed by **w** (remember that **h** always assumes the mouth shape of the following sound). Jespersen considers this also the commoner form of the sound of those in southern England who distinguish between *whales* and *Wales*. A true voiceless **w** (IPA ʍ) with fricative sound added is also used by some speakers. In ʍ the friction of air is in the mouth, and in **hw** it is in the glottis (i.e., it is **h**). See **w** and **hw** in *Consonants in Detail*.[9]

39. The sound **h** is sometimes voiced in English between voiced sounds, as in *behind*. The vocal cords separate a trifle for the **h,** but not enough to stop vibrating. But voiced **h** is not a distinctive sound in English. It is a member of the voiceless **h** phoneme (§§79 ff.)

40. m is voiceless in certain common utterances not usually

---

[9] It is because **hw** and voiceless **w** are often interchangeable, that **hw** is listed as one symbol in the tables of phonetic symbols. Otherwise they should be listed separately only as **h** and **w,** which can be combined like other sounds such as **tr, sl,** etc. On the other hand, the symbols **tʃ** and **dʒ** stand for single speech sounds. Whatever their composition, they function in English as single speech sounds, and single symbols would be better for them. These symbols were devised before the sounds were so well understood as now. The symbols are often ligatured, and may well be written so. See the detailed description of the sounds.

regarded as real words, but often with such meanings as "yes," "no," etc. A devoiced consonant that is usually voiced is shown by a small circle below its symbol, as l̥, m̥. Try to pronounce the following: m m̥ m, m̥ m ? m. Try similar ones with voiced and voiceless n. Represent in symbols the sounds you think are meant by the spelling "*Humph!*", "*Eh?*".

41. The sonorants and the glides are often devoiced at the beginning of their sound when preceded by certain voiceless consonants. Thus in **smɔl, sno, slo, twaɪs, hjudʒ, traɪ,** the **m, n, l, w, j,** and **r** are voiceless at the beginning and voiced at the end. But none of these voiceless forms are distinctive in English. Though really very different acoustically, the **r** in **traɪ** is "the same" **r** as in **raɪ.** Hence the difference is not noticed and need not be expressed. The fricative **r** of **traɪ** belongs to the same phoneme (79 ff.) as the glide semivowel **r** of **raɪ.** But in Welsh there is a voiceless fricative **l** (IPA l̥) which distinguishes words from those with voiced **l.** This l̥ is heard in Welsh place names, as *Llangollen* l̥an'gɒl̥ən.[10]

42. Observe that the voiceless stops have no sound at all while the tongue or the lips are in contact; they are therefore **silent speech sounds,** but just as real and useful as if they had sound. Their silence is "heard" as clearly as other sounds. For fuller explanation, see §46.

The voiced stops have a brief sound of voice during the contact. How can you explain the fact of breath vibrating the vocal cords but not escaping from the mouth or nose?

The voiceless fricatives have the sound of friction only, and the voiced fricatives have the combined sound of friction and of voice.

The sonorants and the glides have no other sound than voice. If they are made voiceless, either there is silence, or the in-

---

[10] Welsh voiceless **l** is strongly fricative. For more exact transcription a special IPA symbol **ɬ** is used. See *PDAE*, §29.

creased breath due to the opened glottis causes friction in the mouth, as in the voiceless fricatives.

43. We make the same distinction between voiceless and voiced sounds in whispering as in speaking aloud. But for the voiced sounds we use, instead of the speaking voice, the whispering voice, which is made by closing the cord glottis altogether and forcing the breath through the cartilage glottis. See §28 (1). The whispering voice can easily be heard and felt by whispering vowels or voiced consonants. Voiceless sounds are alike in whisper and loud speech.

When the voiced fricatives v, ð, z, ʒ, dʒ are final and not followed by voiced sounds, as in **liv, smuð, pez, ruʒ, rɪdʒ,** in ordinary speech the last part of the fricative is whispered, and at the very end is often quite voiceless. Compare the sound of z in *it pays* ɪt **pez** with that in *it pays him* ɪt **pez ɪm.** The same is true to some extent with initial voiced fricatives. When a voiceless sound, or none, precedes, the first part of the fricative is de- vocalized: cf. **fvɛrɪ gʊd** and **ðæts fvɛrɪ gʊd** with **hiz vɛrɪ gʊd.** When voiced fricatives are final after a voiced consonant, they are often wholly devocalized: cf. *pays* with *fills*, or *rouge* with *ridge.* In very distinct utterance this devocalization of final voiced fricatives is avoided by some speakers.

44. Oral and Nasal Consonants. Begin to make the sound **b** without allowing the lips to separate. Then while continuing the effort, allow the breath to pass out through the nose. This results in the sound of **m.** When breath passes through the nose with the mouth passage shut off by the lips or the tongue, the velum is lax and hangs away from the back of the upper pharynx. When the velum is drawn up to contact with the back of the upper pharynx, the breath is prevented from passing through the nose and is forced out through the mouth. When the velum is lax, leaving the passage through the nose open, breath may pass through nose and mouth at the same time, but ordinarily in speaking it passes through only one at a time. Test the other consonants of the list and determine which of them are nasal.

Nasalized vowels are made through the mouth, but with the nasal passage open for some breath to pass out, and also so as to produce resonance from the nasal cavity. Nasalized vowels are regular in French, but are not ordinarily used in English.

45. Stops. The stops need more particular notice. In pronouncing the voiceless stop **p** in *pay*, there is an explosive sound of breath (its aspiration; see §78) between the stop and the vowel just as the lips separate. Likewise in the **t** of *too*, as the tongue point leaves the teethridge, and in the **k** of *key* just as the tongue back leaves the velum. A similar explosive sound can be heard in *stop 'em* **stɑp m̩,** for which the lips do not separate but the velum opens and the explosion, less marked, is made through the nose. So in *battle* **bæt̩l** the tongue point remains on the teethridge while the air bursts out at the sides of the tongue; and in *cotton* **kɑtn̩** the tongue point remains on the teethridge while the breath, by sudden opening of the velum, escapes through the nose. In *I can go* **aɪ kŋ go** the tongue back remains on the velum, the velum opens, and the explosion takes place through the nose. These various manners of explosion after **p, t, k** are varieties of especially prominent transition sounds (§77)—they are not the speech sounds **p, t, k** themselves, which often occur without them with no loss of their practical use in living speech. These transition sounds are absent, e.g., from **p** in *jump back* **dʒʌmp bæk,** from **t** in *outdo* **aʊtdu,** and from **k** in *background* **bækgraʊnd,** yet the **p, t,** and **k** are plainly present.

46. In the three last examples the **p, t,** and **k** are entirely silent from the end of the preceding sound to the beginning of the following sound. In these cases we have speech sounds which are not *sounds* from the point of view of physics; but they make as definite an impression on the speaker and the hearer as if they were accompanied by noise, or physical sound. The same silent speech sounds can be heard when **p, t, k** are pronounced at the ends of words before a pause, as in **sæp, sæt, sæk.** In these cases the **p, t, k** are recognized by the preceding transition sound that leads up to them till the contact of the lips or the tongue is made. This initial contact for any sound that has contact is called the **closure,** or **occlusion,** and the end of the contact is called the **opening,** or **release.**[11] In **sæp, sæt, sæk** the closure is evident to the ear by the sudden cutting off of the preceding vowel **æ,** and the acoustic character of this sudden closure reveals whether the following stop is **p, t,** or **k.**[12] The closure is not heard when the stops are initial, as in **pe, tu, ki.** Between vowels both closure and release are evident, as in *copy, duty, seeking.*

Stops are also called plosives, or explosives, because the explosive release is often a prominent mark of the presence of these sounds. But the closure and release are the transition sounds, not the speech sounds.

47. When the stops are voiced (**b, d, g**) in similar surroundings to those named above for **p, t, k,** as in **be, du, go, rɑb m̩, sʌdn̩, dɔg ŋ gʌn,** the explosion is less marked and is accompanied by voice.[13] It, too, may be absent, as in **kɑb paɪp, saɪdtræk, dɔgkɑrt,** or when **b, d,** or **g** ends a phrase or sentence. When special effort is made to explode final voiced stops, a brief

---

[11] The same terms are also sometimes applied to sounds that have only narrowing, as **s, z.**

[12] Instructive experiments can be made by pronouncing the words given while the mouth of the speaker is concealed from the listener.

[13] Often the voice does not begin till the moment of the release of the voiced consonant, the consonant itself being without sound of voice. But such voiceless **b, d, g** sounds still are members of the **b, d, g** phoneme (§§79 ff.) and are distinguished acoustically from **p, t, k** by the difference in the manner of release. There are also organic differences, as in the position of the glottis.

vowel ə is heard after them. In mistaken efforts to speak clearly radio announcers sometimes use such pronunciations as hi dɪdə, hi traɪdə tu rɑbə, etc.

48. The Glottal Stop. Since this is formed by the firmly closed glottis, it can only be voiceless and silent, though the transition sound before or after it can be either voiceless or voiced. Its presence is evident, like that of **p, t, k,** either by the sudden cutting off of the preceding sound or the explosive release and transition to a following sound, especially a vowel. This explosive release is heard in the common cough. In some languages it is a distinctive speech sound, as in Semitic, where it has a letter to spell it, and in Danish. It also occurs regularly in standard German before initial vowels of accented syllables, though not, except rarely, as a distinctive speech sound.[14]

Though not a distinctive speech sound nor of regular occurrence in English, the glottal stop occasionally occurs in both British and American standard speech. It is used before a vowel at the beginning of a word or syllable for special emphasis, as hiz ʔɔlwɪz let; ɪts ɪnǀʔædəkwɪt; in public speaking to give a staccato effect of clearness; and frequently to make an easy or clear transition from a final vowel to an initial one, as əǀmɛrɪkə ʔən fræns, edə ʔæn, etc., where speakers of some types of English are apt to insert an intrusive **r** (see §241).

In some local British dialects, as that of Glasgow, the glottal stop occurs regularly as a substitute for the stops, especially **t** and **d**, as in gɛʔ ɪʔ for gɛt ɪt, lɛʔər, for lɛtər, etc.

49. Combinations of Stops. When stops are followed by other stops, as in **ækt,** only the closure of the first and the opening, or release, of the second are heard. In **ækt** the tongue back and the velum come into contact, making the closure for **k,** and

[14] Cf. Prokosch, *Sounds and History of the German Language,* N. Y., 1916, p. 34, §36.

then before the tongue is released from the velum, the point makes contact with the teethridge for **t,** so that no release for **k** and no closure for **t** are heard, though they both occur silently. The tongue acts likewise but in reverse order in **tk** of **naɪtkæp.** Follow step by step the action of the lips and the tongue in the following **combinations of voiceless stops: æpt, nʌtpɪk, ʌpkip, rɑkpaɪl.** Do so likewise with these combinations of **voiced with voiced stops: sɑbd, rɛdbɜd, hɛdgɪr, bægdæd, rʌgbɪ, kræb græs.**

50. When a **voiceless stop** is followed by a **voiced stop,** as **pd** in **læp dɔg,** we likewise hear only the closure of the first (**p**) and the release of the second (**d**), but in this case the voice begins somewhere in the second stop (sometimes just at the release). Follow the process in **ˈʌpˈgred, sɛtbæk, fæt gus, brɪkbæt, bæk dor.**

51. When **voiced stops** are followed by **voiceless,** the first closure and the second release only are heard, as in the preceding, but the voice sounds during the first, and then becomes silent at the beginning of the second, or a little after its closure. This may be observed in **bɑbtel, sʌbklæs, tædpol, mædkæp, mægpaɪ, wægtel.**

52. In the **homorganic stops,** voiceless+voiced (**pb, td, kg**) and voiced+voiceless (**bp, dt, gk**), the situation differs in that the speech organs of the mouth keep the same contact from the closure of the first to the release of the second, so that there is only **one closure and one release,** instead of the two closures and two releases of the foregoing groups, in which only one of each was heard. The voice begins or ceases in the midst, as in the other combinations of voiceless and voiced stops. Observe the examples **skræpbʊk, kɑb paɪp; aʊtˈdu, saɪdtræk; bækgraʊnd, dɔgkɑrt,** with lip contact, tongue-point contact, and tongue-back contact.

53. **Lengthened Consonants.** Consonants, like vowels, differ

in length in English. For example, the l of *build* bɪlːd is longer
than that of *built* bɪlt, m is longer in *dumb* dʌmː than in *dump*
dʌmp, and n is longer in *hens* hɛnːz than in *hence* hɛns. It is
likely that consonant length, like vowel length, differs in England and America. The subject is complicated and as yet little
investigated. Reliable results can come only from instrumental
experiment. Important work has been done by E. A. Meyer,
G. E. Fuhrken,[15] and others, chiefly for British speech, but much
remains to be discovered, especially in America. The length of
sounds not only in separate words, but in connected speech of
different styles and by different persons, needs investigation.
The subject is very important for dialect study and the history
of sound changes, but fortunately not so important for the
practical study of speech, in America, at least.

For it is doubtful whether length of consonants by itself is
ever distinctive in English. Possibly the length of n in *hens* hɛnz
is its chief acoustic difference from *hence* hɛns, for the final z
and s of these words are very much alike to the ear. Perhaps
if the word *hens* were pronounced with as short a n as in *hence*,
the two words would be confused, if they occurred in contexts
where confusion of meaning would be likely.

54. Doubled Consonants. Consonants represented by double
letters in present English are seldom double, except in words
joined in compounds and when contiguous in speech, and occasionally when prefixes or suffixes are added, as in *unknown*
ʌn-ˈnon, *wholly* hol-lɪ, *solely* sol-lɪ, *meanness* min-nɪs, etc. Most
words with **doubled letters but single sounds**, as *happy* hæpɪ,
little lɪtl̩, *follow* falo, are merely relics of a time in Middle English when the consonants were really long or double, being
shortened later with the old spelling retained.

---

[15] E. A. Meyer, *Englische Lautdauer*, Uppsala, 1903: G. E. Fuhrken, *Standard English Speech*, Cambridge (Eng.), 1932. See §76.

When **voiceless stops** are combined, as in *hoppole* **hɑp-pol,** *coattail* **kot-tel,** *bookcase* **bʊk-kes,** the lips or the tongue are in contact from the closure of the first consonant to the release of the second, with a moment of silence between. During this silence, after the closure and before the release, Stetson[16] has shown that there is a fall and then a rise in breath pressure due to a chest pulse which marks the division between the syllables and the beginning of a second consonant. The double is also made evident to the ear by the perceptible interval between the closure and the opening of the double consonant.

When the abutting consonants are **voiced stops,** as in *grab -bag* **græb-bæg,** *headdress* **hɛd-drɛs,** *big game* **bɪg-gem,** the voice usually continues from closure to release, with a slight weakening in the middle that likewise indicates the syllable boundary, followed by the pulse of the second consonant.

The situation is similar when **fricatives** or **sonorants** are combined, as in **hæf-fʊl, lɪv-vekənt, boθ-θɪŋz, wɪð-ðɪs, pɜs-strɪŋ, hɪz-zil, wɑʃ-ʃip, fil-laɪk, hom-med, pɛn-naɪf,** though the syllable division is not so sharp as with stops.

55. From the point of view of the continued contact of the lips or the tongue, such abutting consonants as in *coattail* **kot-tel** and the others are lengthened consonants; from the point of view of the syllable division with a chest pulse between the closure and the opening, they are double. Both points of view are suggested by doubling the symbol with a connecting hyphen between (**hɑp-pol,** etc.).

56. When the abutting consonants are **affricates,** which consist both of a contact and a fricative narrowing, both parts must

---

[16] R. H. Stetson, *Motor Phonetics* (in *Archives Néerlandaises de Phonétique Expérimentale*), La Haye, 1928, pp. 67 ff.

be repeated in order to retain the identity of the two consonants, which, if treated like the others, would become either **t-tʃ, d-dʒ** or **tʃ-ʃ, dʒ-ʒ**. Hence they are sounded as stop-fricative-stop-fricative, the tongue passing from the first stop position to the narrowed fricative position, and then to the second stop position without opening to the full open vowel position, as it does after the second fricative position; as in **dʌtʃ-tʃiz, dʒɔrdʒ-dʒonz**.

57. Consonants that do not end words, as **h** and the glides **w, hw, j, r,** and those that do not begin words, as **ŋ** and **ʒ** (except rarely), are not thus doubled. When such combinations occur as *how weak* **hau-wik**, *why yes* **waɪ-jɛs**, *far-reaching* **far-ritʃɪŋ**, we have the abutting of the final **nonsyllabic vowel** of a falling diphthong (**au, aɪ, ar**) with the initial **nonsyllabic glide consonant** of a rising one (**wi, jɛ, ri**). See §20.[17]

58. Doubled consonants are often **distinctive**, as in **aɪ du, aɪd-du; aɪ o nʌn, aɪ on-nʌn; aɪm aɪk, aɪm-maɪk**;[18] **tap ʌp, tap-pʌp; wɪð ə mæn, wɪð-ðə mæn; ʌn|emd, ʌn-|nemd**. Cf. also **ðɪs-sə faɪn de**. But such abutting double consonants do not show that consonant length is distinctive in English; for the consonants are not merely lengthened but are doubled; and it is rather the syllable division that is distinctive in the practical use of English. Syllabic and nonsyllabic consonants are distinctive for the same reason; as in *batlet* **bætlɪt** and *battle it* **bætl̩ ɪt**; *ordnance* **ɔrdnəns** and *ordinance* **ɔrdn̩əns**; *Stop, Mike!* **stap maɪk** and *Stop 'em, Ikel* **stap m̩ aɪk**. The difference is perceived by the extra syllable, though it is true that length of the consonant (not doubleness) is the cause of the syllabicness. The same consonants (but not in the same environment) can, however, be

---

[17] The word *diphthong* is used in this book to include such consonant-vowel combinations as **wa, ja, ju, ra,** etc.

[18] Stetson, p. 67.

long without being syllabic, as in **fɪlɪ, fɪdl̩; bʌnɪ, bʌtn̩;** *Ohm*
omɪ, opm̩.

When it does not give a wrong meaning, doubled consonants
are often made single, as **pɛnaɪf, ˌɪməˈtɪrɪəl, ɪnet;** and in *wholly*,
often pronounced **holɪ** in spite of the homophone *holy* **holɪ,** the
latter not being often used in the same situation in the sentence.

59. Vowels and Consonants. The key to the meaning of
vowel[19] as formed by the speech organs is **shape,** and as heard
by the ear, free **tone** of a certain **resonance.**[20] The key to the
meaning of **consonant** is, organically, **contact or narrowing** and
acoustically, **dampening of sound.** The dampened sound may
vary from a sonorous sound almost as full as a vowel to complete silence. The shape of the whole mouth and throat cavity
is significant for the vowel; for the consonant the determining
(though not the exclusive) feature is contact or opposition of
some particular parts of the speech apparatus, as lips, teeth,
tongue, palate, velum, glottis. Vowels and consonants have
many features in common. It is the predominating features that
are significant for each class by itself. These predominating
features determine the practical use of the vowel and consonant
sounds in actual speech.

60. A vowel is a form of **musical tone.** A voice tone is a com-
plex of sets of regular vibrations of the vocal cords of different
rapidity, or frequencies. These consist of a **fundamental** and of
overtones. The fundamental is the lowest-pitched set of regular
vibrations (lowest frequency) in the tone, and the overtones
(partials) are several sets of vibrations of higher pitch (greater
frequency) in harmony with the fundamental. The mouth and

---

[19] The definitions of vowel and consonant are based on the author's type of
General American.

[20] The term *resonance* is here used, not in its general sense of resounding
power or sonorousness, but in its technical sense of specific tone quality, as
defined above.

throat cavity as shaped for each particular vowel has, like any cavity, a certain **natural resonance,** or "echo." If one hums a tune in an empty room, one of the notes "rings in one's ears." This is the note having the pitch that agrees with the natural resonance of the room. In a similar manner the mouth cavity, shaped with the aid of the tongue and lips for a given vowel, **reinforces those partials** of the voice tone which best fit its particular shape. This gives the resonance of the vowel, the characteristic **quality** that identifies it. For some vowels the mouth and throat are divided by the tongue into two connected compartments, each with its characteristic resonance. Such vowels then have a double characteristic, or resonance.

61. The fundamental tone may be changed in key (pitch), but the mouth cavity, shaped for the same vowel, will still select and reinforce partial tones of the same frequency as before. Hence the same vowel may be sung on different pitches (fundamentals). Whispering the vowel (substituting glottal friction for voice) reveals the characteristic resonance of the mouth shape for that same vowel without the fundamental and partial vibrations of the vocal cords. Hence a vowel can be whispered on only one pitch.[21]

62. A **consonant** depends for its identification, not upon the shape of the resonance cavity, but chiefly on **contact or narrowing** of the speech organs. We know when we are making a vowel chiefly by the shape of the mouth and the resulting resonance, which we know how to make, if not to describe. We are aware of pronouncing consonants chiefly by the sensations of contact or narrowing of particular speech organs, as the lips, the tongue against the teeth or approaching the teethridge or velum, etc. The consonants vary more in variety of sound than the vowels.

---

[21] There are slight variations, within limits, of the characteristic pitches of the different vowels. The above explanation in the main follows the findings of Dayton C. Miller (*The Science of Musical Sounds*, N. Y., 1926).

In the first group, the **stops,** the contacts of lips or tongue and velum make complete closure of the breath passage. In the second group, the **fricatives,** there is either contact together with friction (**f, v, θ, ð**) or narrowing with friction (**s, z, ʃ, ʒ**); in the **affricates** (**tʃ, dʒ**) there are both. In the **sonorants m, n, ŋ,** there is lip or tongue contact together with open velum, and in **l** there is tongue contact with closed velum. The sonorants are the most sonorous of the consonants, and are hence often syllabic (see §87); for this reason they have sometimes been falsely called vowels. Contact, not tone quality, is the essential of their formation (see §63).

63. With the **gliding consonants w, j,** and **r** (**ret, brɛd**) the situation is modified but the same at bottom. These consonants result from an immediate rapid movement of the lips and tongue, or tongue alone, from the positions for the vowels **u, i, ɜ** to a following vowel (see §29). If the voice is uttered while the lips and tongue are held fixed for a perceptible moment in the vowel position, the vowel **u, i,** or **ɜ** is heard. Though the lips are narrowed or the tongue approaches the palate or the velum, yet this is not significant, but incidental to forming the shape for the vowel resonance, which is the predominating feature; but if the lips and tongue immediately move toward a following vowel, the perception of this vowel resonance is prevented, and the sense of narrowing—considerably enhanced by the quick movement—becomes dominant, and we have a consonant **w, j,** or **r.**[22] The difference in feeling at the lips or the tongue is very obvious on comparing the utterance of **u, i,** or **ɜ** with that of **w, j,** or **r.** The close relation of these three vowels to the corresponding consonants, the nearly even balance of the features of resonance and narrowing, is suggested by the name **semivowels** often used of **w** and **j.** But **w, j,** and prevocal **r** are not

[22] Compare the difference in muscular sensation in bending the elbow slowly and then with a jerk.

half vowel and half consonant; they are true consonants, and **u, i, ɜ** are true vowels, for the reasons given. Walker (1791) pointed out that the sounds **w** and **j** were treated popularly as consonants in actual unconscious speech by the use of the indefinite article ə (ə wɔk, ə jok). Likewise today the definite article ðə and the preposition tə are used (ðə wɔk, ðə jok, tə wɔr, tə jʊrəp) as before other words beginning with consonants. But ən, ðɪ, and tʊ are used before **u, i,** and ɜ (ən uzɪŋ sprɪŋ, ðɪ ist, tʊ ɜdʒ, etc.).[23]

64. Resonance form of the mouth cavity is thus the key to the **vowel,** and **contact or narrowing** the key to the **consonant.** But many consonants also show distinct resonance, while they remain consonants; as the voiced consonants, and especially the sonorants **m, n, ŋ, l.** The consonant **l** has very marked resonance quality; **l** sounds can be made that by their tone quality suggest all the different vowels. But the tone quality is not the identifying feature; it is only incidental. None of its various resonances changes **l** into any vowel. It is the point contact and lateral opening of the tongue, with closed velum, that makes and keeps it **l.** Likewise some vowels also have marked contact or narrowing. The contact of the tongue for **i** may be greater than that for **l,** as shown by palatograms,[24] or by rapidly breathing these sounds. But it is not the contact that identifies **i;** it is its tone quality. So the vowel **u** has close narrowing of the lips; but this is likewise incidental to the formation of the cavity for the characteristic resonance of **u.**[25]

---

[23] ðə is sometimes assimilated to ðɪ before **j** (ðɪ jɑrd), and tə to tʊ before **w** (tʊ wɔr); but ə, ðə, and tə otherwise remain unchanged before **w** and **j.**

[24] Cf. Daniel Jones, *Outline of Phonetics,* 3d ed., 1932, pp. 64 and 161, Fig. 85.

[25] For some of the foregoing ideas about vowels and consonants I am indebted to Jörgen Forchhammer (see Bibliography). But some of my conclusions disagree with his.

65. In studying the vowels it is important to get a clear idea of the **positions of the tongue,** especially its position forward or backward, and its height up or down as determined in part by the raising or lowering of the jaw.

Pronounce **i** (*beet*) with the finger held lightly against the tip of the tongue. Then sound **u** (*pool*). The tip of the tongue has receded, and the back of it is raised up in the back of the mouth toward the velum. With reference to these positions of the tongue, then, **i** is a **front vowel** and **u** a **back vowel.** Try the same with the pairs **e** (*bait*)—**o** (*coat*), and **æ** (*bat*)—**ɑ** (*ah*), and it will be evident that **e** is front and **o** back, **æ** is front and **ɑ** back, though the tip of the tongue has receded less from **æ** to **ɑ** than it did from **i** to **u.**

66. Brace the thumb and finger under the bone of the jaw so as to feel any upward or downward movement, and also with a mirror watch the amount of space between the front upper and lower teeth. Then pronounce in succession the vowels **i** (*beet*), **e** (*bait*), **æ** (*bat*). For **i** the jaw is nearly closed, but it drops a little for **e,** and a little lower for **æ.** The body of the tongue goes down with the jaw, the point of it remains on or near the lower front teeth, and for each vowel in turn the front of the tongue is less elevated toward the hard palate. Repeat the experiment till this becomes entirely clear.

67. Of the front vowels, then, **i** is **high-front, e** is **mid-front,** and **æ low-front.** Now try the same for the back vowels **u** (*pool*), **o** (*coat*), **ɑ** (*ah*), and it will be seen that **u** is **high-back, o mid-back,** and **ɑ low-back.** The lips will hide the teeth and the back of the tongue for **u,** but a small flashlight will show that the back of the tongue is high toward the velum for **u,** and successively lower for **o** and for **ɑ.** The back of the tongue is lower than the front is for **i,** and lower for **ɑ** than the front is for **æ** Fig. 9, p. 61. Verify these six tongue positions with the thumb and finger on the jaw as before by pronouncing in succession the

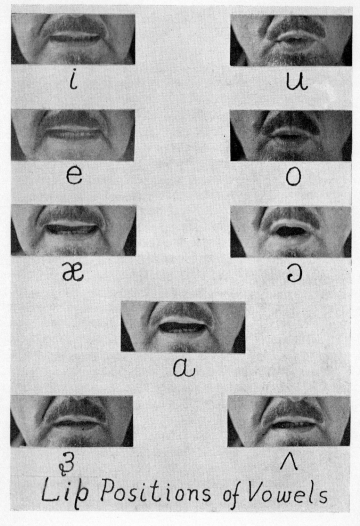

Lip Positions of Vowels

Fig. 8.

pairs **i—u, e—o, æ—ɑ,** observing within each pair the backward movement of the tongue, and the successive lowering of the jaw for the second and third pairs.

68. Watch the separation of the teeth while pronouncing alternately **i** (*beet*) and **ı** (*bit*). The teeth are slightly farther apart for **ı** than for **i.** Hold the butt of a pencil between the front teeth, not inserted far enough to interfere with the tongue. It will be found possible to sound **ı** after **i** without lowering the jaw. In this case the top of the tongue is lowered and retracted a trifle for sounding **ı.** The same may be tried for **e** and **ɛ,** and for **u** and **ʊ,** with a similar result. With some speakers the tongue is tenser for **i, e, u** than for **ı, ɛ, ʊ,** respectively, and some phoneticians regard this as the important difference between them. The difference in tenseness is less certain for the lower vowels. No English vowels are so tense as some of the French and German vowels, and the present author does not regard the distinction by tenseness and laxness as being so important as the difference in the height of the tongue.

69. Pronounce before a mirror the series **u, ʊ, o, ɔ, ɑ** (the back vowels from the highest downward); and **æ, ɛ, e, ı, i** (the front vowels from the lowest upward). For **u** the lips will be seen to be closely **rounded and closed at the edges,** and successively less until for **ɑ** they are **wide open** up and down and **spread to the corners.** Then beginning with **æ** they remain **spread laterally** while they approach each other vertically a little more for each of the front vowels from **æ** to **i.** In English only the back vowels (except **ɑ**) are rounded. The rounding is less marked in familiar connected speech than in sounding isolated vowels and separate words for experiment. It is usually somewhat less in American than in British speech, being often little more than compression of the lips at the corners.[26]

[26] Bloomfield's statement (*Language*, N. Y., 1933, p. 105) that "Different positions of the lips play no part in American English vowels, except for one minor fact [w?]," is somewhat extreme.

None of our front vowels are now rounded, though in Old English and Middle English there were high-front rounded and mid-front rounded vowels that have since been unrounded.[27] Other languages, as German and French, also have front rounded vowels. It is good practice to learn to shape the lips independently of the position of the tongue; as to sound **u** and then without moving the lips from the **u** position try to sound **i**; or to sound **o** and with the lips kept in the **o** position try to sound **e**; or to sound **ɔ** and with the same lip position sound **æ**. These efforts should result in making the high-front-round **y** as in German *kühn* **kyɪn**, or French *dur* **dyɪr**; and the mid-front-round **ø**, as in G. *tönen* **tøɪnən**, or Fr. *peu* **pø**; and the low-front rounded **œ**, as in G. *Völker* **fœlkər**, or Fr. *peur* **pœɪr**. Likewise it is instructive to practice pronouncing the higher back vowels unrounded by holding the lips fixed after sounding **i** and trying to sound **u**; or after **e**, and trying to sound **o**, etc. Some languages (as Indo-Chinese) have such unrounded back vowels.

70. Pronounce **æ** and **ɑ**, and then watch the tongue while trying to stop it halfway back from **æ** to **ɑ**. This gives the **low-central** tongue position. Do the same for **e** and **o**, using for a halfway station the last sound in *sofa* **sofə**. This gives the **mid-central** tongue position.

71. The tongue and lip position for each vowel can thus be indicated by the proper combination of descriptive terms, as **high-front, mid-back-round,** etc. The terms **advanced** and **retracted** may be added for minor variations forward and backward from the main positions, and the terms **raised** and **lowered** for minor variations up and down from them. The following are the designations of the American vowels:

i high-front (hf)	**u** high-back-round (hbr)
ɪ lower high-front (lhf)	**ʊ** lower high-back-round (lhbr)

---

[27] The word *busy* contained the high-front rounded vowel that has since become an unrounded **ɪ**, but the spelling *u* came from the time when it was rounded.

e higher mid-front (hmf)	3, ɘ, ɜ, ə mid-central (mc)	o mid-back-round (mbr)
ɛ lower mid-front (lmf)	ʌ lower mid-central retracted (lmcr)	ɔ higher low-back-round (hlbr)
æ low-front (lf)	a low-central advanced (lca)	ɒ low-back-round (lbr)
		ɑ low-back (lb)

72. In these descriptions it is the position of the highest part of the tongue that is designated, since that is most important for the vowel because it serves to divide the mouth cavity. Notice, e.g., that it is possible to alternate æ and ɑ with the point of the tongue resting on the backs of the lower teeth for both; but the front is raised for æ, and the back (though less) for ɑ.

73. The scientific value of the designation of vowels by tongue position has been questioned. Its uniformity among different speakers of the same dialect has no doubt been exaggerated. Some phoneticians have gained such skill in observing their own tongue positions that they can perceive very slight changes in their vowels by the change of tongue position. Such skill is very valuable for its possessor. But evidence is yet lacking that all speakers of a language pronounce the same vowels with the same tongue positions, and the value of elaborate schemes for indicating tongue positions with mathematical precision may perhaps be doubted. Even x-ray photography does not show uniform results, though excellent technique has been developed for making uniform measurements.[28] On seeing an x-ray photograph of the vowel ɑ, e.g., one may well ask "Whose ɑ,[29] and what ɑ?" There are many different ɑ sounds any one of which would make the word *father* quite intelligible.

---

[28] Cf. C. E. Parmenter, S. N. Trevino, and C. A. Bevans, *A Technique for Radiographing the Organs of Speech during Articulation, Zeitschrift für Experimental-Phonetik*, Leipzig, July, 1931, Band I, Heft 2.

[29] The usual biography of the subject does not answer this question; one must hear him talk.

74. There are other factors than the tongue that enter into the production of the required vocal cavity for a vowel. Mouths are not all shaped alike, and compensating adjustments are made by the walls of the pharynx, by the cheeks, and possibly even by the vocal cords.[30] Yet tongue position is the best means yet discovered for convenient description of the vowels. Of its essential validity there is little doubt. It accounts better than anything else for many vowel changes that have occurred in various languages, and if interpreted with moderation and caution, there is no doubt of its usefulness.

75. The chart (Fig. 9, p. 61) of the tongue positions of the vowels (those of the author except ɜ and ɒ) is intended to represent only approximately the relative positions of the tongue for the different vowels. Its irregular shape is designed to suggest only roughly the successive retraction of the tongue from the high-front to the low-front and low-back vowels, and to show the somewhat larger range of differences in mouth opening for the front vowels than for the back vowels. The left side of the chart represents the front of the mouth of a person facing the left.[31]

76. Vowel Quantity. In phonetics quantity (length or short-

[30] The possibility of such compensating adjustments is shown by the fact that, with a pencil butt inserted between the teeth to hold the jaw rigid, all the vowels can be pronounced recognizably.

[31] The relative nearness of e to ɪ and of o to ʊ, also confirmed by Parmenter and Trevino (*Vowel Positions as Shown by X-rays, Quarterly Journal of Speech,* June, 1932), has important bearings on the historical development of these sounds. For example, ME ɪ when lengthened often became eː and ʊ became oː. A result of this is seen in the present double pronunciation of *creek* as krɪk and krik. Cf. also the variation in the pronunciation of *poor* as pʊə and poə, found in standard British and American. Their close similarity is also suggested by Latin ʊ becoming Italian o (L. **multum,** It. **molto**), and by Germanic ʊ becoming OE o (cf. Gothic **gulþ** with cognate OE **gold**). The author recalls a classroom remark by Professor Edward S. Sheldon of Harvard: "If you prolong ɪ, you may be surprised to find how much it is like eː."

ness) means duration only, and must not be confused with the traditional unscientific distinction such as that between so-called "short *a*" in *sand* and "long *a*" in *late*. The vowels in these two words, though both spelt with the letter *a*, are actually different vowels, one being **æ** and the other **e**. They differ in **quality**—the way they sound to the ear—which is due to the difference in position of the vocal organs. But in **quantity**, or

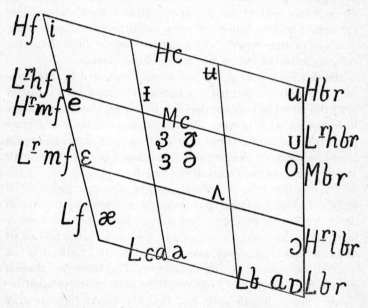

FIG. 9.—Chart of the Tongue Positions for the Vowels.

Hf =High-front	Hc =High-central	Hbr =High-back-round
Lʳhf =Lower high-front		Lʳhbr =Lower high-back-round
Hʳmf =Higher mid-front	Mc =Mid-central	Mbr =Mid-back-round
Lʳmf =Lower mid-front		Hʳlbr =Higher low-back-round
Lf =Low-front	Lca =Low-central	Lbr =Low-back-round
	advanced	Lb =Low-back

length, the "short *a*" in *sand* is actually longer than the "long *a*" in *late*.

The subject of vowel quantity is not yet fully understood. Interesting and valuable facts are presented by E. A. Meyer,[32] Otto Jespersen,[33] and C. H. Grandgent[34]—the first two for British English and the third for American, which differs somewhat in laws of quantity. Professor Grandgent distinguishes four degrees of vowel length; namely, short, half-long, long, and overlong. These terms refer to the relative lengths of vowels uttered by the same speaker under the same conditions, not to absolute duration or time-length, which depends on rapidity of speech, differing with the habits and mood of the speaker.

In this book quantity is not usually indicated in transcriptions. When it is indicated, the International symbol ˑ is placed after the vowel to indicate that it is half-long, and the symbol ː, to indicate that it is long. The combination of the two ːˑ may be used to indicate a vowel that is overlong. Unmarked vowels are to be regarded as short when mentioned in connection with other vowels that are marked for length.

Only a few laws of vowel quantity are here given, since length of vowels, as also of consonants, is seldom distinctive in American English; there are few pairs of words that differ solely in length of the vowel.[35] For example, the words *seat* **sit** and *sit* **sɪt** differ in quality of vowel, and if they differ in length, it is not noticed, because it is not distinctive. The following should, however, be mastered. Note carefully that the signs used indicate relative length only; i.e., that the marks indicate only that the vowels in question are longer or shorter than those mentioned in the same connection. Thus vowels with similar marks may have different absolute lengths.

---

[32] *Englische Lautdauer*, Uppsala & Leipzig, 1903.

[33] *Grammar*, I. (Heidelberg, 1909), §§16.31 ff.

[34] *Die Neueren Sprachen*, II, 463 ff. (1895).

[35] See *PDAE*, §55.

1. The same vowel, if stressed, is **longer when final** or **before a voiced consonant** than it is **before a voiceless consonant:**

siː, siːd—sit   **sɛːd—sɛt**

2. The same vowel, if stressed, is **longer when final** or **before a final consonant** than it is when **followed by an unaccented syllable:**

steː, steːd—ste ɪŋ   **koˑt—ko tɪŋ**

3. The same vowel, if stressed, is **longer when followed by a sonorant** m, n, ŋ, l+a voiced consonant than it is when followed by the **sonorant+a voiceless consonant:**

θʌːmd—θʌmpt   **peːnd—pent**
briːŋz—brɪŋk   **wɔːlz—wɔlts**

4. The same vowel becomes **longer or shorter** as its **stress is increased or decreased:**

ˈdaɪː—ˌdaɪˈɔgˈnosɪs—   **ˈnoːtəbļ—ˌnoˈtəˈbɪlətɪ—**
**   daɪˈægənəl**   **noˈteʃən**

The low-front vowel æ, commonly called "short *a*" (*hat*), and the low-back ɑ, which in General American usually replaces "short *o*" (*hot*), are particularly subject to lengthening under stress. Such words as *sat*, *had*, *lot*, *odd*, when stressed, often have fully long æː and ɑː, respectively. Professor Daniel Jones mentions the lengthening of æ in Southern British speech.[36]

For fuller treatment of vowel length in American English, see *Webster's New International Dictionary, Second Edition*, 1934, *Guide to Pronunciation*, §49.

77. Speech Sounds and Transition Sounds. In living language the speech sounds do not occur separately, but in continuous flow of sound from pause to pause. Thus in the phrase *the most of the book* ðə most əv ðə bʊk there are thirteen suc-

---

[36] *Outline of English Phonetics*, N. Y., 1932, p. 218.

cessive **speech sounds,** each here represented by a phonetic symbol. But there is no break in utterance between them, not even between the words. For each of these speech sounds the speech organs are momentarily in a definite position. But the speech sounds are not the only physical sounds in the group. As the speech organs leave the sound ð in passing to the sound ə, they pass through many intermediate positions, the organs sounding all the time with a continuously changing sound. And so with every two successive speech sounds in the phrase. There are a very great number and variety of these intermediate sounds— depending on the different possible combinations of speech sounds in actual speech. These are called **transition sounds,** or glides, the one leading up to a speech sound being the **on-glide,** and that leading away from it the **off-glide.** So most transition sounds between two speech sounds consist of an off-glide continuing into an on-glide. In some cases the glides are inaudible (see §§49 ff.), but between every two different speech sounds there is invariably an organic glide—a change in position of some speech organ.

78. It is the speech sound that is **significant** in the practical use of language; that is, it serves to identify or distinguish meanings. Thus in the word *till* tɪl there is a very noticeable off-glide after the **t**—a puff of breath (**aspiration**). This, however, is not an essential part of the speech sound **t;** it is much less noticeable in the word *still* stɪl, and entirely absent in *outdo* aʊtdu; but the sound **t,** in the actual use of speech, is the same speech sound in English in all three cases. That is why we notice and recognize the speech sounds: they are employed to identify or to distinguish words (as *till* from *fill, sill, bill,* etc.), while we ignore the transition sounds because they are not significant. But in some other languages (as Chinese) the **t** with the puff of breath and the **t** without it are two different speech sounds, distinguishing from one another words otherwise alike. In such languages the aspiration is a necessary part of the sound.

A transition sound may sometimes be identical with a significant speech sound. Thus *going* **goɪŋ** is often pronounced **go-wɪŋ** with a transition sound **w**. But though identical with the speech sound **w** in *wide* **waɪd,** where it is significant and therefore necessary, in **go(w)ɪŋ** it is nonsignificant and unnecessary.

79. The Phoneme. Above, the term "the same speech sound" applies to a group of slightly varying sounds of **t** that are apprehended by speakers and hearers as the same sound **t.** In the word *till* mentioned above, the aspirated off-glide of **t** affects the auditory impression made by the **t** on a carefully attentive ear. The difference heard between that **t** and the unaspirated **t** in *outdo* is a result of slightly different actions of the speech organs. Other different organic actions also vary the often unconscious effect of the same speech sound. For example, the sound of **k** varies from that in *keep* **kip,** *seek* **sik,** to that in *cot* **kɑt,** *lock* **lɑk,** and to that in *cool* **kul,** *spook* **spuk,** as the back of the tongue touches the roof of the mouth farther and farther back, being attracted by its positions for making the adjacent vowels **i, ɑ,** and **u.** Similarly a difference can be heard between the intervocal **z** in *lazy* and the final one in *adz* (§43). For each of these slightly different varieties of **t,** of **k,** and of **z,** there is a definite position and action of some speech organs. A sound in speech made by such a definite action of speech organs is called a **phone.** Thus there are three different phones of the **k** sound in *keep* **kip,** *cot* **kɑt,** and *cool* **kul,** or in *seek* **sik,** *lock* **lɑk,** and *spook* **spuk.** Likewise there are five different phones of the **l** sound in *lit, feel, play, filth, failure.* All **l** phones have the tongue point in contact on or near the teethridge. But in addition, **l** in **lɪt** has the front of the tongue (Fig. 2, p. 34) near the hard palate; **l** in **fil** has the back of the tongue raised toward the velum; **l** in **ple** is partly devoiced; **l** in **fɪlθ** has the point in contact nearer the teeth (where **θ** is formed); **l** in **feljɚ** has the point in contact nearer the hard palate (where **j** is formed). By careful attention these differences can be heard. Yet in actual use of spoken

English these phonically different sounds are all "the same sound" t, k, z, or l. The phones in each group differ among themselves according to phonetic surroundings or conditions, as preceding or following sounds, or to other varying conditions of utterance such as stress, pitch, length, syllable division, etc.

Such a group, or class, of related, similar phones varying according to changing phonetic surroundings or conditions is called a **phoneme.** When, for example, we speak of the l phoneme, we refer, not to a single phone, but to all the phonic varieties of l sound in the language of a single speaker or in a uniform dialect. These slightly different phones that make up a phoneme are called **allophones.** Thus the different varieties of l heard in the words *lit, feel, play, filth, failure* are allophones of the l phoneme.

80. We have seen (§78), in considering the relation of transition sounds to speech sounds, that some sounds made by the speech organs are distinctive and others are not.[37] This fact is of great importance in understanding the nature and function of the phoneme, and calls for further illustration. For instance, *sink* sɪŋk and *zinc* zɪŋk differ only by s and z; hence s and z are mutually distinctive sounds in present English: they are the sole distinction between sɪŋk and zɪŋk.[38] So *ink* ɪŋk becomes sɪŋk by adding s, or sɪŋk becomes ɪŋk by omitting s, which is

[37] The elementary student is cautioned not to confuse the word *distinctive* with *distinct*. *Distinctive* here means 'serving to distinguish.'

[38] In King Alfred's English z was not mutually distinctive with s; it was only a nondistinctive variety of s occurring between voiced sounds. Such pairs as *sink—zinc* could not then exist. Hence only the letter s was used to spell the two sounds, which belonged to the same phoneme. The same was true of the sounds and spelling of f and v. Since that time z and v have become distinctive speech sounds. The same is true of ŋ in *sing*. Till Early Modern English it was only a nondistinctive variety of n occurring before k and g sounds. When the g sound was dropped from *sing* (i.e., when sɪŋg became sɪŋ) then ŋ became distinctive and a separate phoneme. In Italian and Spanish ŋ is still a nondistinctive variety of n occurring only before k or g. See §218 (1).

therefore a distinctive sound. Or *sing* sɪŋ becomes *sink* sɪŋk by adding **k**, and vice versa; hence **k** is distinctive. Or lɪt becomes kɪt by replacing **l** with **k**; hence **l** and **k** are mutually distinctive. So we say that **s, z, k, l** are different phonemes.

81. But no word containing one of the allophones of **l** shown in the five words above will be changed in meaning to another word by substituting another allophone of **l**. Thus if the variety of **l** heard in lɪt is pronounced in *feel* **fil,** though it may produce an old-style elocutionary effect, it will not change *feel* to another word. Or if the kind of **l** in *filth* fɪlθ is pronounced in *feel* **fil,** though the result may resemble French *fil* (with dental **l** instead of English alveolar **l**), the word will still be *feel* in English. The practical reason why substitution of one allophone for another allophone of the same phoneme does not change one word to another is, that such allophones, though phonically different, are apprehended by the users of English as "the same sound." Only allophones of different phonemes can change meanings, for to the user of spoken English they alone are "different sounds."

So we say that the differences among the varieties of **l** shown above are not phonemic—are not members of different phonemes. But **p** and **b,** for example, though identical in two essential organic features out of three (§29), belong to different phonemes, the difference (voicing) being distinctive, or phonemic, in English, as in *peg* and *beg*. In some languages, however, **p** and **b** are merely allophones of the same phoneme and cannot distinguish words as they do in English.

82. Though we sometimes say, without serious confusion, that, for example, the **l** in lɪt and the **k** in kɪt are different phonemes, strictly we mean that the **l** and the **k** are allophones of different phonemes. For it is to be remembered that a phoneme is not a single sound with invariable organic formation, but is a group, or class, of similar, related allophones commonly regarded as one sound and by the literate usually spelt with the same or equivalent letter. In this connection *similar*, or *related*, sounds are those that have in common one or more organic formations not made in any other phoneme. Thus the five varieties of l shown above all have in common (1) contact of the point of the tongue on or near the teethridge, combined with (2) an opening at one or both sides of the tongue for the free expulsion of breath through the mouth, and (3) the raised velum, closing the passage through the nose—a combination of organic formations found only in the l phoneme, and identifying it to the ear.[39] For the vowel phonemes the chief determining organic formations are the positions of the tongue with the resulting shapes of the oral cavities. See above, §§59–61.

83. In the actual use of English one easily observed function of the phoneme is to contrast with other phonemes, or their absence, in words otherwise identical, thus distinguishing their meanings. For example, the l in lɪt contrasts with the k in kɪt, with the w in wɪt, or with the absence of a contrasting sound in ɪt; the s in sɪŋk contrasts with the z in zɪŋk, or with the absence of a sound in ɪŋk; the t and the d in ɪn|tɛnd contrast, respectively, with the d and the t in ɪn|dɛnt; the æ in læðɚ contrasts with the ɛ in lɛðɚ; the ɑ in fɑrm with the ɔ in fɔrm; the ʊ in pʊl with the u in pul; and so on. Phonemes (groups or classes of allophones), however, contrast with one another in more complicated situations than in words otherwise identical; and in general we may say that the function of phonemes is to help distinguish the meanings of words, and their ability to do this is one of the chief tests of whether two sounds of speech are different phonemes.

---

[39] Some writers on the phoneme have neglected to define the otherwise vague, unscientific terms *similar* and *related*. This defect is remedied by Bernard Bloch and George L. Trager, *Outline of Linguistic Analysis*, Baltimore, 1942, §3.1, pp. 38 ff.

84. In one class of words, however, the phoneme plays no part in distinguishing meanings between pairs of words; namely, in homophones[40]—words of different meanings pronounced alike, as *rite*, *right*, *write*, *wright*, and often spelt alike, as *bear* (n.) and *bear* (vb.). In these words, only context and circumstances show the intended meaning.[41] Such homophones seldom occur in contexts where their meanings would be likely to be confused. When two homophones do occur frequently in situations where their meanings might easily be confused, one of the two tends to disappear from common use. This is illustrated by the homophones *straight* (native English) and *strait* (from Old French; cf. *strict*, from Latin). In the phrase the *strait and narrow path* (cf. Matth. vii, 14: strait is the gate, and narrow is the way), many people unfamiliar with the Bible suppose that the word is *straight*; and *strait* is now only preserved in a few stereotyped phrases, as ˈstrait-ˈlaced, ˈstrait-ˌjacket, strait ʼnarrows.ʼ

Although, strictly, a phoneme is a group of variants (allophones) of a sound of speech as used by a single speaker, the symbols here used can represent with sufficient exactness the phonemes of most of the varieties of English which there is occasion to refer to. The general principle of such transcription as is used in this book is to use one symbol for each phoneme with all its allophones, and in the main this is carried out.

85. The phoneme principle warrants the use of the symbols **i** and **u,** and **e** and **o** in words like *beet*, *boot*; *made*, *mode*; for

[40] Also, less happily, called homonyms.

[41] It is quite possible that the importance of the difference in single speech sounds as a means of distinguishing words from one another has been overestimated, especially by students of the phoneme. When words do come to be sounded alike, it appears to give users of a language no difficulty, for we have no trouble with the numerous homophones of English (see Sir Robert Bridges, "On English Homophones," *Society for Pure English Tract No. 2*). Context and circumstances are the chief aids in understanding the meanings of words that sound at all alike.

although these sounds are of diphthongal ɪi, ʊu, eɪ (or ɛɪ, etc.), oʊ (ɔʊ, ɜʊ, etc.), yet in no case are the simple vowel and the diphthong mutually distinctive. No English word containing i, u, e, or o would be a different word if ɪi, ʊu, eɪ, or oʊ were substituted. Hence it is correct in principle to transcribe such words as *see, do, may, made, go, mode* as si, du, me, med, go, mod, even though these vowels are often diphthongal both in America and England. They are often not so in America, and sometimes not even in standard British.[42] So it must be remembered that such transcriptions as *rate,* ret, *made* med, *note* not, *rode* rod, etc., by no means imply that these words are pronounced only with the simple vowel rather than the diphthong (reɪt, meɪd, noʊt, roʊd, etc.). Of course, if a teacher wishes to show either the monophthongal or the diphthongal character of the vowels in specific cases, the symbols e, eɪ; o, oʊ; i, ɪi; u, ʊu are available, with specific explanation.

On the other hand, in recording dialects for historical or geographical study it is often of great importance to record as many nondistinctive variants as possible, since they often reveal linguistic facts and changes that would not appear in a strictly phonemic transcription, and would thus go unrecorded, though perhaps of great importance to the history of the language and the relations of dialects. For example, a phonemic transcription of American dialects would not record the variation in various isolated parts of the United States and Canada of the diphthongs aɪ and aʊ before voiceless and voiced sounds (since they all belong to one phoneme, respectively) which suggests interesting relations to Scottish speech and throws light on the historical development of the Middle English simple vowels iː and uː into the corresponding modern diphthongs aɪ and aʊ. As seen above (footnote 38) nondistinctive and transition sounds may become distinctive; hence for historical purposes it may be im-

---

[42] See Fuhrken, §§26, 74, 93 f.

portant to record them. The Eng. tʃ and dʒ sounds are instances in which the principal acoustic feature was once a mere off-glide, a transition sound that has now become distinctive and cannot be omitted without changing the sound to another phoneme. So it is convenient and useful to depart somewhat from a phonemic transcription to show, e.g., the frequent difference between standard American and British speech in the vowels e, o and eɪ (ɛɪ, etc.), ou (ɜu, etc.), or especially between the pronunciation of standard English in Scotland and in south England.

86. It is sometimes desirable to show nondistinctive differences in pronunciation, some of which may be differences between standard and substandard, or may be allowable variants worth knowing about. For example, some linguists consider that the syllabic consonants l̩, m̩, n̩ are members of the same phonemes, respectively, as əl, əm, ən. However this may be, it is true that they are not always interchangeable in good use. Such pronunciations as bætəl, lɪtəl, ædəl, fɪdəl, katən, nɪdənt, ʃudənt are not in general cultivated use. In the standard form of these and similar words the tongue does not leave the teethridge between t and l, d and l, t and n, d and n. Differences between standard and substandard speech are often nonphonemic. If one pronounced *little* with the two allophones of l exchanged, the result would be substandard and strange, though the word would remain *little*. Sometimes, however, the difference between n̩ and ən is phonemic. In regions where r is only sounded before a vowel, the word pronounced sætn̩ is *satin*, while that pronounced sætən is *Saturn*, and that pronounced bɪtn̩ is *bitten*, while that pronounced bɪtən is *bittern*.

Again, some linguists consider ʌ to be the same phoneme as ə, and ɜ the same phoneme as ɚ. But for transcribing such words as *pervert* (vb.) pɚˈvɜt, *pervert* (n.) ˈpɜvɚt (not riming with *Herbert* ˈhɜbɚt), *compurgation* ˌkampɜˈgeʃən or ˌkampɚˈgeʃən,

concert **kɑnsɜt** or **kɑnsɚt,** *hiccup* (*hiccough*) **hɪkəp** or **hɪkʌp,**
undone and done up **ʌnˈdʌn ən dʌn ʌp,** *walnut* **wɔlnət** or **wɔlnʌt**—
it seems more convenient to use the symbols ʌ and ə, ɜ and ɚ
than to show the different sounds by means of accent marks or
length signs. This is especially true of monosyllables that have
variant forms (fully illustrated in §137); as *some* **sʌm, səm;**
us **ʌs, əs;** *her* **hɜ, hɚ, ɚ,** in which the difference in vowel quality
is important to good speech, whether phonemic or not, and
must be presented to the student unmistakably.

For a strictly phonemic transcription of unstressed vowels,
I have not yet discovered any wholly consistent theory. However valuable for linguistic analysis, a system that writes
the same symbol in stressed and unstressed positions in teaching that aims to enlighten the student on current cultivated
pronunciation, tends directly to defeat one of the most necessary and difficult achievements—his understanding of vowel
and consonant gradation in its bearing on normal cultivated
speech. Every teacher knows that a major difficulty is to
lead the student to realize that the vowel in the last syllable
of *moment* is not phonically the same as in *mental*. A system of
transcription that declares to his eye that they *are* the same
creates the same obstacle to his understanding that is now
found in the ordinary alphabet.

It is, of course, idle to claim that a phonic system accurately
represents sounds. It does, however, serve to fix in the mind of
the student distinctions and resemblances between sounds he is
already familiar with, and so serves further to point out to him
variations and distinctions he had not before noticed.

I therefore continue for the present the use of the form of
the IPA alphabet found in this book. It is the best form of the
alphabet for American English that I have seen. It serves, with
no serious variation in the phonic values of the symbols, to
represent all the historical stages of English and all the dialects

of American and British English with sufficient accuracy to give the student an intelligent view of them.

87. The Syllable. In spelling, the division of words into syllables is conventional, and does not always correspond to the actual division made in speech. For the rules of syllable division in writing, see *Webster's New International Dictionary, Second Editio.* p. lviii.

According to the theory probably now most widely accepted, the division of words into syllables in actual speech depends upon the principle of **sonority** or degree of audibility, of speech sounds. Vowels are the most sonorous of the speech sounds, the sonorants **m, n, ŋ, l** are next, then the other voiced consonants, the voiceless fricatives, and least of all the voiceless stops, **p, t, k,** which, apart from their on-glides and off-glides, have no sonority at all. The phonetic center, or "peak" of a syllable is its point of greatest sonority.

Another theory is that the syllable is begun, and thus marked off, by a muscular pulse from the chest, or in some cases by the force of the consonant movement in the mouth. See §54, footnote 16. The two theories are perhaps not contradictory, the one dealing chiefly with the center of the syllable and the other with its boundaries.[43] In spite of the uncertainty as to the nature of the syllable, it is perhaps the most easily perceived unit of speech.

88. Usually a vowel is the center of a syllable, alone or with a consonant. But certain consonants, the sonorants **l, m, n, ŋ,** can form syllables, alone or with other consonants, without any vowel whatever, as in *cattle* **kæt-l̩,** *saddle* **sæd-l̩,** *open* **op-m̩,** *mob 'em* **mɑb-m̩,** *cotton* **kɑt-n̩,** *sudden* **sʌd-n̩,** *Jack and Gill* **dʒæk ŋ dʒɪl,** *crag and cliff* **kræg ŋ klɪf,** *settled* **sɛt-l̩d,** *handled* **hæn-dl̩d,** *battled* **bæt-l̩d.** If any vowel whatever, no matter how obscure

---

[43] For fuller discussion, see *Webster* (1934), *Pronunciation,* §59.

or short, intervenes, it becomes the syllabic sound, and the consonant is no longer syllabic.

No vowel can intervene if (1) the speech organs, the lips or the tongue, hold the same position from one consonant to the next, as in the above examples, the tongue point remaining on the teethridge for **tl̩, dl̩, tn̩, dn̩**; the lips remaining closed for **pm̩, bm̩,** and the tongue back remaining on the velum for **kŋ̩, gŋ̩.**

89. When the lips or tongue must change position from one of the consonants to the next, if (2) the opening is not made wider than for either of the consonants, the opening will be too narrow to form a vowel, and the second consonant will still be syllabic; as in *castle* **kæs-l̩,** *prison* **prɪz-n̩,** *chasm* **kæz-m̩,** *Jonathan* **dʒɑnəθ-n̩,** *mason* **me-sn̩.** Sometimes (3) the organs can reach the second position before the first is released, as in *maple* **me-pl̩,** *bubble* **bʌb-l̩,** in which the tongue point reaches the teethridge before the lips open from **p** or **b**; or in *buckle* **bʌk-l̩,** *straggle* **stræg-l̩,** in which the tongue point reaches the teethridge before the back leaves the velum; or in *slogan* **slo-gn̩,** *beacon* **bi-kn̩,** in which the same is true.

90. In the first class of cases, when the consonants are homorganic, if the contact is broken, a vowel **ə** or **ɪ** intervenes, as in *Boston* **bɔstən,** *London* **lʌndən,** *mountain* **mauntɪn.** Syllabic consonants are the rule in the first sort of cases. But in the other two classes, the opening for the transition may be wide enough, or the second position may not be reached till after the first, so that **ə** or **ɪ** is more likely to intervene and the second consonant cease to be syllabic. Such pronunciations are very common in these words, as **mesən, dʒɑnsən, mepəl, ɔfən, ivən, bekən, slogən.**

91. Observe that, in English, no consonants except the sonorants **m, n, ŋ, l** can be syllabic and only in unaccented syllables; and that these are syllabic only after certain consonants. Thus the nasals are not syllabic after nasals. Hence such transcriptions as kɑmn̩ for *common*, vɛnm̩ for *venom* are wrong; without a slight vowel, there would be but one syllable. In some cases, too, where a syllabic consonant is *possible* it is very unlikely, as in *bottom*, where the pronunciation bɑtm̩ would be unusual. When a sonorant l is syllabic after a nasal as in *channel* tʃænl̩, *trammel* træml̩, the nasal remains nonsyllabic if their order is reversed, as in *Milne* mɪln, *elm* ɛlm. Hence the contracted form *swoln* is pronounced either swoln̄ (one syllable), as in Milton, or swolən, not swoln̩. So too consonants are unlikely to be syllabic after vowels. Though it is possible by special effort to pronounce bærl̩, vaul̩, in ordinary speech they are bærəl, vauəl. Such words are often also monosyllabic (see further, §355). The combinations θm̩, ðm̩, sm̩, zm̩, as in *rhythm*, *prism* are not usual, though here the current spelling often leads to regarding these as syllabic. The usual pronunciation of these words is probably rɪθəm, rɪðəm, prɪzəm, blɑsəm, kæzəm, etc., as recognized by Hempl long ago.[44]

92. British practice differs in some words in regard to syllabic consonants from that in America. Words in *-tion* appear to be there more commonly pronounced with n̩ (neʃn̩, kən'dɪʃn̩, etc.) which in America usually have -ən (neʃən, kən'dɪʃən, etc.). So with vɪʒən, dɪ'sɪʒən, etc.

93. The boundary between two syllables may fall between two consonants, as in rɛd-nɪs, between two vowels, as in krɪ-ˈet, ɪndɪ-ən, or it may fall within a consonant, or be doubtful, as in hæ-p-ɪ. This uncertainty has sometimes led to the unconscious transfer of a sound from one word to another, as when *a norange* ə nɔrɪndʒ became ən ɔrɪndʒ, or ə nepɚn became ən epɚn; or vice versa, *an eke name* became *a nickname;* or Middle English *at ten Oakes* ɑt tən ɔːkəs "at the oaks," became *atte Noakes* ɑttə nɔːkəs "at Noakes," and then *Noakes* noks, a place in Hereford-

---

[44] Pierce. Cf. also Wyld, *Universal English Dictionary*, London, 1932.

shire. Likewise the ME *at ten Ash* became *atte Nash*, place name
and personal name (from the place name).

94. Assimilation. Assimilation is the phonetic process by
which one sound is made to resemble a neighboring sound. For
example the word *open* **opən** is often pronounced **opm̩**. Here **n**
is assimilated, or made like, to **p**; i.e., the tongue-point alveolar
nasal is changed into the lip nasal under the influence of the lip
sound **p**. In this case the combination **pm̩** is made with one
position of the lips, whereas **pən** or **pn̩** requires a position of the
lips followed by a position of the tongue. Thus there is a degree
of economy of effort in the assimilation of **n** to **p**.

95. All assimilation is based on the tendency of the organic
positions for one sound to become the same in part or entirely
as the organic positions for a neighboring sound. Thus when
opn̩ is changed to **opm̩**, the tongue-point alveolar closure, the
open velum, and the vibrating vocal cords of **n** change only to
lip closure, in conformity to the lip closure of the neighboring **p**,
retaining the open velum and vibrating vocal cords. This combination produces **m**. When **kɑnkwɛst** is changed to **kɑŋkwɛst**,
the tongue-point alveolar contact of **n**, with open velum and
vibrating cords, changes to tongue-back velar contact, in conformity to **k**, retaining the open velum and vibrating cords.
This combination produces **ŋ**. When the word *class* **klæs** is
(as often) pronounced **tlæs**, the tongue-back velar contact of **k**,
with closed velum and open (silent) vocal cords, is changed to
the tongue-point alveolar contact that the following **l** has, the
closed velum and open vocal cords being retained. This combination makes **t**. When ˈ**gus**ˌ**bɛrɪ** is changed to ˈ**guz**ˌ**bɛrɪ**, the
tongue-blade alveolar narrowing of **s**, its fricative sound of
breath, and its closed velum, are retained in **z**, but the open
vocal cords of **s** are changed to ˈthe vibrating vocal cords of
z in conformity to those of the voiced **b** (and also of the preceding vowel).

96. For brief descriptions of such assimilative changes, mention may be omitted of those organs that remain unchanged, and such an assimilation as the change from **klæs** to **tlæs** may be briefly described as the assimilation of a tongue-back velar **k** to the tongue-point alveolar **l**, which produces **t**. Then, since the vocal cords are independent of the oral speech organs, it is practically convenient to speak of the change of position in them as voicing or devoicing. Hence for practical description we may speak of two kinds of assimilation—**place assimilation** (opn to opm) and **voice assimilation** (ˈgusˌbɛrɪ to ˈguzˌbɛrɪ), though, strictly, all assimilation is place assimilation.

97. In the example opn—opm the position of the lips for **p** was continued, or carried forward, replacing the tongue-point position of **n** by the closed lips of **m**. Such effect of a preceding sound on a following one is called **progressive assimilation,** the second sound being assimilated (made like) *to* the first. On the other hand, when **grænpɑ** becomes, as usually, **græmpɑ,** the lip closure for **p** is anticipated and taken during the **n** or in place of it, thus putting **m** in place of **n**. Where a following sound is thus anticipated and changes a preceding one, the process is called **regressive assimilation.** In this case the first sound is assimilated *to* the second.

98. Frequently assimilation is only partial, as in opm, in which **n** becomes **m,** more like **p** than **n** is, but not identical with **p**. Complete assimilation is seen in the pronunciation ðɪʃ-ʃo for *this show*. But the distinction is not of great importance, as Jespersen has shown,[45] for the same change may be partial in one case and complete in another. Thus when **s** becomes ʃ in *this year* ðɪʃ jɪr, the likeness to **j** is partial; but the likeness to the following sound is complete in ðɪʃ-ʃo.

99. Some assimilations have become permanent, as the change of **d** to **t** in *looked* **lʊkt,** while others occur only occasion-

[45] *Lehrbuch,* p. 169.

ally, as in **opm̩ ð͡ə dor,** especially when they are the result of the occasional juxtaposition of sounds in varying groups of words, as in *meet you* **mitʃu** (cf. *meet me* **mit mɪ,** *saw you* **sɔ ju**).[46]

100. Assimilation applies to vowels as well as to consonants; but the principal influence of vowels is in voicing neighboring consonants, especially those between vowels (where the assimilation is both regressive and progressive). In the past, however, vowels have changed extensively by assimilation. The result of such a change is seen in *fill* beside *full*, the back vowel **ʊ** of older **fʊljan** being changed to front **ɪ** by front **j.**

101. Consonants that have changed by assimilation are sometimes lost later, but their former existence is often shown by the spelling, as in the place name *Defford* **dɛfəd,** formerly **dɛf-fərd,** *cupboard* **kʌbəd,** *raspberry* **ræzbɛrɪ.**

102. In the following examples explain the consonant assimilations shown in transcription, and where ordinary spelling is used, state what assimilations are usual in current colloquial speech. Show whether there is voice assimilation, or place assimilation, or both together; and explain the changes in the position of the speech organs for the place assimilations. The examples do not all belong to the same level of usage.

hæŋkətʃɪf, ˈræz͡ɪbɛrɪ, **græm-ma,** ˈbaɪmˈbaɪ, **hi jus tə du ɪt, hil hæf tə go,** *walked, chopped, wished, hissed, puffed, frothed, eighth,* **kʌp m̩ sɔsɚ, sɪˈdaʊn,** *husband* (housebond), *huzzy* (housewife), *cupboard, conquest, conquer, Concord* (Mass.), *gosling, Goswell* **gazwɛl,** *Gosbeck* **gazbɛk,** *East Riding* (from East Thriding = "third"), *blackguard* **blægard, blægɚd,** *clapboard* **klæbɚd,** *cats*

---

[46] Professor Daniel Jones distinguishes between **assimilation**—the change of a sound due to a neighboring sound, as in **opm̩**—and **similitude**—the permanent resemblance of certain neighboring sounds, as of the partly voiceless **l** to voiceless **p** in *please*. It is not possible to know in all cases whether the particular resemblance always existed, or was the result of assimilation at some time in the past. The organic principle appears to be the same in both.

(late Middle English kɑt-təz), *robes* (ME rɔːbəz), *ropes* (ME rɔːpəz), pʌŋkɪn (18th c. pumkin), ˈnɪʊsˌpepɚ, *I can go*, gɪm(m)ɪ əˈnʌðɚ, sɛbm̩, lɛbm̩, tlæs, dlæs, bæg ŋ bægɪdʒ, *wives, worthy* (cf. worth), *heathen* (cf. heath), aɪ don-no, aɪ domp bl̩ˈiv ɪt, *fippence* fɪpəns, hwɑdə jə wɑnt? dɪdʒʊ si ɪm? sɔrɪ tə mɪʃ ʃu, dʌʒ ʃɪ no ɪt? aɪʃt θɪŋk so, ʃʌtʃɚ aɪz, ɪt kæmp bɪ dʌn, ðɪʃ jɪr, læstʃɪr, sɪks mʌnts əgo, lɛs go! ju məʃ ʃo mɪ hɑʊ, æst tɑm, ðə sɛkənt taɪm, gʌvɚmənt, *wristband* rɪzbənd, ˈhɔrʃ ˌʃu, *he hit it* "*pime blank*," "*Saddy*" (Saturday), *vamp* (Fr. avant-pied), *count* (Lat. comitem), *tense* (L. tempus), *subscription* (cf. sub-scribe), *complete* (L. con-), *suppose, illegal, immense, oppose* (cf. obˈject), *announce* (cf. adopt), *Retford* (red ford), *Shefford* (sheep ford), *Defford* (deep ford), *Sampford* (sand ford), *Mitford* (mid(dle) ford), *Stafford* (ford situated at Stath), *Ratcliff* (red cliff), *Bedlam* (Bethlehem), *Suffield* (south field), *Sheffield* (York-shire—field on the river Sheath, now called the Sheaf), *Sheffield* (Sussex—sheep field), *Glenfield* (clean field), *Smithfield* (from ME smeːðə feld, smooth field), *Metfield* (mead(ow) field), *Sutton* (south town = "farm"), *Wootton, Wotton* wutn̩ (wood town), *Ditton* (dike town), *Pigdon* (pike down = "hill"), *Whaddon* (wheat down), *Shibden* (sheep den = "valley"), *Ogden* (oak den), *Debden* (deep den), *Brogborough* (brook borough), *Aggborough* (oak borough), *Sudbury* (south bury), *Suffolk* (south folk), *Waltham* wɔltəm (wald ham = "forest home"), *cobweb* (from *cop* = "spider"), *hobman blind*. A girl on the telephone gave a name that was heard as Bernie Skipson. What was her name? It was a common one. Explain the assimilations. For Dissimila-tion, see §243 and *PDAE*, §121.

103. Study of the foregoing list shows some assimilations that would be looked upon by many as careless, while others are in undoubted good use. The *tendency* to assimilation as a result of the various sound junctions that are made in daily speech is always present. The necessity of making ourselves understood, as well as a conservative desire not to "mispronounce," exercises a restraining influence on the tendency, and prevents many changes that would otherwise proceed more rapidly in the language, tending to obscure the identity of some words. Our attitude toward assimilations must be determined by judgment, by observation of the actual habits of people who are accepted as speaking well, and by a desire to speak clearly without being artificial. Too much avoidance of the common assimilations of current good usage, such as the insistence on **mit ju, dont ju, netjʊr, ˌɛdjuˈkeʃən,** instead of the normal **mitʃu, dontʃu, netʃɚ, ˌɛdʒəˈkeʃən,** is pedantic; while too liberal surrender to the tendency results in careless or slovenly utterance.

104. Stress in English may be defined as the **prominence** given in speech to a syllable or a word which makes it stand out to the attention above the syllables or words next to it. Stress, like quantity, is relative—not a fixed degree of prominence, but one greater or less than that of adjacent syllables. Stress may be of two kinds—**accent** and **sense-stress.** The term **accent** is used to indicate the stress given to a syllable above that of the preceding or the following syllable in a word of more than one syllable.[47] Thus in *going*, **go** is more prominent than ɪŋ, in *today*, **de** is more prominent than tə and in *invention*, vɛn is more prominent than ɪn and ʃən. The term **sense-stress** applies to the prominence given to a word over the preceding or following word in a group that makes sense. Thus in *I will do it now*, **aɪ, du,** and **naʊ** receive higher stress than wɪl and ɪt. Hence monosyllabic words, which by themselves have no accent, when joined in sense-groups—phrases, clauses, or sentences—take varying degrees of sense-stress, or none, according to the meaning expressed. When plurisyllables are so joined in sense-groups, they take sense-stress only on the syllables that would be accented if the words stood by themselves, so that accent and sense-stress coincide. Thus in the sentence *His father promised to reflect over it*, each of the words *father*, *promised*, *reflect*, and *over* takes a sense-stress on its accented syllable, that on *reflect* being the strongest, those on *father* and *promised* being next, and that on *over* being weaker.

105. The chief means of making a syllable or a word prom-

[47] A **Monosyllable** is a word of one syllable; a **Plurisyllable** is a word of more than one syllable. Plurisyllables of two syllables are called **Dissyllables,** of three syllables, **Trisyllables,** and of more than three, **Polysyllables.** Another term for *plurisyllable* is *pleiosyllable*. *Plurisyllable* is a hybrid of Latin and Greek, like *bicycle; pleiosyllable* is pure Greek, like *megalophonous*.

inent by accent or sense-stress is increased force of utterance, or loudness, caused in part by more forcible expulsion of air from the lungs through the vocal organs. But besides this, the prominence of a syllable is sometimes increased by lengthened duration of the syllable, and by changing the pitch of the voice.

The exact relations among force, time, and pitch as affecting stress are not yet known, but the ear in acquiring speech has learned to interpret the results of their combination in practice, so that, though we may not know, in such a word as *horseshoe*, ˈhɔrsˌʃu, whether pitch, force, or time is the most important in differentiating the two syllables, we all easily recognize in practice that the first syllable is more prominent than the second. In some syllables of nearly equal force, either pitch or time, or both, may help in producing a sense of difference in their relative prominence.

The same marks may be used to indicate sense-stress that are used for word accent, with the same relative values (see §13). There are, of course, more distinguishable degrees of stress than the four here recognized, but these are sufficient for most practical study of English pronunciation.[48]

106. Plurisyllables have at least one main stress, called **primary accent,** as in *beating* ˈbitɪŋ, *followed* ˈfɑlod, *into* ˈɪntu. But not all primary accents are equal to each other. Primary accent means merely the strongest accent on the word. When plurisyllables occur in sense groups, their primary accents can be seen to be of different degrees. Thus in the sentence *he* ˈfollowed me ˈquickly ˈinto the house, each of the words *followed, quickly, into* has a primary accent; but that on *quickly* is slightly stronger than that on *followed*, and both are noticeably stronger than that on *into*. This difference is due to sense-stress (§§124 f.).

107. Even accent. A large number of more or less fixed combinations have what is called even accent, though the second

---

[48] The term *stress* in its narrower sense means "force," and in strictness should be applied only to force accent. But the word has gained a more general sense by usage, and is here used as a general term for accent or prominence of all kinds, without regard to its constituent elements.

accent of such groups is usually a trifle stronger than the first; as ˈJames ˈBrown, ˈMrs. ˈWhite, ˈNew ˈEngland, ˈKing ˈAlfred, ˈWilson ˈAvenue, ˈfifˈteen, ˈtwenty-ˈfive, ˈwhite-ˈhot, ˈwell-ˈmade, ˈunderˈfed, ˈupˈstairs, ˈapple ˈpie, ˈsquare ˈrod, ˈfall ˈdown, etc. These bear a close relation to similar combinations under the influence of sense-stress; in fact, this accentuation is a kind of sense-stress. (See §125.)

108. Secondary accent, or half stress, occurs in three principal types of words.

(1) It occurs in **compounds** such as *milkman* ˈmɪlkˌmæn, *childlike* ˈtʃaɪldˌlaɪk, *outrun* ˌautˈrʌn. In **compound nouns and adjectives** the first element of the compound regularly has primary accent and the second element secondary accent. In **compound verbs** the reverse is true. This is a law of stress that has descended to us from the time of Old English. In this first type the primary and secondary accents may be **adjacent,** as in ˈmɪlkˌmæn, or **separated** by one or more syllables, as in ˈθɜoˌfær.[49]

109. The English habit of accenting compound nouns (or adjectives) and verbs thus differently has been also frequently applied to foreign loan-words whether compounds or not, the noun or adjective having first-syllable accent, and the verb second- or third-syllable accent (the secondary accent being sometimes omitted). Thus noun and verb: ˈconˌtract—conˈtract; ˈexˌtract—exˈtract; ˈdiˌgest—diˈgest; ˈinˌsult—inˈsult; ˈobject—obˈject; ˈattriˌbute—atˈtribute; or adjective and verb: ˈperfect—

---

[49] In present usage there is no settled and consistent practice in the manner of writing compound words. Sometimes they are written as one word (*milkman*), sometimes with hyphen (*morning-glory*), and sometimes as separate words (*corn law*). The unsettled state of usage in this matter may be seen by noting in the *Oxford Dictionary* the recent quotations illustrating the last-named compounds and others. It is probably impossible at present to devise any entirely consistent and logical practice in the manner of writing compounds. The laws governing the meaning and stress of compounds are not yet fully known. For various types of compound stress, see *Webster* (1934), *Pron.* §63.

*per*ˈ*fect;* ˈ*frequent—fre*ˈ*quent.* But there is some interference with the operation of this habit, partly by the tendency to recessive accent, partly by the modern English tendency to use the same word as noun, adjective, or verb without change of accent, and partly by other causes, such as the influence of sentence rhythm in connected speech (see *Shifting Accent,* §123).

110. In some cases the same habit of accentuation takes the form of omitting the secondary accent in the noun or adjective and keeping it in the verb. Note the parallel accentual scheme in ˈ*over*ˌ*flow* (noun)—ˌ*over*ˈ*flow* (verb) and in ˈ*separate* (adj.) ˈsɛpərɪt—ˈ*sepa*ˌ*rate* (vb.) ˈsɛpəˌret. Hence we find pairs like the following:

Spelling	Noun	Adjective	Verb
alternate	ˈɔltɚnɪt	ˈɔltɚnɪt	ˈɔltɚˌnet
appropriate		əˈpropriɪt	əˈpropriˌet
animate		ˈænəmɪt	ˈænəˌmet
aspirate	ˈæspərɪt	ˈæspərɪt	ˈæspəˌret
compliment	ˈkamplɪmənt		ˈkamplɪˌment
consummate		kənˈsʌmɪt	ˈkansəˌmet
deliberate		dɪˈlɪbərɪt	dɪˈlɪbəˌret
elaborate		ɪˈlæbərɪt	ɪˈlæbəˌret
estimate	ˈɛstəmɪt		ˈɛstəˌmet
moderate		ˈmadərɪt	ˈmadəˌret
ornament	ˈɔrnəmənt		ˈɔrnəˌment
separate		ˈsɛpərɪt, ˈsɛprɪt	ˈsɛpəˌret
supplement	ˈsʌpləmənt		ˈsʌpləˌment

111. (2) **Secondary accent** also occurs in words not usually considered as compounds, such as *ambush* ˈæmˌbʊʃ, *convoy* ˈkanˌvɔɪ, *conflict* ˈkanˌflɪkt, *accent* ˈækˌsɛnt, *pathos* ˈpeˌθɑs, etc., in which primary and secondary accent are **adjacent**. The syllable next to the main accent receives secondary accent for various reasons: (**a**) Sometimes the half-stressed syllable is mentally **associated with an identical syllable** that is fully stressed

in a related word; e.g., the last syllable of the noun *conflict* ˈkɑnˌflɪkt, with secondary accent, is associated with the last syllable of the verb *conflict* kənˈflɪkt with primary accent, and so retains a part of its stress in the noun. Other examples of this are ˈconˌtract (noun) and conˈtract (verb); ˈabˌstract (n.) and abˈstract (vb. and adj.); ˈconˌtrast (n.) and conˈtrast (vb.); ˈcomˌpact (n.) and comˈpact (adj.); ˈimˌpost and imˈpose; ˌcashˈier and cash; ˈloˌcate and loˈcation. (b) Sometimes a word from a foreign language which is less popular may receive something of its **foreign stress**; e.g., *program* ˈproˌgræm; compare the more popular form ˈprogrəm, in which the secondary accent is lost. So ˈsynˌtax, ˈcliˌmax, ˈvorˌtex. (c) Sometimes **importance of meaning** in the half-stressed syllable leads to a secondary accent. Thus in *re-make* ˌriˈmek, *re-* has a sharper meaning than it does in *return* rɪˈtɜn; cf. *re*ˈact, "respond to stimulus," with ˌre-ˈact, "act over again"; *re*ˈcover, "get back," with ˌre-ˈcover, "cover again." In such cases emphasis leads to even accent: ˈre-ˈact. Some other causes also probably operate in giving a secondary accent to the syllable next to the primary in words not felt as compounds.

112. (3) Secondary accent occurs in a third type of words of **three or more syllables,** mostly borrowed from Latin or French, such as ˈdesigˌnate, ˈintelˌlect, ˌascerˈtain, ˌcircumˈvent, ˌdeviˈation, ˌfundaˈmental, ˌperpenˈdicular, ˌuninˈtentional, which are accented on alternate syllables with differing degrees of stress. In some longer words there are two stressless syllables between accented ones, as in ˌcrystalliˈzation, ˌrealiˈzation.[50] This accentuation is due to the natural **rhythm of speech.** When a series of three or more syllables are pronounced with one impulse of the

---

[50] Such accent on first and fourth syllables instead of alternating first and third is probably due to the combined analogy of two groups of words—one like ˈcrystalˌlize, ˈminiˌmize, ˈrealˌize, with strong accent on the first, and the other like ˌcombiˈnation, ˌdenoˈtation, asˌsociˈation and others in ˈ-ation, with accent on the -ˈa-.

breath, they naturally fall into a rhythm of alternating higher and lower stresses. One or more of these is apt to be a secondary accent, as in the first syllable of ˌperpenˈdicuˌlar, and sometimes a third one is a light accent, as in the last syllable of the same word. Rhythmical accent is most frequently found in words derived from Latin or French, owing to their greater length, but occasionally is found in a native English word, as ˈlovliˌness.

113. Sometimes this law of rhythmic accent coincides with the old law of English accent in compound nouns, as in the native word ˈthoroughˌfare, which is accented on the first and last according to rhythm, and takes primary accent on the first, and secondary on the last, by the ancient law of compounds.

114. Free Accent, and Recessive Accent. In some long words the law of alternating rhythmical accent is interfered with by another ancient law of accent. In the Indo-European language, from which both English and Latin descended, the accent was originally **free**; i.e., it rested in some forms of a word on one syllable, and in other forms of the same word on a different syllable. This method of accenting continued to some extent in Latin, and is preserved in some English words taken from Latin. Note, for example, the variable position of the accent in the Latin derivatives ˈfamily, faˈmiliar, faˌmiliˈarity. On the other hand, at a prehistoric period in the English branch of the Indo-European family of languages, this movable accent gradually **receded** and became fixed on the first syllable of all forms of a word. This is seen in native English words, as in love, ˈlovely, ˈloveliness, ˈlovableness. This **recessive** accent is so firmly imbedded in English, that many words borrowed from Latin or French, at first with their foreign accent, have gradually succumbed to the native English law, and so receive their main stress at or near the beginning of the word. This law sometimes proves stronger than that of rhythmic alternation, so that while such a word as ˌgeneˈration follows the rhythmic law, the word ᴵ*generally* follows the law of recessive accent, with a strong accent on the first syllable, and none on the others. This law of recessive accent accounts (1) for the large number of English words accented on the first syllable, (2) for the large number of monosyllables in English, one or more syllables having been lost from the end of the word by gradual obscuration from the loss of accent after it had been shifted to the first syllable, and (3) for the loss of one or more syllables from words with only primary accent on the first syllable, as in Southern British ᴵɔdɳrɪ as compared with American ᴵɔrdɳˌɛrɪ (see §116).

British and American Accent

115. The treatment of secondary accent in one group of words requires particular notice because of the difference between American and British practice. In words ending in *-ary*, *-ery*, *-ory*, such as *necessary*, *monastery*, *territory*, which are derived from Latin through Old French, the main accent in Old French was usually on what is now the next to the last syllable. After these words were taken into English in the Middle English period, the accent shifted to the fourth syllable from the last in accord with the native English tendency to accent words near the beginning; but, owing to the principle of alternating rhythm mentioned in §112, a distinct secondary accent remained where the main accent had been. Thus Middle English ˌ*neces*ᴵ*sarie* became ᴵ*neces*ˌ*sary*, and ˌ*terri*ᴵ*torie* became ᴵ*terri*ˌ*tory*. This secondary accent remained on these words till comparatively recent times in England, and it still remains in American English, constituting one of its most noticeable differences from British. Whitney (*Orient. and Ling. Stud. 2d Ser.*, 1874, p. 232) and later Jespersen (*Gram.* §§5.63, 9.77) pointed out that this originally British accentuation has been preserved in America.

There are hundreds of these words in English. Here are a few examples with their usual American and British pronunciation:

Spelling	American	British
adversary	ˈædvɚˌsɛrɪ	ˈædvəsərɪ
commentary	ˈkɑmənˌtɛrɪ	ˈkɒməntərɪ
imaginary	ɪˈmædʒɪnˌɛrɪ	ɪˈmædʒɪnərɪ
January	ˈdʒænjʊˌɛrɪ	ˈdʒænjʊərɪ
missionary	ˈmɪʃənˌɛrɪ	ˈmɪʃn̩ərɪ
momentary	ˈmomənˌtɛrɪ	ˈmoməntərɪ
secondary	ˈsɛkənˌdɛrɪ	ˈsɛkəndərɪ
stationary (adj.)	ˈsteʃənˌɛrɪ	ˈsteʃnərɪ
voluntary	ˈvɑlənˌtɛrɪ	ˈvɒləntərɪ
millinery	ˈmɪləˌnɛrɪ	ˈmɪlɪnərɪ
presbytery	ˈprɛzbəˌtɛrɪ	ˈprɛzbɪtərɪ
stationery (n.)	ˈsteʃənˌɛrɪ	ˈsteʃnərɪ
auditory	ˈɔdɪˌtorɪ	ˈɔdɪtərɪ
oratory	ˈɔrəˌtorɪ	ˈɒrətərɪ
preparatory	prɪˈpærəˌtorɪ	prɪˈpærətərɪ
territory	ˈtɛrəˌtorɪ	ˈtɛrɪtərɪ

116. The natural effect of omitting the secondary accent in British pronunciation is the loss of one or more unaccented syllables (see §114, above). Note the following British pronunciations given in Jones's *Pronouncing Dictionary:* ˈdɪkʃənrɪ, ˈdɪkʃn̩rɪ; ˈmɪlɪtərɪ, ˈmɪlɪtrɪ; ˈɔdn̩rɪ, ˈɔdɪnərɪ, ˈɔdɪnrɪ, ˈɔdnərɪ, ˈɔdn̩ərɪ; ˈsɛkəndərɪ, ˈsɛkn̩drɪ; ˈsɛkrətrɪ; ˈsɛdn̩tərɪ, ˈsɛdn̩trɪ; ˈtɛmpərərɪ, ˈtɛmprərɪ, ˈtɛmpr-rɪ; ˈvɛtn̩rɪ, ˈvɛtərɪnərɪ, ˈvɛtrɪnrɪ; ˈsɛmɪtrɪ; ˈmɒnəstrɪ; ˈdɔmɪtrɪ.

117. In some words British avoids an accumulation of obscure syllables, not by preserving the original secondary accent as in America, but by shifting the main accent onward; as in *capillary* Amer. ˈkæpəˌlɛrɪ, Brit. kəˈpɪlərɪ; *centenary* Amer. ˈsɛntəˌnɛrɪ, Brit. sɛnˈtinərɪ; *corollary* Amer. ˈkɔrəˌlɛrɪ, Brit. kəˈrɒlərɪ; *laboratory* Amer. ˈlæbrəˌtorɪ, Brit. ləˈbɒrət(ə)rɪ, also ˈlæb(ə)rət(ə)rɪ; *obligatory* Amer. əˈblɪgəˌtorɪ, ˈɑblɪgəˌtorɪ, Brit.

ˈɒblɪgət(ə)rɪ, ˈɒblɪgetərɪ, əˈblɪgət(ə)rɪ; in *necessary*, Brit. sometimes has ˈnɛsɪsɛrɪ (with enough subordinate accent on -sɛrɪ to
preserve the full vowel ɛ).

118. In the retention of the secondary accent in these words,
as in many other respects, American English preserves from an
earlier stage of the language a feature that has become archaic
in Southern British. At what period the secondary accent in these
words ceased to be used in England is not quite certain. The
practice of the poets in this respect is not wholly decisive, since
they may use for the verse-stress archaic accent that has been
abandoned in current speech. At any rate, the secondary accent
in these words regularly appears in British verse down to the
present time. Note, e.g., Spenser, *Fairie Queene*, I.iii.3.2:

> For|saken, |woful, |soli|tarie |mayd.

Shakespeare, *Hamlet*, I.ii.78:

> Nor |Custom|ary |suites of |solemne |Blacke.

Sidney, *Astrophel*, 15.5:

> |Ye that do |diction|ary's |method |bring
> |Into your |rimes.

Pope, "Eloïsa," 18:

> Re|pentant |sighs, and |volun|tary |pains.

Wordsworth, "Intimations of Immortality," 56:

> |Whither is |fled the |vision|ary |gleam?

Tennyson, *Queen Mary*, 4.2.4:

> I |found it |all a |vision|ary |flame.

Bridges, "Eros and Psyche," May, 2:

> The |soli|tary |rock where |she was |left.

Noyes, "Niobe," 4:

> No |weeping |cloud, no |momen|tary |rain.

As early as Spenser, however, we find an occasional example,
which may or may not represent contemporary colloquial practice, like the following from *Fairie Queene*, IV.ix.19.6:

> She |was as |safe as |in a |sanctua|ry.

(rimes, |divers|ly:|privi|ty).

Keats, "Eve of St. Agnes," 16:
> Knights, ˈladies, ˈpraying ˌin dumb ˈoraˌtries

(rimes, *knees:freeze*).

Tennyson, "Dream of Fair Women," 22:
> And ˌI saw ˈcrowds in ˈcolumn'd ˈsanctuaˌries

(rime, ˈpalaˌces).

119. The superficial methods by which school pupils are taught "correct" pronunciations in America are well illustrated by the frequent treatment of the word *dictionary*. Some teachers, and others equally ill-informed of the actual practice of cultivated American speakers, for one reason or another have adopted the British pronunciation ˈdɪkʃənərɪ (or ˈdɪkʃn̩rɪ, ˈdɪkʃnərɪ) as the supposed elegant form of the word. Having no background of historical knowledge of the English language, ignorant that the usual American pronunciation ˈdɪkʃəˌnɛrɪ represents a living and once universal tradition only recently abandoned in Southern British, they fail to recognize that the pronunciation ˈdɪkʃənərɪ in America is an isolated exception to the very large class of words it belongs to, as *adversary, millinery, territory*, and innumerable others, which they innocently continue to pronounce in the American (and historical) way, but which the Englishman pronounces in the British way without secondary accent (ˈædvəsərɪ, ˈmɪlɪnərɪ, ˈtɛrɪtərɪ). Probably few educated Americans would adopt this sole foreign pronunciation if they knew the relevant facts.

120. Some other words than those ending in *-ry* show a secondary accent in American pronunciation that is absent in British. Such are words in *-ative*, as *accumulative* əˈkɪumjəˌletɪv, British əˈkjumjələtɪv, *administrative, communicative, imaginative, nominative, operative, remunerative, significative*, etc. In these, America regularly has the secondary accent. In *administrative, imaginative*, and *operative*, British has both pronunciations, and perhaps in some of the others.—Words in *-ony*, as *ceremony* A. ˈsɛrəˌmonɪ, B. ˈsɛrɪmənɪ, *matrimony, patrimony;* in *-ature*, as *legislature.* But American and British usage agree in omitting the secondary accent from *temperature, miniature,* and *literature.*

Others in which American usage differs from British are: *circumstance* ˈsɜkəmˌstæns, ˈsɜkəmstəns, *controversy, holiday,* British ˈhɒlədɪ, -de, *miscellany,* British ˈmɪsɪlənɪ, mɪˈsɛlənɪ.

121. In other groups of words also secondary accent has disappeared in American English. Among these are words in *-able* (*-ible, -uble*), as *amicable, comparable* ˈkɑmpərəbl̩, *lamentable* ˈlæməntəbl̩, *preferable* and many others, in which American and British pronunciation are alike. So with words in *-acy,* as *accuracy, confederacy, delicacy, intimacy, legitimacy, magistracy, obduracy* ˈɑbdjʊrəsɪ, əbˈdɪur-; in *-ancy, -ency,* as *elegancy, relevancy, significancy; impotency, innocency, presidency;* with adverbs in *-ly* formed on adjectives accented on the antepenult, as *accurately, delicately, exquisitely* ˈɛkskwɪzɪtlɪ (see *PDAE*) *permanently, principally,* etc.

122. Light accent is heard in certain syllables—a stress that is below secondary accent and perceptibly above that of stressless syllables. This can be plainly detected in a word like ˌmisˌunderˈstanding. It is clear that the main accent is on the syllable ˈstænd, and the next highest on ˌmɪs. The syllables dɚ and ɪŋ are the lowest, being without stress. Hence ˌʌn has light accent, for it is lower than ˌmɪs and higher than dɚ. So in the word *complimentation* ˌmɛn shows an accent lower than the secondary ˌkɑm and higher than the stressless plɪ. In the foregoing words, light accent is fixed by the neighboring accents. In other instances light accent is somewhat variable in strength, and often can be detected only by the quality of vowel sound in the syllable. For example, note the very light accent on **-æp-** in ˌædæpˈteʃən, absent in the pronunciation ˌædəpˈteʃən; or on the first syllable of veˈkeʃən, absent in vəˈkeʃən.

123. Shifting Accent. Certain words and phrases, chiefly adjectives and adverbs, are stressed on the last syllable when they stand alone, as *sixˈteen;* or with no following word, as *she is sixˈteen, years sixˈteen;* but when followed by an accented syllable, the accent of the preceding word shifts, owing to the principle of rhythm; as, ˈsixteen ˈboys and ˈgirls. Compare *he is very* *ex*ˈ*pert* with *an* ˈ*expert* ˈ*workman; he is here, al*ˈ*most*, with *he is* ˈ*almost here.* This is especially common in adjectives accented on the last syllable, as *ex*ˈ*pert*, and in compound adjectives with even accent, as ˈ*long-*ˈ*armed, a* ˈ*long-*ˌ*armed* ˈ*man;* ˈ*close-*ˈ*fisted,* *a* ˈ*close-*ˌ*fisted* ˈ*miser*, where the second accent is changed from slightly stronger than the first to noticeably weaker, and may thus be marked with the secondary accent. For fuller treatment of shifting accent, see *Webster* (1934), *Pronunciation*, §66, where it is shown that hundreds of English words have no fixed accent in actual speech. See also *PDAE*, §§53–54.

124. Sense-Stress. Sense-stress, defined in §104, in popular language is "putting the emphasis on the right words." The term applies, however, not only to the more prominent words in a statement, or any group of words that makes sense, but to all of the words, to their relative prominence or lack of prominence. We learn it from childhood, and it forms as essential a part of the expression of meaning as the words themselves. It is also closely connected with intonation, the rise and fall in pitch of the voice in speech, it being sometimes difficult to distinguish stress of force from stress of pitch.

125. The underlying principle of sense-stress is the fact that words are more prominent or less prominent according to the nature of the ideas they express. In general it is true that words which present to the mind a definite picture or idea, such as *tree, run, slow, wagon, walking, swiftly*, have relatively strong sense-stress, and words that represent vague ideas or mere relations, such as the prepositions *in, for*, etc., or conjunctions, as *and, but*, etc., or auxiliaries, as *can, has, shall*, etc., have relatively weak sense-stress. (For a few apparent exceptions, cf. §138.)

It would be difficult to formulate all the laws of sense-stress in English, and only a few illustrative examples will be given.

Certain combinations regularly have so-called **level stress** (see §107), in which, however, the second stress is slightly stronger than the first; as **verb+adverb** (*He* ˈ*went* ˈ*far*), **adverb+participle** (ˈ*quickly* ˈ*made*), **adverb+adjective** (ˈ*hardly* ˈ*wise*), **adjective+noun** (ˈ*long* ˈ*days*) and **attributive noun+noun** (ˈ*gold* ˈ*ring*), **genitive+noun** (ˈ*stone's* ˈ*throw*), **noun subject+verb** (*the* ˈ*house* ˈ*burned, the* ˈ*ladies* ˈ*came*), **subject+noun or adjective predicate** (*The* ˈ*trees are* ˈ*maples, The* ˈ*trees are* ˈ*tall*). In general any predicate is slightly stronger than a noun subject (*The* ˈ*trip was in* ˈ*vain, The* ˈ*man was a*ˈ*way*). Pronoun subjects and objects have less stress than nouns (cf. ₁*He* ˈ*sent* ₁*it* with ˈ*Carrie* ˈ*sent* ˈ*Burt*).

Fortunately it is not necessary to know all the laws of sense-stress in order to perceive it. All that is needed is a sharpened sense of accent and stress. For fuller treatment and examples of sense-stress, see *Webster* (1934), *Pronunciation*, §69.

126. In some instances sense-stress and the accent of compound nouns or adjectives come into conflict. For example, the sense-stress of the adjective+noun ˈ*golden* ˈ*sun* is level stress; the accent of the compound noun ˈ*gold*₁*smith* is, as regularly, primary+secondary. But in ˈ*gold* ˈ*ring* we have level stress because *gold*, though a noun, is used as an adjective, and so takes adjective+noun sense-stress. When the idea of the noun as one unit predominates, as in ˈ*red*₁*bird*, we have compound noun stress; when the idea of adjective followed by noun predominates, we have adjective+noun sense-stress, level stress, as ˈ*red* ˈ*bird*.

127. So the chief factor that distinguishes real compounds (whether written solid or with hyphen or separately) from adjective+noun phrases is the stress. Thus ˈ*gold* ₁*dust* is a compound noun whether hyphenated or not. But since there are cases in which the idea wavers between single compound noun and adjective+noun, some cases show either accentuation; as

ˈoak ˈtree or ˈoakˌtree; cf. ˈapple ˈpie with ˈappleˌtree. Can you think of a plausible reason why we can say either ˈoakˌtree or ˈoak ˈtree, but cannot say ˈapple ˈtree, but only ˈappleˌtree?

128. Sense-stress is the foundation of English poetry—not merely of "accent" or "meter," but of the essence of poetry. Poetry is speech—a fact sometimes forgotten. The sense-stresses of speech determine the movements and contrasts of speech— the movements and contrasts of the thought and feeling. The poet selects and arranges those thoughts and feelings whose stress movements and contrasts make up the particular pattern of verse he has chosen. Thus the rhythm and the thought and feeling are one. The stress movements and contrasts are present, not because it is verse, but because it is speech. It is verse because the speech stresses are what they are. The verse-beats are simply the beats of the thought and feeling—the sense-stresses. There is exactly the same variety in the strength of the successive stresses of poetry that there is in the sense-stresses of living speech. Those systems of marking verse scansion that mark the verse-beats all alike obscure that fact and mislead the student. The same general statements apply to "free verse." If it has any rhythm, it is the rhythm of speech and is based on sense-stress.[51]

129. Emphasis. The term emphasis is often loosely used of various kinds of stress. Though in its physiological and psychological nature it is the same as any stress, the term will here be limited to what may be called unusual stress, or stress for special purposes, in contrast to sense-stress, which is the normal stress of words to show the relations of meaning, and is never absent from a group of words that makes sense.

[51] For the relation of sense-stress to poetry, see Mark Harvey Liddell, *An Introduction to the Scientific Study of English Poetry*, N. Y., 1902, and *A Brief Abstract of a New English Prosody based upon the Laws of English Rhythm*, Lafayette, Indiana, 1914.

H. O. Coleman[52] has pointed out a valuable distinction in emphasis as the **emphasis of prominence** and the **emphasis of intensity.** The emphasis of prominence gives special prominence to an idea among other ideas, and hence is most commonly used for contrast, expressed or implied; as He is *rich* but *discontented.*[53] The emphasis of intensity, on the other hand, heightens the idea of a word in itself without regard to other ideas; as We're *lost!* The emphasis of prominence might be called **logical emphasis,** and the emphasis of intensity, **emotional emphasis.**

130. Gradation. It is a characteristic of English, deeply imbedded in its long history, that the vowels of unaccented syllables have gradually become obscured to a sound quite different in resonance, or quality, from what they had formerly been, and from the present-day vowels that have preserved their full quality under accent.[54] This fact escapes the attention of many because the same spelling is kept for the obscured vowel that was used to spell it before it became obscured in course of time, and the same spelling that is also used for the accented vowel that takes its place when its syllable is accented. Thus the quite different vowel sounds in *a'part* are each spelt with *a;* so in *a'las* ə'læs, *ap'pal* ə'pɔl, ₁*appa'ratus* ₁æpə'retəs. It is only when they are expressed in phonetic symbols that it becomes clear that the vowels are really different though spelt alike.

The following tables show in the accented syllable (primary or secondary) of the first column a full vowel, and in the cor-

---

[52] *Miscellanea Phonetica* (IPA, 1914), pp. 6–26.

[53] The examples cited by Coleman of emphasis of prominence that are not for contrast seem to be normal sense-stress on the most important word, as in his example, I am feeling *ill*. If this is given additional emphasis, it becomes the emphasis of intensity; as Oh! I'm *ill!*

[54] The historical change of quality in unaccented vowels must not be confused with the historical change of past accented vowels to present accented vowels, the "Great Vowel Shift," as of ɔː to o (ME stɔːn. ModE ston). (§244.)

responding unaccented syllable of the second column the obscured vowel that takes its place when unaccented. (After reading them through carefully, read the explanations at the end and then look them through again.)

Gradation of Vowels According to Stress

Accented syllable or stressed monosyllable	*Unaccented syllable or unstressed monosyllable*
(1) Full Vowel	Reduced Vowel

i	ˈri ˌflɛks (ˈreˌflex)	ɪ	rɪ ˈflɛkt (reˈflect)	
	kəm ˈpit (comˈpete)		ˌkɑm pɪ ˈtɪʃən (ˌcompeˈti-tion)	
	ˌdi noˈteʃən (ˌdenoˈtation)		dɪ ˈnot (deˈnote)	
	ˈmi tɚ (ˈmeter)	ə	daɪ ˈæm ə tɚ (diˈameter)	
	kwaɪ ˈi təs (quiˈetus)		ˈkwaɪ ət (ˈquiet)	
ɪ	hə ˈbɪt ʃʊəl (haˈbitual)	ɪ	ˈhæb ɪt (ˈhabit)	
	pə ˈzɪʃ ən (poˈsition)		ˈɑpə zɪt (ˈopposite)	
	tə ˈrɪf ɪk (terˈrific)	ə	ˈtɛr əˌfaɪ (ˈterriˌfy)	
	ˈdɪv ə ˌdɛnd (ˈdiviˌdend)		də ˈvaɪd (diˈvide)	
e	ˈde lɪ (ˈdaily)	ɪ	ˈmʌn dɪ (ˈMonday)	
	ə ˈwe (aˈway)		ˈɔl wɪz (ˈalways)	
	ˈedʒ (ˈage)		ˈnɑn ɪdʒ (ˈnonage)	
	ˈsent (ˈsaint)		sɪn ˈklær (Sinˈclair)	
	ˈsɛpə ˌret (ˈsepaˌrate)		ˈsɛpə rɪt (ˈseparate)	
	ˈste bl̩ (ˈstable)	ə	stə ˈbɪlətɪ (staˈbility)	
	ˈtʃes (ˈchase)		ˈpɜ tʃəs (ˈpurchase)	
ɛ	ˈdɛf ənɪt (ˈdefinite)	ɪ	dɪ ˈfaɪn (deˈfine)	
	dɪ ˈstrɛs (disˈtress)		ˈmɪs trɪs (ˈmistress)	
	ən ˈlɛs (unˈless)		ˈnid lɪs (ˈneedless)	

ɛ	prɪn ˈsɛs (*prɪnˈcess*)	ɪ	ˈprɪn sɪs (ˈ*princess*)
	mo ˈmɛn təm (*moˈmen-tum*)	ə	ˈmo mənt (ˈ*moment*)
	ˈlɛnt (ˈ*Lent*)		ˈsaɪ lənt (ˈ*silent*)
	ˈkɑmplɪ ˌmɛnt (ˈ*compli-ˌment*)		ˈkɑmplɪ mənt (ˈ*compli-ment*)
æ	ˈmæn lɪ (ˈ*manly*)	ə	ˈpost mən (ˈ*postman*)
	ˈlænd ˌlɔrd (ˈ*landˌlord*)		ˈɪŋ glənd (ˈ*England*)
	ˈæn ˌɛks (ˈ*anˌnex*)	ə	ˈnɛks (*anˈnex*)
	ˈæd ˌɛpt (ˈ*adˌept*)	ə	ˈdɛpt (*aˈdept*)
	ˈhæmp tən (ˈ*Hampton*)		ˈwɪnd əm (ˈ*Windham*)
ɑ	ˈmɑ mə (ˈ*mama*)	ə	mə ˈmɑ (*maˈma*)
	hi ˈwɑz (*he ˈwas*)		ˈðæt wəz ˈraɪt (ˈ*that was ˈright*)
	ˈɑb dʒɪkt (ˈ*object*)		əb ˈdʒɛkt (*obˈject*)
	ə ˈpɑs ḷ (*aˈpostle*)		ˌæp əs ˈtɑlɪk (ˌ*aposˈtolic*)
	ˈkɑn ˌdʌkt (ˈ*conˌduct*)		kən ˈdʌkt (*conˈduct*)
ɒ	hi ˈwɒz (*he ˈwas*)	ə	ˈðæt wəz ˈraɪt (ˈ*that was ˈright*)
	ˈɒb dʒɪkt (ˈ*object*)		əb ˈdʒɛkt (*obˈject*)
	ə ˈpɒs ḷ (*aˈpostle*)		ˌæp əs ˈtɒlɪk (ˌ*aposˈtolic*)
	ˈkɒn ˌdʌkt (ˈ*conˌduct*)		kən ˈdʌkt (*conˈduct*)
ɔ	ˈɔ θɚ (ˈ*author*)	ə	ə ˈθɔr ətɪ (*auˈthority*)
	ɪn ˈstɔl (*inˈstall*)		ˌɪn stə ˈleʃən (ˌ*installˈla-tion*)
	ˈɔ fɚ (ˈ*offer*)		ə ˈfɛnd (*ofˈfend*)
	ˈbɔld lɪ (ˈ*baldly*)		ˈrɪb əld (ˈ*ribald*)
	ˈθiə ˌbɔld (ˈ*Theoˌbald*)		ˈtɪb əlt (ˈ*Tybalt*)

o   ɪm ˈpoz (*im*ˈ*pose*)   ə   ˌɪm pə ˈzɪʃən (ˌ*impo*ˈ*sition*)

     ɪn ˈvok (*in*ˈ*voke*)   ˌɪn və ˈkeʃən (ˌ*invo*ˈ*cation*)

     mɪl ˈto nɪən (*Mil*ˈ*tonian*)   ˈmɪl tən (ˈ*Milton*)

     ˈrop (ˈ*rope*)   ˈstɝ əp (ˈ*stirrup*)

     ˈfok (ˈ*folk*)   ˈnɔr fək (ˈ*Norfolk*)

ʊ   ˈfʊl nɪs (ˈ*fullness*)   ə   ˈkær fəl (ˈ*careful*)

     ˈʃʊd ṇt (ˈ*shouldn't*)   ˌwi ʃəd ˈgo (ˌ*we should* ˈ*go*)

     ˈæmˌbʊʃ (ˈ*am*ˌ*bush*)   ˌæm bəs ˈked (ˌ*ambus*-ˈ*cade*)

u   ˈtu ən ˈfro (ˈ*to and* ˈ*fro*)   ə   tə ˈnaɪt (*to*ˈ*night*)

     ˈru mɪ (ˈ*roomy*)   ˈbɛd rəm ˈdor (ˈ*bedroom* ˈ*door*)

     ˈdu ˈɔl (ˈ*do* ˈ*all*)   ˈhaʊ də jə no? (ˈ*how do you know?*)

     ˈdum (ˈ*doom*)   ˈkɪŋ dəm (ˈ*kingdom*)

ɜ   kən ˈvɜs (*con*ˈ*verse*)   ɚ   ˌkɑn vɚ ˈseʃən (ˌ*conver*-ˈ*sation*)

     ˈpɜ sṇ (ˈ*person*)   pɚ ˈsɑn əˌfaɪ (*per*ˈ*soni*ˌ*fy*)

     ˈsɜ ˌve (ˈ*sur*ˌ*vey*)   sɚ ˈve (*sur*ˈ*vey*)

     ˈfɜm (ˈ*firm*)   ˌkɑn fɚ ˈmeʃən (ˌ*confir*-ˈ*mation*)

ɜ   kən ˈvɜs (*con*ˈ*verse*)   ə   ˌkɒn və ˈseʃən (ˌ*conver*-ˈ*sation*)

     ˈpɜ sṇ (ˈ*person*)   pə ˈsɒn əˌfaɪ (*per*ˈ*soni*ˌ*fy*)

     ˈsɜ ˌve (ˈ*sur*ˌ*vey*)   sə ˈve (*sur*ˈ*vey*)

     ˈfɜm (ˈ*firm*)   ˌkɒn fə ˈmeʃən (ˌ*confir*-ˈ*mation*) ʌ   ˈʌpɚ (ˈ*upper*)   ə   ə ˈpɑn (*up*ˈ*on*)

kən ˈsʌlt (*con*ˈ*sult*)   ˌkɑn səl ˈteʃən (ˌ*consul-*ˈ*tation*)

sɚ ˈkʌm fərəns (*cir*ˈ*cum-*   ˌsɝ kəm ˈskraɪb (ˌ*cir-*
ference)   *cum*ˈ*scribe*)

ˈkʌm pənɪ (ˈ*company*)   kəm ˈpænjən (*com*ˈ*pan-*
ion)

ˌʌn ˈles (ˌ*un*ˈ*lace*)   ən ˈlɛs (*un* ˈ*less*)

aɪ   ˈmaɪ ˌgret (ˈ*mi*ˌ*grate*)   ə   ˌɛm ə ˈgreʃən (ˌ*emi*ˈ*gra-*
tion)

ə ˈblaɪdʒ (*o*ˈ*blige*)   ˌɑb lə ˈgeʃən (ˌ*obli*ˈ*ga-*
tion)

ˈbaɪ ˌpæθ (ˈ*by*ˌ*path*)   ˈtu bə ˈtu (ˈ*two by* ˈ*two*)

aʊ   ˈfaʊnd (ˈ*found*)   ə   ˌnɪu fənd ˈlænd (ˌ*New-*
*found*ˈ*land*)

ˈmaʊθ ˌfʊl (ˈ*mouth*ˌ*ful*)   ˈports məθ (ˈ*Portsmouth*)

ˈtaʊn (ˈ*town*)   ˈwaʃɪŋ tən (ˈ*Washing-*
ton)

ˈwɑtɚ ˌhaʊs (ˈ*Water-*   ˈwɑtrəs (ˈ*Watrous*)
ˌhouse

ɪu, ju   ˈtɪun (ˈ*tune*)   ə   ˈfɔr tʃən (ˈ*fortune*)

ˈdɪuk (ˈ*duke*)   ˈɛdʒ ə ket (ˈ*educate*)

ˈsɪu pɚfaɪn (ˈ*superfine*)   sə ˈpɪr ɪɚ (*su*ˈ*perior*)

sə ˈlɪut (*sa*ˈ*lute*)   ju   ˌsæl jʊ ˈteʃən (ˌ*salu*ˈ*ta-*
tion)

ˌkɑntɪ ˈnɪu ətɪ (ˌ*conti*ˈ*nu-*   kənˈtɪn jʊ (*con*ˈ*tinue*)
ity)

ˈjun jən (ˈ*union*)   jʊ ˈnaɪt (*u*ˈ*nite*)

	(2) Full Vowel		Lost Vowel
i	ˈfor ˈtin (ˈfourˈteen)	( )	ˈfɔrt ˌnaɪt (ˈfortˌnight)
ɪ	ə ˈbɪl ətɪ (aˈbility)	( )	ˈe bḷ (ˈable)
	sɪ ˈvɪl jən (ciˈvilian)		ˈsɪv ḷ (ˈcivil)
	ju ˈtɪl ətɪ (uˈtility)		ˈju tḷ ˌaɪz (ˈutiˌlize)
	læ ˈtɪn ətɪ (Laˈtinity)		ˈlæt ṇ (ˈLatin)
e	rɪ ˈmen (reˈmain)	( )	ˈrɛm nənt (ˈremnant)
	rɪ ˈten (reˈtain)		ˈrɛt ṇˌɪu (ˈretiˌnue)
	ˈtwidˌdel (ˈTweedˌdale)		ˈtwi dḷ (ˈTweedle)
ɛ	po ˈten ʃəl (poˈtential)	( )	ˈpo tṇt (ˈpotent)
	rɪ ˈbɛl (reˈbel)		ˈrɛb ḷ (ˈrebel)
æ	fe ˈtæl ətɪ (faˈtality)	( )	ˈfe tḷ (ˈfatal)
	se ˈtæn ɪk (saˈtanic)		ˈse tṇ (ˈSatan)
ɑ	ˌæp əs ˈtɑl ɪk (ˌaposˈtolic)	( )	ə ˈpɑs ḷ (aˈpostle)
	tɪu ˈtɑn ɪk (Teuˈtonic)		ˈtɪu tṇ (ˈTeuton)
	kʊd ˈnɑt (could ˈnot)		ˈkʊd ṇt (ˈcouldn't)
	pɚ ˈsɑn əˌfaɪ (perˈsoniˌfy)	( )	ˈpɝ sṇ (ˈperson)
ɔ	ˈfɔl (ˈfall)	( )	ˈɔf ḷ (ˈoffal)
	ˈstɔl (ˈstall)		ˈpɛdɪs tḷ (ˈpedestal)
o	ˈmɑn ə ˌton (ˈmonoˌtone)	( )	mə ˈnɑt ṇ əs (moˈnoto-nous)
	ˈblækˌston (ˈBlackˌstone)		ˈblæk stṇ (ˈBlaxton)
	dʒɑn ˈso nɪən (Johnˈson-ian)		ˈdʒɑn sṇ (ˈJohnson)

ʊ	ˈfʊl (ˈ*full*) ˈtɜnˌbʊl (ˈ*Turn* ˌ*bull*)	( )	ˈɔ fḷ ɪ (ˈ*awfully*) ˈtrʌm bḷ (ˈ*Trumbull*)[55]
ʌ	ˈsʌn (ˈ*son*) kənˈsʌlt (*con*ˈ*sult*)	( )	ˈwɪl sṇ (ˈ*Wilson*) ˌkɑnsḷˈteʃən (ˌ*consul*ˈ*ta-* *tion*)
aʊ	ˈtaʊn (ˈ*town*)	( )	ˈbraɪ tṇ (ˈ*Brighton*)
ɪu	ˈtɪun (ˈ*tune*)	( )	ˈfɔr tʃṇ ɪtlɪ (ˈ*fortu-* *nately*)

131. Not all of these pairs of stressed and stressless vowels represent the same historical stage of obscuration of the unaccented vowel. The most of them show what each accented vowel at the present time becomes when it loses its accent; as ˈde lɪ—ˈmʌn dɪ, or mo ˈmɛn təm—ˈmo mənt. But in some cases the obscure vowel represents a reduced pronunciation of the corresponding accented vowel at an earlier period, as in ˈtaʊn—ˈwɑʃɪŋtən, in which the unaccented vowel began to be obscured at a time before the accented vowel became aʊ, while it was still uː. The stages of obscuration then were ˈtuːn—tun—tʊn—tən. But when ˈtuːn kept its accent it became ˈtaʊn by the Great Vowel Shift. So in the pair ˈmæn—ˈpost mən it is probable that mən is the reduced form, not directly of ˈmæn, but of its earlier stage ˈmɑn. In loan-words from French or Latin the correspondence of the stressed and unstressed vowel may in some cases go back to a period before they were taken into English. But the principle is the same in all cases, the difference in vowel being a

---

[55] If *Turnbull* was changed to *Trumbull*, as is possible, account for the **m**. For the shifting of **r** (metathesis) compare *grass* with OE *gærs*, *bird* with OE *brid*, and *worked* with *wrought*.

regular accompaniment of the difference in accent, the same original vowel developing differently when accented and when unaccented.[56] In some examples a different word is used, but the vowels correspond. Thus in *unless* the ending *-less* is not the same as that in *needless;* but the vowels (accented ɛ, unaccented ɪ) correspond. So *Lent* is not the same word as the last syllable of *silent*, or *bald* as that of *ribald;* but the vowels correspond. If the accent were put on the last syllable of these words, they would be sə'lɛnt and rɪ'bɔld.[57]

132. Our custom of spelling with the same letter such vowel sounds as the second one in *momentum* and the last one in *moment*, the first in *manly* and the last in *postman*, the last in *re'cord* (vb.) and '*record* (noun), the first in '*object* (noun) and *ob'ject* (vb.), has firmly fixed in our consciousness the entirely erroneous idea that they are the same vowel sound in each pair of words. In reality they are as different as if they were spelt with different letters. The last vowel in *moment* is more different from the second vowel in *momentum* than the vowel of *feel* is from the vowel of *fate*.

133. In the examples given, the corresponding syllables have virtually the same quality of vowel sound under secondary accent as under primary. In most cases, too, a similar quality of vowel sound is found under light stress, but with greater laxness and brevity; though under very light stress some vowels tend to become obscure with loss of their distinctive quality.

[56] It is not entirely certain that accent or the lack of it *causes* the change in vowel quality. It is possible that the accent is as much a result of the difference in vowel quality as a cause of it; i.e., that vowel quality is a constituent of accent (prominence). It has not, I think, yet been shown that full vowel quality exists in English under the lowest grade of stress. Such so-called unaccented vowels as ɑ in 'kænɑt, ʊ in ¡sæljʊ'teʃən, the second æ in ¡ædæp'teʃən, can be pronounced with less prominence, as obscure vowels: 'kænət (cf. kænt), ¡sæljə'teʃən, ¡ædəp'teʃən; and even ¡sɪtʃʊ'eʃən can be reduced to ¡sɪtʃə'weʃən.

[57] A radio announcer introducing grand opera said rɪ'bɔldrɪ.

134. But when the vowel is without stress, we find, e.g., that the sound which is e when accented, as in *daily* ˈdelɪ, is ɪ when unaccented, as in *Sunday* ˈsʌndɪ; or the vowel that is o when accented, as in *revoke* rɪˈvok, is replaced by ə when unaccented in *advocate* ˈædvəˌket; or what is æ in the accented syllable of *manly* ˈmænlɪ, becomes ə in the unaccented syllable of *postman* ˈpostmən; or what is ɔr in the accented syllable of *record* rɪˈkɔrd, becomes ɚ in the unaccented syllable of *record* ˈrɛkɚd. In the examples given, note that all accented vowels (with a few exceptions to be noted below), when they lose their accent, become one of the three unstressed vowels ɪ, ə, ɚ. In regions where *r* is silent except before vowels the accented vowels of words like *re*ˈ*cord*, ˈ*person*, which are there pronounced rɪˈkɔ(ə)d and ˈpɜsn̩, are replaced in ˈ*record* and *per*ˈ*soni*ˌ*fy* by the unaccented ə, ˈrɛkəd, pəˈsɒnəˌfaɪ.

135. In general it is seen that the high-front vowels i, ɪ, the mid-front e, and usually ɛ, when they lose their accent are replaced by the front vowel ɪ, and that the low-front æ, all the central vowels, and all the back vowels are replaced, when unaccented, by the mid-central ə. There is a further tendency in popular speech for the high-front vowels, when unaccented, also to become retracted and lowered beyond ɪ to ə. This has found its way into general cultivated speech in some words, as in *possible, enough*, etc., and the tendency seems to be increasing.

136. It is sometimes thought that the substitution in unaccented syllables of ɪ for i, e, ɛ of accented syllables, as seen in comparing *decompose* ˌdi kəmˈpoz with *define* dɪˈfaɪn, or the substitution of ə for other accented vowels, as seen in comparing *object* ˈɑbdʒɪkt with *object* əbˈdʒɛkt, or *revoke* rɪˈvok with *advocate* ˈædvəˌket, is an evidence of slovenly and vulgar pronunciation. This idea is erroneous, resulting partly from our imperfect system of spelling, and partly from the misguided

efforts of some well-meaning teachers not sufficiently acquainted
with the history and laws of the English language. Not only are
the unaccented sounds ɪ, ə, ɚ universally in actual use in the
unaffected speech of cultivated people of England and America,
but this fact is an instance of one of the most interesting and
important laws of the branch of the Indo-European language to
which English belongs. The tables show three grades of vowel
quality corresponding to differences in accent—(1) **Full grade**
(as ɛ in mo ˈmɛn təm), (2) **Reduced grade** (as ə in ˈmo mənt),
and (3) **Lost grade** (as shown in ˈbraɪ tn̩, where syllabic n̩ replaces the vowel; sometimes the syllable also is lost, as in ˈfɔrt-
ˌnaɪt compared with the full grade in ˈfor ˌtin ˈnaɪt). These
grades correspond in a general way to different grades in the
early stages of Indo-European of what is called **ablaut** (ˈɑbˌlaʊt,
German ˈɑpˌlaʊt). The results of IE ablaut as it operated in
verbs can now be seen in the parts of the verb *sink, sank, sunk,*
of which the forms *sink, sank* represent the full grade, with
accented vowel, and *sunk* (earlier *sunken*) represents the lost
grade (formerly with the first syllable unaccented and without
vowel, the ŋ being syllabic)

137. **Words Having Both Stressed and Unstressed Forms.**—
Owing to the principle of gradation of vowels according to
stress, a group of short words, chiefly monosyllables, frequently
used as connectives, prepositions, auxiliaries, etc., **though having
only one spelling form, in actual speech exist in two or more
forms** according to whether or not they have sense-stress. Thus
in *He has money,* *has* is the main verb of the sentence, and
therefore has strong sense-stress. Hence it has its full vowel
hæz. But in *John has gone,* *has* is a mere auxiliary, the meaning
of the main verb being contained in *gone,* which therefore has
the sense-stress of the verb while *has* is without any. In speech,
therefore, the second *has* is not **hæz,** but **həz, əz, z: hi həz gɔn,
hi əz gɔn, hiz gɔn.** The student should rid himself of the prevalent notion that these are merely careless pronunciations. On

the contrary, they are universal in cultivated speech that is not artificial.

Following is a list of stressed and unstressed forms. It should be remembered that the unstressed forms are those of unconscious speech. The moment we try to pronounce some of the unstressed forms consciously and out of their place in the sentence, we stress them, thus restoring the full vowel of the strong form. It is customary, when mentioning isolated words, to pronounce their stressed form, as *a* e, *an* æn, *the* ði. These are rare forms in actual speech, and the mistake must not be made of pronouncing the isolated form either in ordinary speech or when mentioning them in phrases or sentences, unless the sense requires the stressed form. Students are advised to read aloud carefully every item in the following list. The time will be well spent, for there is no more important feature of correct cultivated speech than the treatment of unstressed vowels.

Stressed and Unstressed Monosyllables of Speech

Spelling	Stressed Form		Unstressed Form	
a	e	(rare) ˈe ˌmæn, nɑt ˈtu ˌmɛn	ə	ə ˈtɔl ˈmæn
an	æn	(rare) ˈæn ˌɛg, nɑt ˈtu ˌɛgz	ən	ən ˈold ˈmæn
			n̩	ˈgɑt n̩ ˈæpl̩?
am	æm	ɪnˈdid, aɪ ˈæm	əm	ˌaɪ əm ˈrɛdɪ
'm			m	aɪm ˈrɛdɪ
and	ænd	ˈænd, ɪnˈdid, aɪ ˈʃʊd	ənd	ˈsno ənd ˈaɪs
	æn	ˈboθ ˌdʒɑn ˈæn ˌdʒemz	ən	ˈkʌp ən ˈsɔsɚ
			n̩d	ˈhɛd n̩d ˈɑrm
			n̩	ˈrɑd n̩ ˈgʌn
			ŋ	ˈdʒæk ŋ ˈket
			m̩	ˈʌp m̩ ˈdaʊn
are	ɑr	ˈjɛs, ðe ˈɑr	ɚ	ˈɔl ɚˈmɔrtl̩
're		(nonsyllabic)	r	ˌðer ˈhɪr
as	æz	ˌæz i ˈkem	əz	ˈdʒʌst əz ˈgʊd
			z	ˈnɑt sə ˈgʊd z ɪt ˈwɑz
			s	ˈnɑt sə ˈlaɪt s ɪt ˈlʊks

Spell-ing	Stressed Form		Unstressed Form	
at	æt	ˈmed tə ˈlʊk ˌæt	ət	ˈlʊk ət ðə ˈhaʊs
be	bi	ˈhaʊ kən ɪt ˈbi?	bɪ	ɪt ˈkʊdn̩t bɪ ˈdʌn
but	bʌt	ˈbʌt, ju ˌsi, aɪ ˈdɪd	bət	ˈɔl bət ˈtu
by	baɪ	ðe ˈdroʊv ˈbaɪ	bəɪ	bəɪ ˈɔl ˈmɪnz
			bə	ˈtu bə ˈtu (chiefly+cons.)
			bɪ	(occas. Brit. form; cf. *my*)
can	kæn	du ˈɔl ju ˈkæn	kən	ˌhi kən ˈsi ɪt
			kn̩	ˌaɪ kn̩ ˈdu ɪt
			kŋ	ˌaɪ kŋ ˈkɔl ɪm (esp.+k, g)
could	kʊd	ɪf ju ˈonlɪ ˈkʊd	kəd	ˌhi kəd ˈdu ɪt əˈlon
do	du	ˈhaʊ ʃəl aɪ ˈdu ɪt?	du	ˈhaʊ du ˈaɪ ˌno? (+vowel)
			də	ˈhwɑt də ðe ˈwɑnt? (+cons.)
does	dʌz	aɪ səˈpoz i ˈdʌz	dəz	ˈhaʊ dəz ɪt ˈgo?
'em	No stressed form. For a stressed form a different word, *them*, is used. See *them*, below.		əm	hi ˈtold əm tə ˈkʌm
			m̩	ˈkip m̩ ˈwɔrm
for	fɔr	ˈhu ɪz ɪt ˈfɔr?	fə	ˈwet fə ˈælɪs
from	frɑm	ˈhwær dɪd i ˈkʌm ˌfrɑm?	frəm	hi ˈkem frəm ˈtaʊn
had	hæd	ɪt wəz ˈɔl i ˈhæd	həd	ðe həd ˈgɑn ɔlˈredɪ
			əd	ðə ˈmæn əd ˈgɑn
'd			d	hid ˈgɑn hwɛn aɪ ˈkem
has	hæz	hi ˈhæz ðə ˈbʊk	həz	ˈmɑrθə həz ˈfaʊnd ɪt
			əz	ˈdʒɔrdʒ əz ˈkʌm; ˈgres əz ˈkʌm; ˈtʃstʃ əz bɪˈgʌn; ˈroz əz ˈkʌm (after sibilants)
's			z	(after voiced sounds exc. sibilants) hiz ˈdʒʌst ˈkʌm; ˈdʒɑnz ˈdʒʌst ˈkʌm
			s	(after voiceless sounds exc. sibilants) ˈdʒæks ˈkʌm
have	hæv	ˈlɛt mɪ ˈhæv ɪt	həv	ˌðe həv ˈʃʊrlɪ ˈkʌm
			əv	ðe ˈwʊdn̩t əv ˈgɑn
've			v	aɪv ˈlɔst ɪt

NOTE: The unstressed form ə is heard in rapid familiar speech before consonants; as ˌhi kəd ə ˈgɑn. In Early Modern it was common in cultivated speech and writing.

Spell-ing	Stressed Form		Unstressed Form	
he	hi	ˌhiənd aɪ ˈwɛnt	i	ðe ˈθɪŋk i ˈɪz
			ɪ	ðe ˈθɔt ɪ ˈdɪd

NOTE: *He, her,* and *his* are never entirely unstressed at the beginning of a phrase: hi ˈsɛd i ˈwʊd.

her	hɝ	ðæts ˈhɝ ˌbaks, nat ˈhɪz	hɚ	hɚ ˈmʌðɚ wəz ˈglæd
			ɚ	ʃi ˈmɛt ɚ ət ðə ˈsteʃən
him	hɪm	ˈgɪv ɪt tə ˈhɪm, nat ˈmi	ɪm	aɪ ˈmɛt ɪm ɪn ˈtaʊn
his	hɪz	ɪts ˈmaɪn, nat ˈhɪz	ɪz	ˈɔl ɪz ˈfrɛndz wɚ ˈhɪr
I	aɪ	ˌaɪ ˈsɔ ɪm ət ˈtʃɝtʃ	ə	(in rapid speech) ˌaɪ ˈdɪd ˌɔlə ˈkʊd
in	ɪn	ˈlɛt mi ˈɪn	n̩	ˈbrek ɪt n̩ ˈtu (occasional)
into	ɪntu	ɪt ʃəd bi ˈlʊkt ˈɪntu	ɪntʊ	ɪt ˈlɛd ɪntʊ ən ˈælɪ
			ɪntə	hi ˈwɔkt ɪntə ðə ˈgardn̩
is	ɪz	aɪ ˈθɪŋk i ˈɪz	ɪz	ðə ˈgræs ɪz ˈwɛt; ðɪ ˈɛdʒ ɪz ˈdʌl
's			z	(after voiced sounds exc. sibilants) ˈdʒanz ˈhɪr; ˈdʒoz ˈhɪr
			s	(after voiceless consonants exc. sibilants) ˈdʒæks ˈhɪr

NOTE: After s or z, instead of the unstressed form ɪz, sometimes the final sound of the preceding word is lengthened; as ðɪs s ə faɪn de; roz z ə laɪvlɪ gɔl. After ʃ, s is added in the same syllable; as, ðɪs dɪʃs hat; and after ʒ, z is added likewise; as, ðə gəraʒz ɛmptɪ. Apparently this does not happen after tʃ and dʒ.

Observe that two unstressed forms of *is* (s and z) are identical with two of *has* (s and z). In hiz kʌm, dʒæks kʌm, it is impossible to tell whether the auxiliary verb is *has* or *is*. Originally, with the verbs *come, go, lie, sit,* and other intransitive verbs of motion, the auxiliary was *is. Has,* which was originally used only with transitive verbs, came later to be used also with intransitives.

it	ɪt	ˈjɛs, ˈðæts ˈɪt	ɪt	ˌhwat ˈav ɪt?
't			t	ɪf twɚ ˈmaɪn, aɪd ˈsɛl ɪt

NOTE: The form *'tis* tɪz is used only under some stress. The usual unstressed combination is *it's* ɪts; as, ɪts ə ˈgʊd ˈθɪŋ. ˈjɛs, ˈtɪz. tɪz ə ˈgʊd ˈθɪŋ is now archaic or dialectal. The same distinction holds for stressed *'twill* twɪl and unstressed *it'll* ɪtļ; ɪtļ bi ə ˈgʊd ˈθɪŋ. ˈjɛs, ˈtwɪl. However, the form *t'll* tļ is common in familiar speech; as, tļ bi ə ˈgʊd ˈθɪŋ. Apparently unstressed *'twould* twʊd and *it'd* ɪtəd are interchangeable; as, twʊd bi ə ˈgʊd ˈθɪŋ, or ɪtəd ˈbi ə ˈgʊd ˈθɪŋ. For other similar combinations, see *Webster* (1934), *Pronunciation* §71.

may	me	ɪt ˈme bɪ ˈso		mɪ	ˈju mɪ ˈæsk ɪm
				mə	ju mə ˈgo ˌnaʊ
me	mi	ˈgɪv ɪt tə ˈmi, nat ˈhɪm		mɪ	hi ˈtraɪd tə ˈsi mɪ
must	mʌst	wil ˈdu ɪt ɪf wɪ ˈmʌst		məst	ju məst ˈæsk ɪm (+vowel)
				məs	wi məs ˈgo ət ˈwʌns (+cons.)
my	maɪ	ðæts ˈmaɪ ˌbʊk		məɪ	(+vowel) aɪ ˈsɔ məɪ ˈʌŋkļ
				mə	(+cons.) ˈpliz gɛt mə ˈkot
				mɪ	(occasional British; an archaic form, shortened from *my* when it was pronounced mi:)[58]
no (adj.)	noː	ˈno ˈren ˌfɛl		no, nə	(adv.) no lɔŋgɚ tru; hiz ˈgat nə ˌmor ðən ˈwi
nor	nɔr	ˈnɔr, æz ɪt ˈɪz, kən ˈwi		nɚ	niðɚ ˈfɪʃ nɚ ˈflɛʃ
not	nat	hiz ˌnat ˈhɪr jɛt			
n't				ņt	(after cons.) dʌzņt, dəsņt, dɪdņt, hædņt, hævņt, hæzņt, ɪzņt, kʊdņt, maɪtņt, mʌsņt, nidņt, ɔtņt, ʃʊdņt, wazņt, wʊdņt
				nt	(after vowels) arnt, dærnt, dont, ment, ʃænt, wɜnt, wʌnt, wont
't				t	kænt
				ņ	(occas.+cons.) hi hæzņ ˈkʌm; hi kʊdņ ˈdu ɪt; hi wʊdņ ˈtraɪ

NOTE: In the combination of auxiliary and *not*, sometimes the auxiliary is unstressed, and sometimes the negative; as ðɛv ˌnat ˈgɔn jɛt, or ðe ˌhævņt ˈgɔn

---

[58] See Daniel Jones's interesting note on *my* (*Phonetics*, 1932, §473).

jɛt; hiz ˌnɑt ˈhɪr, or hi ˌɪzn̩t ˈhɪr. The unstressed n̩t seems to be more informal. The two ways are traditional and utilized by poets; cf. Keats:

> She ˈcannot fade, though thou hast ˈnot thy bliss.

| of | ɑv | ˌhwɑt ˈɑv ɪt? | əv | ðɪ ˈɛnd əv ðə ˈwik |
| *'o* | | | ə | ˈtɛn əˈklɑk (frequent+ cons. in very informal speech; as, ə ˈlod ə ˈwʊd; ə ˈglæs ə ˈmɪlk) |

NOTE: Observe that one unstressed form of *have* (əv) in cultivated speech is exactly like the usual unstressed form of *of* (əv). Hence when the schoolboy writes *I wouldn't of gone*, he is not making a mistake in grammar, but merely in spelling. The two expressions *I wouldn't have gone* and *I wouldn't of gone* are exactly alike in standard pronunciation. To pronounce *have* and *of* differently in sentences that require the unstressed forms, would be a worse blunder than to misspell *have*. Some writers try to give a dialect tinge to the speech of their characters by representing them as saying "I wouldn't of gone." This is silly, and shows ignorance of standard English pronunciation. The same statement applies to the use of such pseudo-dialect spellings as *sez, wuz, iz, kumz*, etc., which are good (though unconventional) spellings for as good pronunciations as such authors themselves could muster.

on	ɑn	ðə ˈbæt̩z ˈɑn; ˌɑn ə ˈrʌn; ˌɑn ˈfɑɪr; hi ˈwɛnt ˌɑn ə ˈhʌnt		
a-			ə	ðe ˈkem ə ˈrʌnɪŋ; ðə ˈhaʊs ɪz əˌfɑɪr; hi ˈwɛnt əˈhʌntɪŋ
one	wʌn	ˈhwɪtʃ ˈwʌn?	wən	aɪ ˈwɑnt ˈðæt wən
or	ɔr	ˈɔr, ɪf ˈnɑt, ˌtek ˈðɪs	ɚ	ˈwʌn ɚ ðɪ ˈʌðɚ
pretty	prɪtɪ	ə ˈprɪtɪ ˈgɜl	pɚtɪ	pɚtɪ ˈwɛl, ˌθæŋk ju (the vowel ɚ here is practically a retroflex ɪ)
Saint	sent	ˈsent ˈpitɚ	sənt, sən	sənt ˈæn; sən ˈdʒemz
			sɪnt, sɪn	sɪnt ˈɔdrɪ; sɪn ˈdʒɒn
			sn̩	sn̩ ˈdʒɒn (unstressed forms chiefly British)
shall	ʃæl	aɪ ˈθɪŋk aɪ ˈʃæl (formerly ʃɒl, riming with *all* in "John Gilpin's Ride")	ʃəl	ˌwi ʃəl bi ˈrɛdɪ
			ʃl̩	ˌaɪ ʃl̩ bi ˈglæd tə ˈgo

Spelling	Stressed Form		Unstressed Form	
she	ʃi	aı ˈsɔ ɪm bɪfor ˈʃi dɪd	ʃɪ	aı ˈθɔt ʃɪ ˈmɛnt ɪt
should	ʃʊd	aı ˈθɪŋk jʊ ˈʃʊd	ʃəd	ˌaı ʃəd bɪ ˈglæd ˌtu
			ʃd	(familiar) aı ʃd–ˈdu ɪt
			ʃt	(familiar) aı ʃt ˈθɪŋk so
sir	sɝ	ˈno, ˈsɝ!	sɚ	sə ˈrɑbət; ˈθæŋk jʊ, sɚ
so	so	ˈso ðe ˈsɛd	sə	ɪts ˌnɑt sə ˈkold təˌde[59]
some	sʌm	ˈsʌm ɚ ˈbɛtɚ ðən ˈʌðɚz	səm	ˈlɛts ˈhæv səm ˈaɪsˈkrim
			sə	(before m) ˈhæv sə ˈmor

NOTE: Observe the correspondence between the stressed form of *one* wʌn and stressed sʌm: (sg.) ˈwʌn ˌmæn ˈsmoks, əˈnʌðɚ ˈdʌznt: (pl.) ˈsʌm ˌmɛn ˈsmok, ˈʌðɚz ˈdont; and between ə (historical unstressed form of *one*) and səm (unstressed form of sʌm): (sg.) aı ˈmɛt ə ˈmæn: (pl.) aı ˈmɛt səm ˈmɛn. The form səm is also used with mass-words that do not take ə; as, səm ˈti, səm ˈhwɪt. səm never stands alone; cf. ˈhæv səm ˈti. ˈθæŋks, aıl ˈhæv ˌsʌm, and ˈhæv ə ˈkek. ˈθæŋks, aıl ˈhæv ˌwʌn. But wən can stand alone (ˈðæts ə ˈfaın wən), and its plural is wənz (ˈðoz ɚ ˈnaıs wənz).

than	ðæn	(rare) əz ˈgʊd ˌæz, ɚ ˈbɛtɚ ˌðæn	ðən, ðņ	ˈmor ðən ˈɛvɚ; ˈmor ðŋ ˈɛvɚ
			ņ	(familiar) ɪts ˈlɛs ņ ne ˈɪntʃ
			n	(familiar) ˈðæts ˈmor n ˈaı no
that	ðæt	(demonstrative) ˈðæts ˈɔl	ðət	(conjunction) hi ˈsɛd ðət i ˈsɔ ɪt
				(relative) ˈhiz ðə ˈmæn ðət ˈdɪd ɪt
the	ði	(rare) ˈe ˌmæn, nɑt ˈði ˌmæn	ðə	(+cons.) ðə ˈtri; ðə ˈrod; ðə ˈwɔl
			ðɪ	(+vowel) ðɪ ˈ3θ; ðɪ ˈɛnd

NOTE: ðɪ is also sometimes used before j by assimilation (§§94 ff.); as, ðɪ ˈjɪr; and before h followed by a front vowel; as, ðɪ ˈhit, ðɪ ˈhɪlz, ðɪ ˈhɛdʒ. What fact in the formation of h explains this?

[59] *So* has been weakened several times in the course of its history. It was originally swaː, and successively saː, sɔ, sə, s, z. The last form is preserved in *as* æz, əz, formerly ɑlˈswaː, ɑlˈsɔ, ˈɑlsə, ɑls, ɑz, æz, əz.

Spell-ing	Stressed Form		Unstressed Form	
there	ðær	(adv.) ˈðær ðe ˈɑr	ðɛr	(expletive) ðɛr wə ˈtwɛntɪ ˌðær
			ðɚ	ðɚ ˈɑr ˌnʌn
them	ðɛm	ˈgɪv ɪt tə ˈðɛm, nɑt ˈʌs	ðəm, ðm̩	wi ˈmɛt ðəm ət ˈtu ə ˈklɑk (see §205)
to	tu	ˈhwɑt ɪz ɪt ˈkʌmɪŋ ˌtu?	tʊ	(+vowel) frəm ˈhɛvən tʊ ˈɪθ
			tə	(+cons.) ˈɪzɪ tə ˈdu; ˈgo tə ˈtaʊn

NOTE: Many cultivated speakers frequently use tə also before vowels; as ˌhi hæd ˈnʌθɪŋ tə ˈɔfɚ. In such cases the ə is very short.

up	ʌp	ˈmek jɚ ˈmaɪnd ˌʌp	əp	ˈmek əp jɚ ˈmaɪnd
upon	əˈpɑn	ˈhwɑt wəz ɪt ˈbest əˌpɑn?	əpən	(chiefly Brit.) ˈlaɪn əpən ˈlaɪn
us	ʌs	ˈgɪv ɪt tu ˈʌs, nɑt ˈðɛm	əs	ðe ˈæskt əs tə ˈdʒɔɪn ðəm
's			s	ˈlɛts nɑt ˈgo ˌjɛt

NOTE: In the phrase *let's see*, the word *us* was originally not present; *let see* was later transformed to *let's see* by analogy of *let's go*, etc.

was	wɑz	ˈðær i ˈwɑz	wəz	ˌhi wəz ˈðær; ˌhi wəz ˈnɑt ˈhɪr
we	wi	ˈso dʊ ˈwi	wɪ	ˌwil dʊ ˈɔl wɪ ˈkæn
were	wɜ	ˈðær ðe ˈwɜ	wɚ	ˌðe wɚ ˈðær; ˌðe wɚ ˈnɑt ˈhɪr

NOTE: In England the stressed form wɛə, wæə is not uncommon. It is archaic or dialectal in America. wɛr, wær is the historical stressed form, and wɜ is a restressed form (§ 139).

what	hwɑt	hi ˈnoz ˈhwɑts ˈhwɑt	hwət	(in rapid speech) ˈsi hwət ˈaɪ ˌhæv
will	wɪl	aɪ bɪˈliv ðe ˈwɪl	wl̩	ˈno ˌwʌn wl̩ ɛvɚ ˈnotɪs ɪt
'll			əl	ˈfɑðɚ əl ˈbi ˌhɪr ˈsun
			l̩	ˈnɛd l̩ ˈbi ˌhɪr ˈsun; ˈhwɑt l̩ jʊ ˈdu?
			l	ˌðel ˈkʌm; ˌwil ˈθɪŋkəˌbaʊt ɪt

Spell-ing	Stressed Form		Unstressed Form	
would	wʊd	aɪ ˈwɪʃ ðe ˈwʊd	wəd	ˈdʒɑn wəd ˈlaɪk tə ˈgo
'd			əd	ɪt əd bi ˈfʌn, ˈwʊdn̩t ɪt?
			d	ˌðed bi ˈrɛdɪ baɪ ˈfor
you	ju	ˈðɪs ɪz fɚ ˈju	jʊ	pɚˌhæps jʊ ˈɔt tu
	jʊ	ˈjʊr ðɪ ˈonlɪ ˈgɛst	jə	ˈhaʊ də jə ˈdu?
			jɪ	ˈhaʊ də jɪ ˈdu?

NOTE: The unstressed form **jɪ**, occasionally heard in very familiar speech, is probably the unstressed form of *ye* **ji**, now obsolete in speech in its stressed form.

| *your* | jʊr | ɪz ˌðɪs ˈjʊr hæt, ɚ ˈmaɪn? | jɚ | aɪ ˈθɪŋk aɪ ˈsɔ jɚ ˈbrʌðɚ təˌde |

NOTE: Unstressed *your* **jɚ**, in addition to its usual personal possessive meaning, has acquired a special sense, not personal or possessive, but referring to something as familiar, often with a connotation of contempt; as, "That's a sample of your practical education!" So Hamlet says to Horatio,

> "Ther are more things in heauen and earth, Horatio,
> Then are drem't of in your (**jɚ**) philosophie [natural science]."

138. Certain common verbs with full meaning (in contrast to auxiliaries) occur in familiar phrases, such as *come ˈin*, *go ˈout*, *go ˈdown*, *see ˈhere*, *said ˌhe*, which in actual speech are like single words of two syllables with the first unaccented, and hence often have obscured vowel; as, **kəm ˈɪn, gʊ ˈaʊt, gə ˈdaʊn, sɪ ˈhɪr, səd ˌi.** In familiar speech the word *have*, ordinarily stressed when it means "possess" and unstressed when it is auxiliary, sometimes has its unstressed form with full meaning "possess"; as, **jʊv no əbdʒɛkʃən, hæv jʊ? hid no kɔz tə kəmplen; dʒɪm həz no taɪm tə du ɪt.** It is possible that this use is due to the analogy of the auxiliary use of *have* with *got* in the sense of "possess"; as, **hiz gɑt no taɪm tə du ɪt.**

139. In connection with these relation words, which are stressed in different degrees with corresponding gradation of vowels, we have to observe the phenomenon of **restressing.** It

has been seen in the discussion of gradation, that several different vowel sounds all reduce to ə or ɪ when unstressed. Now
since this, like most processes of language development, is unconscious, it sometimes happens, especially in popular speech,
when a word like *from*, which is more often unstressed **frəm,**
for some reason is stressed, that it does not return to its less
familiar original stressed form **fram,** but takes the form **frʌm.**
Hence some speakers, when they have occasion to stress *from*
pronounce it **frʌm** instead of **fram.** Similar instances are seen in
what, with unstressed form **hwət** and restressed form **hwʌt;** *was*,
unstressed **wəz,** restressed **wʌz;** *for*, unstressed **fɚ,** restressed **fɜ;**
of, unstressed **əv,** restressed **ʌv.**

In the foregoing the restressed form has not always replaced the older form. But in the case of *were*, unstressed **wɚ,**
the restressed form **wɜ** has become the standard form, while
the historical form **wær** has virtually disappeared in America,
though it remains **wæə, wɛə** in England. Likewise with *does*,
unstressed **dəz,** restressed **dʌz.** We should expect the form **duz**
from **du,** and this perhaps remains in the dialect stressed form
dʊz which is sometimes heard. See § 322.[30]

140. In some instances the consonant also has been affected
by lack of stress. It has long been a tendency of voiceless consonants in English to become voiced by loss of stress in unstressed syllables. Words like *as, was, is, his*, were formerly
pronounced **as, was, ɪs, hɪs** with **s**, not **z**. The original **s** is still
seen in *it's a fine day*, where the influence of the voiceless **t** has
preserved the **s** from changing to **z** as it has in *it is* **ɪt ɪz.** But
as these words are usually unstressed, they have become **əz,**
wəz, ɪz, (h)ɪz. So now, even when they are occasionally stressed,
the **z** of the usual unstressed form has been transferred unconsciously to the stressed forms, and the **s** has disappeared
from the words. In the case of the word *of*, the older stressed
form **ɒf, ɔf,** now spelt *off*, now remains chiefly as an adverb, and

the unstressed form əv, spelt *of*, is used as a preposition. But when the preposition occasionally is stressed, it becomes ɑv, and is now regarded as a different word from ɔf. So ɔf is the originally stressed form, and ɑv a restressed form, of the same word.

141. In the words *of* ɑv, əv, and *with* wɪð, wɪθ, formerly pronounced ɒf, wɪθ, the voiced v and ð now heard are due to lack of stress. But *there'of* and *there'with* are still often pronounced ðær'ɑf, ðær'wɪθ, because of the accent on the second syllable, which has preserved the f and θ voiceless. When these words are pronounced ðær'ɑv, ðær'wɪð, the voiced v and ð are due to the analogy of ɑv and wɪð.

The word *with*, however, often preserves its older pronunciation wɪθ, especially before voiceless consonants, as in wɪθ'stænd, wɪθ'hold, wɪθ tɑm, wɪθ kærɪ, wɪθ pitɚ; and some speakers regularly use wɪθ in all positions. It is a common form in the North of England and in Scottish standard English.

Spelling-Pronunciation

142. It has been emphasized that phonetic change is concerned primarily with the spoken language, and not with the written or printed representation of it. Most phonetic change is unconscious, and some of it has begun with the illiterate and afterwards found its way into cultivated usage. As a rule the changes that have occurred have either never found their way permanently into the spelling—as seen in the word *use*, which has gained an initial **j** that has not appeared in the spelling; or if the spelling has been changed to express the new sound, as it was in the word *you* (formerly without *y* or **j** sound), this has always happened long after the new pronunciation has become firmly fixed in speech. Thus it was two or three hundred years after the final syllable ceased to be sounded on words like *sunne*, *runne, houre, seeme, heare,* and hundreds of others, before the spelling was changed to *sun, run, hour, seem, hear,* to correspond with the sound; and in numerous cases the spelling has not even yet conformed to changes in sound made hundreds of years ago, as in such words as *have, love, make, cause, tell, said,* etc. Reflection on this aspect of the development of English shows how entirely without foundation is the reasoning frequently heard when a question is raised about the pronunciation of a word: "It is spelt so and so; therefore it should be pronounced so and so." E.g., it is argued that *clerk* and *sergeant* cannot properly be pronounced **kla(r)k** and **sa(r)dʒənt** because they are spelt with *er*. Yet *clerk* is regularly so pronounced in England, and *sergeant* so generally. Such reasoning puts the cart before the horse. The logical reasoning would be, since *clerk* and *sergeant* are pronounced **kla(r)k** and **sa(r)dʒənt,** they should be spelt with *a* instead of *e*.

It happens that the spelling of most words like *star, carve, smart, hart, far, farm,* has, in fact, conformed to the pronunciation. These words, like *clerk* and *sergeant,* formerly were all spelt with *er*, and continued to be so written long after the sound had changed from **ɛr** to **ar**. See §365.

143. (1) Those who reason that words should be pronounced as they are spelt scarcely realize what a revolution would be wrought in present English if they carried out their rule to any extent. Transcribe the following words in a spelling-pronunciation; that is, with the pronunciation they would have if all the letters were sounded in what would seem to you their most usual way:

Among, slough, brought, anxious, said, nothing, worst, people, pretty, brief, fiend, friend, money, could, bargain, road, abroad, scarce, farce, mouse, rouse, famous, where, here, hear, heard, beard, treat, great, leak, break, steak, ever, fever, done, gone, tone, none,

whose, those, whole, whale, poor, moor, door, floor, seven, even,
early, nearly, pearly, pear, fear, goer, doer, swear, answer, swore,
sword, word, ford, form, worm, though, thought, tough, bough,
through, home, some, mere, there, pays, says, gown, grown, down,
mown, eight, height, caught, laughed, draught, evil, devil, double,
doubtless, beeches, breeches, been, cloven, oven, bother, other, honor,
honest, host, heir, weir, shelf, self, half, Ralph, revived, lived, power,
mower, finger, singer, longer, anger, hanger, sorehead, forehead,
hew, sew, county, country, grove, above, move, prove, over, cover,
mover, all, shall, believe, sieve, wholly, jolly, surmise, promise,
dully, gully, fully, pullet, mullet, goes, toes, does, shoes, frowned,
owned, cross, gross, toward, coward, hearing, bearing, pouch, touch.

(2) Find several English words whose pronunciation you can
know for certain from their spelling.

144. (1) The influence of spelling on standard pronunciation
has been especially important since the middle of the 18th c.,
and especially owing to the influence of Dr. Johnson, who,
though he recognized both a colloquial and a formal style of pronunciation, stated this principle: "For pronunciation, the best
general rule is to consider those as the most elegant speakers
who deviate least from the written words." This statement was
made in apparent disregard of the utter impossibility of carrying it out in the state of English spelling then and since. His
influence was strengthened by the prevailing idea of the time
that the written form of the language was the language itself.
This appears clearly in the dictionaries of John Walker (1791
and on), in which letters are treated as the elements of language,
with "powers" of sound, as if they were a kind of seed from
which the spoken language sprouted and grew, and therefore
the original source to which all questions of correct pronunciation were to be referred back.

(2) This point of view is still current and influential. Its ad-

herents cry in triumph, "Isn't there a *t* in *often?* Why should
we neglect to pronounce it?" As Dr. Fuhrken has aptly expressed it, they are willing to mispronounce words in order to
show that they know how they are spelt. In addition to being
fundamentally in error about the nature, origin, and growth of
all language, they strangely ignore the fact that they neither
do nor can carry out their own rule, as the exercise above is
sufficient to show.

(3) A spelling-pronunciation that departs from the traditional pronunciation (the one that is transmitted by word of
mouth and learned by ear) is a blunder, of the same kind that
it would be to pronounce *many* as **mænɪ** or **menɪ** instead of
mɛnɪ. But when such a blunder is adopted into general good
use, as was **swun,** formerly by regular sound-law pronounced
sun (cf. *sword* **sord**), or ₁**æsɪgˈneʃən** (cf. *sign* **saɪn**), and a large
number of others, it is accepted and supersedes the correct
traditional form. So a very considerable number of words—
though a very small proportion of all—have conformed in some
respect to the spelling which happened to be current when the
change was made. Such changes are, however, apt to be isolated
ones, leaving unchanged many other words spelt in the same
way. Thus the pronunciation **kɑnstəbḷ,** a spelling-pronunciation
for the traditional **kʌnstəbḷ,** or **kɑmræd** for traditional **kʌmræd,**
have become isolated in pronunciation from the many other
words in which **ʌ** is spelt with *o,* as *honey, love, above, some,
come,* etc. In two groups, however, (1) words like *host, human,
hospital,* etc., which all came into English from OF without a
h sound (see **h,** §203), and (2) words like *theater, author, apothecary,* etc., which came into English with **t** spelt *th*—spelling-
pronunciation has changed nearly all the words to pronunciations with the **h** sound and the **θ** sound (see **t,** §157).

145. On comparing *host, human, hospital* with *hour, honest,* *honor,* and *theater, author, apothecary* with *Thomas, Thames, Esther,* an underlying principle of spelling-pronunciation is revealed. The words that have resisted spelling-pronunciation (*hour, Thomas*) are more common words, and therefore more likely to be thoroughly learned by children before they learn to read and write. On the other hand, if we first learn words from books, or if we see them in print oftener than we use them, we are more apt to guess at the pronunciation from the spelling. As a great many people are apt to do this, and many even cultivated and influential people unconsciously reason that words should be pronounced as they are spelt, many such spelling-pronunciations get into good use, and older traditional and phonetically natural pronunciations are gradually abandoned.

146. Spelling-pronunciation is especially apt to affect proper names—particularly names of places pronounced from the spelling by people who do not live in them and hence do not know the traditional pronunciation. So *Greenwich, Woolwich,* and *Norwich* in England are pronounced by the inhabitants of those towns **grınıdʒ, wʊlıdʒ, nɒrıdʒ** (the latter riming with "cold pease porridge"). But people not personally familiar with the places themselves and seeing the names in print are likely to call them **grinwıtʃ, wʊlwıtʃ, nɔrwıtʃ.** So *Cirencester* **sısıtɚ** is apt to be called elsewhere **saırənsɛstɚ.** *Concord* **kɒŋkəd** and *Chelmsford* **tʃɛmzfəd** are usually called **kɑnkɔrd** and **tʃɛlmzford** outside of New England. The student can easily find other examples of the same sort.

147. Evidence that the influence of spelling on pronunciation is increasing with the advance of popular education is seen in that in recent times in some of the places themselves the traditional pronunciation is giving way to the spelling-pronunciation. Thus the inhabitants of Cirencester and others in England are beginning to call the place **saırənsɛstə, -tɚ.** *Ravenna* (Ohio)

is called by its old residents rɪˈvænə, but it is now commonly
rəˈvɛnə. *Mantua* (Ohio) is locally ˈmæntəˌwe, but sometimes
called ˈmæntʊə or ˈmæntʃʊə by those who depend on the
spelling.[60]

The comparatively recent increase in the influence of spelling on pronunciation has resulted in the fact that certain places
in England have the traditional name, often widely separated
from the fixed spelling, while places in America with the same
names have the more theoretical pronunciation according to the
spelling. Thus we have grɪnɪdʒ in England, but grinwɪtʃ in
Connecticut; the river tɛmz in England, but θemz in Connecticut, except as the English name is imitated; *Waltham* wɒltəm
in England, but wɒlθəm, wɔlθæm in Massachusetts; *Edinburgh*
ɛdn̩bʌrə in Scotland, and ɛd(ɪ)nbɝg, various American towns;
Marlborough mɔlbərə, England, and *Marlboro* ˈmɑ(r)lˌbɝo,
Massachusetts.

148. In some cases, compounding of names brings together
certain letters so as to suggest sounds not found originally in
the name. Thus the name *Waltham* is composed of *Walt*+*ham*
('home,' 'dwelling'), in the same way as *Windham* wɪndəm,
Durham dʒəm; so we should expect wɔltəm, as we find in England. But the spelling *th* has suggested the sound θ, which is
used in the American name wɔlθæm. *Chatham*, however, remains
tʃætəm, and is often ˈtʃætˌhæm in the Ohio town and on Cape
Cod, being also a spelling-pronunciation, but with a different

---

[60] Regarding the correctness of the different pronunciations, it should be
remembered that a different law governs in personal and place names from that
of speech in general. In the latter, general usage of the cultivated determines
correctness. But in personal and place names, it is personal and local usage that
determines the pronunciation. For example, all the rest of the country cannot
properly change the name of Concord, Massachusetts, to ˈkɑnˌkɔrd so long as
the local inhabitants regularly call it ˈkʊŋkəd. The same principle holds in
family names. See Allen W. Read, *Amer. Speech*, Feb. 1933, pp. 42–46.

result. *Windham*, Vermont, is locally often ˈwɪndˌhæm. Similar
to *Waltham* are *Eltham* in England ɛltəm, ɛlθəm, *Bentham*
bɛntəm, bɛnθəm, *Walsham* wɒlsəm, wɒlʃəm, *Lewisham* luɪsəm,
luɪʃəm, *Feversham* fɛvəzəm, fɛvəʃəm.

In personal names spelling-pronunciation is seen in *Leopold*,
formerly lɛpḷd (cf. *leopard*), now, from the spelling, liəpold;
Ralph, formerly, and still in England **ref**, now rælf; *Theobald*,
formerly tɪbḷd, now θiəbɔld; *Walter*, formerly wɔtɚ, now wɔltɚ.
Personal names, being applied to many individuals and families,
often split up into several different forms. Thus the name *Theobald* is represented by the various forms of the older pronunciation tɪbḷd in the names *Tibbits*, *Tibalt* (*Tybalt* in *Romeo &
Juliet*), *Tibbals*, and the spelling-pronunciation θiəbɔld. *Walter*
shows relics of its earlier pronunciation in the derivatives *Watt*,
Waters, *Watson*, *Watkins*. See §§221 ff.

149. Sometimes the spelling of a name has conformed to the
earlier traditional pronunciation. So in the name *Ker*, *Kerr*
kɑr, changed in spelling to *Carr* to correspond to the sound; and
vice versa, the pronunciation of other instances of the same
name has conformed to the spelling *Kerr*, becoming kɝ. So with
Berkeley and *Barclay*. *Berkeley* was formerly pronounced
bɑ(r)klɪ, as still in England, and accordingly sometimes spelt
Barkley, *Barclay*, while in other cases the pronunciation conformed by spelling-pronunciation to the form *Berkeley* and became bɝklɪ.

150. Of words other than names, spelling-pronunciation has
changed some that have become less familiar than formerly.
Often both pronunciations are used—the older traditional one,
and the newer spelling-pronunciation. So it is, frequently, with
a class of words having the sound ʌ spelt with *o*, such as *love*,
dove, *above*, *come*, *shove*, etc. (§325). The commoner words have
retained the ʌ sound. But the word *wont* wʌnt, 'custom,' 'ac-

customed,' is now often pronounced **wont** from the spelling. Words which formerly had ʌ but now have ɒ, ɑ from the spelling are *dromedary* ˈdrʌmə₁dɛrɪ, ˈdrɑmə₁dɛrɪ, *comrade, constable, bomb, groveling*. The old pronunciation with ʌ is still heard in these, and commonly in some of them.

A group of words like *fault, vault, falcon*, borrowed from French, in which the spelling with *l* is due to imitation of their Latin originals, had no **l** sound when they became English, and for long afterwards. But most of them have now conformed to the spelling; *fault* was fɔt in the 18th century. This accounts for the pronunciation of *Walter* mentioned above, §148.

Miscellaneous examples of spelling-pronunciation are: *steelyards*, formerly **stɪljəˌdz**, now sometimes ˈstilˌjɑrdz; *registrar* formerly **rɛdʒɪstrəˌ**, now ˈrɛdʒɪsˌtrɑr; *nephew* **nɛvju**, now mostly **nɛfju**; *apothecary*, formerly əˈpɑtɪˌkɛrɪ, now əˈpɑθəˌkɛrɪ; *author*, formerly ɔtəˌ, now ɔθəˌ; *soldier*, formerly sodʒəˌ, now soldʒəˌ; *Wandsworth*, formerly **wɒndzə**, now **wɒndzwəθ**; *Southwark* **sʌðək**, sometimes now **saʊθwək**.

Transcribe the names of the letters of the alphabet.

Write their names in ordinary spelling.

Consonants in Detail

The Stops

p

151. (1) Repeat the organic description and give the descriptive name of **p**.

(2) Comment on the **p** sound and its spelling in *apple, appear; sheeppen, hoppole; hiccough, corps*.[60a]

[60a] In finding answers to these questions and others the student will often find the Index useful.

(3) What is the acoustic difference (including on-glides and off-glides) in the sounds of **p** in *pen, copy, rope?* in *stamp, stopped?*

152. (1) In the past history of English, speakers have tended unconsciously to insert a **p** between **m** and any of the sounds **t, k, f, θ, s, ʃ**; as in *empty,* formerly *emty; Tompkins,* formerly *Tomkins; glimpse,* formerly *glimse; presumption,* cf. *presume.* In some cases *p* has been adopted in the spelling, and sometimes the **p** still remains unspelt, though plainly heard; as in *Thompson* or *Thomson; Sampson* or *Samson;* in *comfort, something, warmth, dreamt,* and some others spelt without *p,* a **p** is often sounded. **kʌmpfɚt, sʌmpθɪŋ, wɔrmpθ, drɛmpt.** This is a natural phonetic development. In forming **m** the lips are already in position to form either **p** or **b.** The next sound being oral, the velum rises to close the nasal passage; but if this is closed before the lips open, the stoppage of the breath forms a **p** if the next sound is voiceless.

(2) What will happen to the word *jumped* **dʒʌmpt** if the lips open from **m** as soon as the velum rises for **t?**

(3) What is the relative timing of the lip opening and the velum closure when *glimpse* is pronounced **glɪms?**

In British speech **p** is often omitted after **m,** whether spelt (*empty, prompt, tempt*) or not (*warmth, dreamt*).

For the aspiration of **p,** which is similar to that of **t,** cf. §§78, 45.

b

153. (1) Repeat the organic description and the descriptive name of **b.**

(2) State the relation of **b** to **p.**

(3) While the lips and the velum are closed for **b,** what becomes of the breath that vibrates the vocal cords?

(4) Comment on the **b** sound and its spelling in *rabbit, ebb; subbase, curb bit.*

(5) Point out the acoustic and organic differences in the **b** of *bee, Toby, rob*.

154. (1) In some words a **b** has developed between **m** and **l**, **r**, or **ɚ**; as in *thimble* **θɪmbl̩**, formerly **θɪml̩**; *nimble* **nɪmbl̩**, formerly **nɪm(ə)l**; *humble* **hʌmbl̩**, Lat. *humilem; bramble* **bræmbl̩**, formerly **bræːm(ɛ)l**; or in *slumber* **slʌmbɚ**, formerly **slʊm(ə)r**; *timber* **tɪmbɚ**, formerly **tɪmr**. Explain the excrescent **b** as **p** in *empty* was explained.

(2) In *dumb, climb, comb, jamb, lamb, plumb* the silent *b* was formerly **b** (**dʊmb, kliːmbən, kɔːmb**, etc.). But no **b** was ever sounded in *limb*, **lɪm**, *numb* **nʌm**, which are derived from OE *lim* **lɪm** and *numen* **nʊmɛn**. After the **b** had ceased to be sounded in *dumb* **dʌm**, *climb* **klaɪm**, *comb* **kom**, etc., the words *lim* and *num* also added a silent *b*. This kind of imitation in spelling is called **reverse** (or **inverse**) **spelling,** and the spelling *numb* shows that the *b* in *dumb* had become silent by the time it was added to *num*. Why does it show this?

Thus reverse spelling becomes valuable evidence about early pronunciation. For example, what does the spelling *garding* for *garden* **ɡɑrdɪn,** found in an old letter, show about the writer's pronunciation of *running, coming*, etc.?

t

155. (1) Repeat the organic description and the descriptive name of **t**.

(2) Observe the effect of sounding **t** with the tongue point placed on the very front edge of the teethridge. Try it also on the backs of the upper front teeth. These observations will be useful in pronouncing German and French **t**.

(3) Comment on the **t** sound and its spelling in *tool, seat; attend, outtalk; Thomas, Tom, Anthony, Tony; indict, victuals, mortgage; eighth, ninth*. Does the organic description of **t** in §29 fit the **t** in *eighth, ninth*?

156. In words in *-tion* (*nation*), *-tial* (*partial*), *-tient* (*patient*),

-*tious* (*cautious*), derived from Latin, either directly or through Old French, the **t** sound was not used in French or in English. The Latin **t** in -*tion*, etc., had become, first **ts** (an affricate, cf. §33) and then **s**. The spelling was usually -*cion*, -*sion*, etc., in Old French and Middle English. The spelling -*tion*, etc., was later substituted in imitation of Latin spelling (especially at the revival of learning in the 16th c., when scholarly reverence for Latin and Greek greatly increased), but without affecting the sound **s**. This **s** sound in Early Modern further changed to **ʃ**, by the influence of the following **ɪ** (later **j**); see §195 (3).

157. The spelling *th* represents the **t** sound in a few English words, as *Thomas*, *Thompson*, *Anthony* **æntənɪ** (cf. *Tony*), *thyme* **taɪm**, *Esther* **ɛstɚ**. These are spelt in imitation of Latin, in which there was no **θ** or **ð** sound and *th* was pronounced **t** (Latin borrowed the spelling from Greek, where there had once been a **h** sound after the **t**). Observe that in the derived Romance languages (French, Spanish, Italian, etc.) there is also no **θ** or **ð** sound descended from Latin. Cf. §183 (3).

In many cases, however, the **t** sound spelt thus with *th* was in English later changed to a **θ** sound through the influence of the spelling (cf. *Spelling-pronunciation*, §§142–150), so that many words with *th* now pronounced **θ** were formerly in English pronounced with **t**.

(1) What is suggested about earlier pronunciation by the nicknames *Kate, Betty, Marty, Ted, Art, Bart, Matt, Nat, Tad, Berty* (girl's name), *Dot, Dorrit?*

158. (1) What is the natural tendency of the **t** sound in *postmaster, must be, you must do it, next month, next door, last night, half past five, sit down, I don't know, perfectly, exactly, facts?*

(2) Would you consider it correct to pronounce **t** in the foregoing expressions? Would you consider it correct to pronounce **t** in *chasten, christen, fasten, glisten, hasten, listen, moisten?* in

bristle, castle, hustle, thistle, trestle, whistle, wrestle? in *chestnut, mustn't?* in *soften?* Would you recommend t in *often?*

159. Some words ending in -*st* formerly ended in -*s* only; e.g., *against*, formerly *agains; amongst*, formerly *amongs; midst*, formerly *mids*. Compare also the dialectal pronunciation wʌnst for *once*, twaɪst for *twice*, əkrɔst for *across*. The t was added to *once* wʌnst for the same phonetic cause as to *against*. Why is one incorrect and the other correct?

A similar addition of t is found in some cases after final n. It has become accepted English in *peasant*, from Old French *paysan; pheasant*, OF *faisan; pennant*, OF *pennon* (which is also in use). Forms not now in accepted use, but once in good standing are: *margent* for *margin* (regular in Shakespeare); *varmint* for *vermin; orphant* for *orphan* (cf. Riley's "Little Orphant Annie"). What is there in the tongue positions for articulating s and n that easily leads to the unconscious addition of t in such cases?

160. A t has also developed very generally in America between n and s, ʃ, θ, as in *sense* sɛnts, *fence* fɛnts, *answer* æntsɚ, *mention* mɛntʃən, *ninth* naɪntθ. Can you detect any difference in sound between *sense* and *cents, tense* and *tents, presence* and *presents?* Explain the organic reason for the addition of a t sound in *sense* sɛnts, etc. See §152.

161. The words *debt, doubt, receipt* have never sounded the *b* or *p* in English. These words were taken into English in their spoken forms from Old French in the 13th and 14th cc. At that time the written forms were usually *dette, doute, receite*, in agreement with their pronunciation. But scholars frequently inserted the letter *b* in the spelling of *debt* and *doubt*, and *p* in *receipt*, as if the English words had been taken directly from the Latin forms *debitum, dubitare, recepta*. In Latin the *b* and *p* had been sounded, but had become silent in the French descendants of the words long before they were adopted by speakers of English. The artificial Latinized spelling has not resulted in restoring the lost sounds in these words; compare *receipt* with *conceit, deceit*. In the word *bankrupt* the letter *p* was first wrongly added and then later pronounced. Look up its etymology. How does this exemplify the third paragraph of §144?

162. In the phrase *at all* when it means "in any respect," "to any extent," the **t** is normally carried over to the following word and sounded exactly as it is in *a tall man* ə ˈtɔl ˈmæn. This phrase differs in pronunciation and meaning from the phrase *at all* as in *There are signs at some crossings but not at all* (nɑt ət ˈɔl). Compare *I saw no signs at all* (ə ˈtɔl).[61] In England the phrase *at home* is treated likewise, being often pronounced əˈtoʊm. The phrase *at all events* is also there pronounced əˈtɔl ɪˌvɛnts. The last two pronunciations are not usual in America. *At home* possibly exemplifies a difference between British and American **h**. In America the aspiration of **t**, even when strong, is quite distinct from the speech sound **h**. For the aspiration of **t**, cf. §§78, 45.

163. In American English **t** is often voiced between voiced sounds, as in *better* bɛt̬ɚ, *battle* bæt̬l̩. Yet voiced **t** is not the same as **d**, and does not belong to the **d** phoneme, since Americans do not confuse such words as *latter* læt̬ɚ—*ladder* lædɚ, or *putting* pʊt̬ɪŋ—*pudding* pʊdɪŋ. It never occurs at the beginning or end of a phrase, nor at the beginning of an accented syllable. For example, it may be voiced in the word *at* in nɑt ət̬ ˈɔl, but not in nɑt ə ˈtɔl.

Voiced **t** occurs most commonly between vowels (pɪt̬ɪ), sometimes between a vowel and certain of the voiced consonants (mɔlt̬ɪd, twɛnt̬ɪ) when it is at the end of an accented

---

[61] Teachers or parents who correct children for saying aɪ dɪdn̩t go əˈtɔl are forbidding them to use a standard pronunciation, current both in England and in America among the cultivated classes. Cf. §250 (4).

syllable before an unaccented one (**bɛt-ɚ**), or sometimes, when it is at the beginning of an unaccented one (**mɔltɪd, twɛnti, ɔltə'gɛðɚ, wantə'go**—where there is some doubt which syllable the **t** is pronounced with); and when between unaccented syllables (**dʒɔɪn əs ət ɪ'lɛvən**).

Voiced **t** does not occur (1) at the beginning of syllables initial in the phrase, whether accented (**'tɛbl̩, 'traɪ**) or unaccented (**tə'de**); nor (2) at the end of syllables final in the phrase, whether accented (**rɪ'pit, ɪg'zɔlt**) or unaccented (**'rɪvɪt, 'tɪbl̩t**); nor (3) at the beginning of accented medial (**mɪl'tɑnɪk**) or final syllables (**rɪ'tʒn, əb'ten**).

It occurs after nonsyllabic **l** (**mɔltɪd**) and before syllabic **l̩** (**rætl̩**); after nonsyllabic **n** (**twɛnti, sɛntɚ**), but not before syllabic **n̩** (**mʌtn̩**), nor before nonsyllabic **l** or **n** (*settler* **sɛtlɚ**, *Putney* **pʌtnɪ**). Cf. *settle her* **sɛtlɚ**, with voiced **t**.

Voiced **t** is often described as a single-tap **r**. To the author's ear the two are quite distinct. Even when the voiced **t** has repeated taps (trilled **t**) it is acoustically distinct from trilled **r**, as in *pottage* **pɒtɪdʒ**, *porridge* **pɒrɪdʒ**.[62]

In the author's speech, the chief difference between voiced **t** and **d** is that **t** is less than half as long as **d** in a given utterance, and the tongue contact for **t** is much less firm than for **d**.

d

164. (1) Repeat the organic description and the descriptive name of **d**.

---

[62] All the examples and statements above are supported by kymograms of the author's speech (occasionally that of others). Some American teachers of speech treat voiced **t** as a defect to be corrected. In theory this is perhaps desirable, since it is one of those features that impair distinctiveness in speech, like the loss of distinction between *hoarse* and *horse*, *rumor* and *roomer*, the loss of **r**, of the secondary accent in *dictionary*, etc. Like these losses, also, it chiefly disturbs those to whose speech it is alien. American scholars testify to the wide distribution of voiced **t** in America.

(2) Try for **d** the positions of the tongue suggested for **t** in §155 (2). Apply to **d** in *breadth*, *width* the question in §155 (3).

(3) Apply to **d** the question asked in §153 (3).

(4) Comment on the sound and spelling of **d** in *ready*, *ladder*, *add*, *headdress*.

(5) Point out the difference in the sound of **d** in *day*, *lady*, *sad*.

(6) Is there a difference of meaning expressed by a difference of pronunciation in *a good deal?* In *used*, in *The cane was used to walk with* and *He used to walk with a cane?*

(7) What pronunciations do you know of *second*, *seconds?*

165. (1) What is the tendency of the **d** sound in *hands*, *pounds*, *friendship*, *landscape*, *handful?*

(2) Compare the tendency to drop **d** in the following, observing in which cases the omission of **d** would sound slipshod, and in which it would be apt to pass unnoticed in ordinary speech: *grandfather*, *grand time*, *grand old man*, *old year*, *old wall*, *old rat*, *old horse*, *windmill*, *wild grapes*, *wild animal*, *sound sense*, *good sense*, *sound idea*, *sound lumber*, *groundhog*, *wild west*, *sand ridge*.

(3) Considering the nature of the sounds before and after **d** in the foregoing, formulate and write rules showing when the **d** is most likely to be dropped in ordinary speech.

(4) Discover and write the phonetic law for the sound of the ending *-ed* of the following "regular," or weak, verbs: *dropped*, *talked*, *puffed*, *frothed*, *hissed*, *wished*, *watched; stated*, *needed; robbed*, *dragged*, *lived*, *smoothed*, *raised*, *rouged*, *dodged*, *shamed*, *sinned*, *clanged*, *filled; freed*, *stayed*, *pawed*, *showed*, *wooed*, *purred; carried*, *subpoenaed; barred*, *sighed*, *plowed*, *enjoyed*, *viewed; rattled*, *pardoned*.

(5) Try to find weak verbs whose present tense ends in other sounds than those found in the foregoing list. What accented vowels are notably absent from the ends of words?

166. In some words a **d** has developed after **n**; as in *thunder*, formerly *thunor; sound*, from *soun; astound*, from *astoune* (cf. *astonish*); *hind*, from *hine*. Note also the dialectal *gownd* for *gown*, *drownd* for *drown*, *drownded* for *drowned*. Cf. *Hendry* and *Henderson* from *Henry*. (1) Account for the **d** in *thunder* by reference to §152. (2) The **d** was added in *gownd* from the same phonetic cause as in *sound*. Why is *sound* correct and *gownd* incorrect?

k

167. (1) Repeat the organic description and the descriptive name of **k**.

(2) What is the difference in the position of the tongue contact for **k** in *keep* and in *coop?*

(3) Comment on the spelling and sound of **k** in *keel, character, quick, accord, bookcase, acquire, liquor, six, accent, luxury, strength*.

168. The verb *ache* **ek** used to be spelt *ake*, and the noun *ache* was spelt as now but pronounced **etʃ**, the spelling agreeing with the pronunciation. Note the following in Shakespeare's *Tempest:*

(1)   I can goe no further, Sir,

      My old bones akes.   —III.iii.1.

(2) Fill all thy bones with Aches, make thee rore. —I.ii.370. Observe that in the second passage the rhythm requires the pronunciation **etʃɪz**. Compare the pair *ake*, verb—*ache*, noun, with the following pairs of verbs and nouns: *bake—batch; break—breach; drink—drench; speak—speech; stick—stitch; stink—stench; wake—watch*. State just what changes have been made since Early Modern in verb and noun *ache*. (Dr. Johnson was partly responsible for the mix-up by falsely deriving the word from Greek *achos*, with which it has no connection. The result is an example of his great influence in the latter 18th c. See §144 (1).)

169. What is the sound of *x* in *tax, exact, luxury, luxurious* (two pronunciations), *anxious, anxiety?*

170. A Latinized spelling has become established in *indict* (Early Modern *indite*), *victuals* (EM *vittails*), *verdict* (EM *verdit*), *perfect* (EM *perfit*, Milton, *Lycidas, perfet*). On Latinized spellings, see §156. What effect has the mistaken spelling had on each word? See also §144 (3).

171. For *asked* the pronunciation is often **æst**. Give a reason for the loss of the **k** sound. Cf. §49. The present tense *ask* is also sometimes pronounced **æst**. How would you account for it in such a frequently occurring phrase as *ask the man*, or *ask the teacher?* Consider the preceding and following sounds, and apply the laws of place assimilation.

172. Initially before **n, k** was pronounced in *knee, knit, knot, knight, knife, knead, knowledge,* etc., till the 17th c. The **k** sound is preserved in *acknowledge* (from *a-knowledge*).

For the aspiration of **k** before vowels, which is similar to that of **t** and occurs under the same conditions, cf. §§78, 45.

g

173. (1) Repeat the organic description and the descriptive name of **g**.

(2) What is the difference in the position of the tongue contact for **g** in *geese* and *goose?*

(3) Apply to **g** the question asked in §153 (3).

(4) Comment on the spelling and sound of **g** in *guest, ghost, agree, aggressive, egg-glass, exist, luxurious*.

(5) Look up the pronunciation of *suggest*, and cf. *Webster* (1934), *Pron.* §143. For the pronunciation **dlæs** for *glass*, see **tlæs** in §95.

174. (1) Initial **g** before **n**, as in *gnat, gnaw, gnash, gnarled*, was pronounced till the 17th c.

(2) In *sing, hang, going, coming,* and other words with final

-*ng*, the *ng* was pronounced ŋg, with both ŋ and g, till Early
Modern, as it still is when not final as in fɪŋ-gɚ, æŋ-gɚ, hʌŋ-grɪ,
lɔŋ-gɚ, strɔŋ-gɪst. When final g was lost from the combination
ŋg, this left ŋ alone, as in sɪŋ, kʌmɪŋ, though the spelling *ng*
continued to be used. Note that this was actually dropping a g
sound, not what was later falsely called "dropping the *g*." For
further results, and the subsequent change of -ŋ to n, see under
ŋ, below §§217 f.

The Fricatives

f

175. (1) Repeat the organic description and the descriptive
name of f.

(2) Comment on the spelling and sound of f in *defend, affect,
half-fed, off, rough*. Look up *diphtheria* in *Webster, Pron.* §277.

(3) Some languages have a bilabial f (IPA symbol ɸ), the
"candle-blowing" sound.

(4) When p is followed by f, as in *stop for it, cupful*, the p is
often assimilated to the lip-teeth f and so becomes a labiodental
stop. A labiodental m likewise can be made, and may be heard
in *comfort* kʌmfɚt, *symphony* sɪmfənɪ. Both are often heard
together in *camphor* kæmpfɚ, *campfire* kæmpfaɪr.

176. The f sound in *rough* was an Early Modern substitute
for an older voiceless tongue-back velar fricative spelt *gh* in
Middle English. Its sound may be approximated by first sounding k and then, with the tongue back slightly loosened from the
velum, forcing the breath through. There were two varieties,
one farther forward like the k in *keep*, and one farther back like
the k in *coop*. The IPA symbol for the fronter sound (occurring
next to front vowels) is ç, and that for the backer (next to back
vowels) is x. These are the sounds heard in German *ich* ɪç, *ach* ɑx.
Most words now spelt with medial or final *gh* once had one of
these two sounds. E.g., the ME pronunciation of *high, light, rough*,

taught was **hiːç, lıçt, ruːx, tauxtə**, spelt as now. The fronter **ç** disappeared in Early Modern, and words like *high* **hiːç, lıçt** became **haɪ, laɪt**. (The ME pronunciation is preserved in modern Scottish dialect **hiç, lıçt**.) The backer sound **x** either (1) disappeared like the fronter, so that **tauxtə** became **tɔt**, and so with *bought* **bɔt**, *daughter* **dɔtɚ**, *aught* **ɔt**, etc.; or (2) another voiceless fricative, **f**, was substituted for **x**, and **ruːx** became **rʌf**; and so with *laugh* **læf**, *draught* **dræft**, *enough* **ɪˈnʌf, əˈnʌf**, *tough* **tʌf**, *cough* **kɔf**, *trough* **trɔf**, etc. Some words wavered between pronunciations (1) and (2); the obsolete **drɔt** for *draught* is no longer standard. Dialect pronunciations preserve the old alternate forms in *daughter* **daftɚ**, *through* **θruf**, and some others. *Dwarf* (ME *dwergh*) and often *draught* are now spelt with *f* (*draft*).

177. Similar substitutions for fricative sounds that were unfamiliar to Modern English speakers are seen in *Floyd* and *Fluellen*, in which **fl** is substituted for the Welsh voiceless fricative **ḷ** in *Lloyd, Llewellyn;* in **buθtḷ**, formerly heard for *Buchtel* (German **bʋxtəl**) *College*, Akron, Ohio, in which the dental fricative **θ** is substituted for the velar fricative **x**; and likewise in the pronunciation **trɔθ** for *trough* **trɔf**, widespread in America and not confined to local dialect. Such substitutions exemplify the important phonetic principle that a sound unfamiliar to a speaker or hearer will be spoken or heard by him as one of the nearest familiar sounds. This accounts for the fact that people often "hear" different sounds from those actually spoken.

178. In *delight* and *haughty*, *gh* is a reverse spelling (§154 (2)) and was never sounded. Chaucer's form of *delight* was *delit* **deˈliːt** and Milton's form of *haughty* was *hautie* **haːtɪ**, now **hɔtɪ**. Look up the origin of the word *sleigh* (cf. *Webster, Pron.* §144).

v

179. (1) Repeat the organic description and the descriptive name of **v**.

(2) State the relation of **v** to **f**.

(3) Comment on the spelling and sound of **v** in *navy, navvy, flivver, slave-vessel, leave vacant, of, Stephen*. As there is a bilabial **f** (IPA ɸ), so there is a bilabial **v** (IPA β). This sounds to English ears much like **w**.

(4) A foreigner in the author's boyhood (probably South German) was accused by his Yankee neighbors of calling a *grapevine* "*grape wine*." How does this exemplify the principle stated in §177?

(5) As **p** or **m** followed by **f** often becomes labiodental, so **b** or **m** followed by **v** is often formed with lip and teeth instead of both lips, as in *subvert, obvious*, or in *triumvirate* **traɪˈʌmvərɪt**. Labiodental **p, b,** and **m** are not distinctive sounds in English, and so need not be represented in phonetic symbols.

180. (1) What is your pronunciation of *nephew*? See *Webster, Pron.* §208.

(2) Is there a difference of meaning expressed by a different pronunciation in the word *have* in (1) *That's* ˈall I ˈhave to ˈgo ˌon, and (2) *That's* ˈall; I ˈhave to go ˈon? Cf. §164 (6).

181. Transcribe the following groups: *life, lives, live; wife, wives, wive; strife, strive; thief, thieves, thieve; belief, believe; shelf, shelves, shelve; self, selves*. The change of **f** to **v** in these words took place at a time before the *e* of *lives, live*, etc., became silent, so that **f** was between vowels; and the *e* of *wife, life*, etc., was never sounded, and formerly not written. In view of these facts, under what circumstances did the **f** of these words become voiced to **v**? Cf. §96 and give the right name to the change.

182. (1) The **v** of unstressed *of* əv was formerly dropped before consonants (in speech and sometimes in spelling), as the **n** of *an* still is. Cf. Shakespeare, *Merch. of Ven.* III.i.101: "No sighes but a my breathing, no teares but a my shedding," in which *a*=ə for *of*. But in present standard speech the **v** has been restored except in the most familiar style, and in *o'clock*.

(2) Forms like *e'er* ɛr, *o'er* or, *e'en* iːn for *ever, over, even* were not originally merely poetic contractions, but were natural pronunciations, once general in colloquial speech, now common in local dialect, and preserved in poetry. The forms heard in American dialect, "*nary*," "*ary*," as in "*nary man*," "*ary man*," are *ne'er a man*, "never a man," and *e'er a man*, "ever a man."

θ

183. (1) Repeat the organic description and the descriptive name of θ.

(2) Though spelt with two letters, the sound θ is a single sound, as much so as **s** or **f,** made with a single position of the tongue on the teeth. This position varies somewhat with different speakers. The tip and blade of the tongue may be lightly against the backs of the upper front teeth, usually near their points, or it may be protruded slightly between the upper and lower teeth.

(3) The diagraph *th* for the single sound θ came from the Latin spelling *th* for Greek θ in words borrowed from Greek to Latin. At first θ spelt the sound **t**+**h**, i.e. **t**+aspiration (§78). The Romans pronounced this *th* as simple **t** (§157). But in later Greek, θ [**t**+**h**] became a simple fricative (*ether* iθɚ) as in modern Greek. English printers from Caxton on used this Latin spelling *th* with the later, fricative value of Greek θ to spell our fricative sounds in *ether* iθɚ and *either* iðɚ. The Greek letter θ provides our IPA symbol for the voiceless fricative.

184. The word *drought* is pronounced **draʊt,** and the word *drouth* is pronounced **draʊθ.** The attempt to schoolmaster the word *drouth* **draʊθ** out of use by representing it as a mispronunciation of the other word *drought* has not succeeded in driving it out of good American usage. The two words are normal phonetic variants of the same OE word and have lived side by side, though in England *drought* **draʊt** is preferred in the South, while *drouth* **drauθ** is common in the North and Scotland, and probably prevails in America as a whole.

A somewhat similar situation is seen in *height* and *highth*. The pronunciation **haɪθ**, and in America **haɪtθ**, is less common, but not absent from cultivated use. *Highth* was Milton's form. The form **haɪtθ** for **haɪθ** may be due to the crossing of **haɪt** and **haɪθ**, assisted probably by the analogy of **wɪdθ, brɛdθ, lɛŋkθ, dɛpθ** and perhaps **etθ**. A similar analogy has produced the θ sound on the ordinals **fɪfθ, sɪksθ, ɪˈlɛvən(t)θ, twɛlfθ**, which were formerly **fɪft, sɪkst**, etc., later changed in imitation of **forθ, sɛvənθ, etθ**, etc. In the Bible of 1611, Joab smote Abner "vnder the fift ribbe," but Deuteronomy is "the fifth booke of Moses."

ð

185. (1) Repeat the organic description and the descriptive name of **ð**.

(2) Observe the pronunciation of *th* between vowels in the following foreign loan-words: *ether, method, catholic, atheist, sympathy, author, pathetic*, and compare it with the *th* in these native words: *either, brother, father, mother, fathom, feather, weather*. What difference appears?

(3) In words like *bath, oath, mouth* the singular forms in Middle English were pronounced **baθ, ɔːθ, muːθ**, and the plural forms **baːðəz, ɔːðəz, muːðəz**.

(4) Note likewise that the present-day words **nɔrθ, sauθ, hiθ, wзθ**, show a similar correspondence to **nɔrðɚn, sʌðɚn, hiðən, wзðɪ**; and

(5) That the nouns **brɛθ, bæθ, ʃiθ**, correspond thus to the verbs **brið, beð, ʃið**, which in ME were **brɛːðən, baːðən, ʃɛːðən**. By what native English phonetic law does **ð** replace **θ** in groups (2), (3), (4), (5)?

(6) In these changes there was much interference of analogy with phonetic tendency. No single rule without exceptions can

be given for the pronunciation of *th* in the plural of nouns ending in the sound θ in the singular. (**a**) When a consonant precedes *th*, the plural has θ: hɛl(t)θs, fɪfθs, sɪksθs, etθs, naɪn(t)θs (etc.), mʌn(t)θs, brɛdθs, lɛŋkθs, etc. (**b**) When r (formerly a consonant r) precedes: forθs, harθs, etc. (**c**) When ɜ (formerly a vowel+a consonant r) precedes: bɜθs, wɜθs, ɜθs, etc. (**d**) Of the remaining words the following have -θs: brɛθs, dɛθs, drauθs, groθs, feθs, frɔθs, and usually rare plurals and loan-words (pɪθs, mɪθs). (**e**) The following have -ðz: bæðz, pæðz, mauðz, oðz. (**f**) The following waver: riθs, -ðz, ʃiθs, -ðz, læθs, -ðz, brɔθs, -ðz, mɔθs, -ðz, troθs, trɔθs, -ðz, juθs, -ðz, truθs, -ðz (order of preference not indicated). In all cases where the singular has -ð, the plural, of course, ends in -ðz, as buθ, buð, pl. buðz.

(7) What four pronunciations of the plural of *cloth* correspond to three different meanings? See *PDAE*.

186. The voiced sound ð is found in all the pronominal words *than, that, the, thee, their, them, then, thence, there, these, they, thine, this, thither, those, thou, though, thy,* where a former θ has been voiced by lack of stress in the sentence (cf. §§140, 141). The word *thither* is often heard pronounced θɪðɚ. The word is not in actual current use, and θɪðɚ is probably a spelling-pronunciation as regards the initial sound. It may be noted that the spelling-pronunciation of *th* is regularly θ, not ð (*Waltham, Gotham, Thames* (§147), *Thame*). The preservation of ð in the middle of the word may be due to the analogy of familiar forms like *weather, whether, rather, further, father,* etc.

187. For a long time in OE and ME the sound θ (*thick*) and its voiced correlative ð (*that*) were expressed by the symbols þ (called "thorn" from the ancient runic alphabet) and ð. But þ was not confined to spelling the voiceless sound and ð to the voiced, both being used for either. The sounds did not then distinguish from one another words otherwise alike, as they now do in *thigh* θaɪ and *thy* ðaɪ. They were thus like the other fricatives in OE, **s, z** and **f, v.** Though both voiceless and voiced existed, they were not distinctive. Hence the letters *s* and *f* were used to spell both **s, z,** and **f, v.**

In late ME *th* came into general use to spell the sounds, and are still used to spell both **θ** and **ð** sounds. In the IPA alphabet **θ** (Greek) represents the voiceless, and **ð** (OE) the voiced sound.

The other OE letter *þ* in late ME and Early Modern came to resemble in manuscripts the letter *y*, and later the printed *y* often represented it, especially in abbreviation for *that* (*y*ᵗ) and in *the* (*y*ᵉ). The modern fad of using *ye* in shop signs to give an air of antiquity to things not ancient matches the ignorance displayed in pronouncing it **ji.**

s

188. (1) Repeat the organic description and the descriptive name of **s.**

(2) Comment on the spelling and the sound of **s** in *sent, cent, scent, schism, assail, hiss, except, practice.*

(3) Ascertain in which of the words *isle, island, aisle* the *s* was once pronounced, and in which it is a reverse spelling.

(4) Account for the sound of *s* in *it's good, Jack's got home, what's wrong, what's been done, quick's a flash, used to do it.*

189. Speakers differ somewhat in their tongue position for **s, z.** In the author's speech the two sides of the tongue are pressed against the upper teeth as far forward as the eyeteeth. The front edges of the blade on each side of the point touch the gums, and the point is flattened back upon itself so as to leave a small ditch, forming with the central ditch of the teethridge an aperture smaller than a pencil. Through this aperture a thread of air is forced out and makes a hissing sound across the edges of the teeth.[63] Some speakers make **s** with the tongue

---

[63] Apparently the sound is chiefly made by the lower teeth. If the jaw is lowered with the tongue point still in proper position, the hiss disappears. It can be restored without raising the jaw by substituting a card with upper edge cut in shape of the lower teeth.

against the backs of the lower teeth. With the aid of a mirror study your own tongue position in making **s**.

z

190. (1) Repeat the organic description and the descriptive name of **z**.

(2) State the relation of **z** to **s**.

(3) Comment on the spelling and the sound of **z** in *desire, dessert, scissors, discern, lazy, dizzy, his zeal, sacrifice, sons, son's, sons', Xerxes, anxiety, exhibit, Mrs., newspaper.*

(4) Compare *house* and *husband*, *goose* and *gosling*, and comment.

191. (1) Compare the following pairs: **jus, juz; əbɪus, əbɪuz; klos, kloz; lus, luz; bræs, brez; glæs, glez; haus, hauz; ˈrɛfjus, rɪˈfɪuz.** In Middle English, **s** in these words was final in nouns and adjectives; in verbs it was followed by a vowel. How does this account for the **z**?

(2) How do you pronounce *to grease* and *greasy*?[64]

(3) Transcribe the following groups, with primary and secondary accents marked: (1) *exercise, execute, exhibition, exhortation;* (2) *exert, executive, exhibit, exhort.* State what you discover about the influence of accent on the sound of *x*. Compare also *luxury, anxious* with *luxurious, anxiety.*

192. (1) Arrange the following regular nouns in three groups according to the sound of the plural ending. Then transcribe the plural forms and discover what phonetic condition determines each of their endings. (The sounds **s, z, ʃ, ʒ, tʃ, dʒ** are called "sibilants.") *Glass, rib, tree, sofa, robe, ship, beam, fox, month, sky, city, rose, cliff, bed, shoe, bush, cow, hat, stone, duke, garage, saw, file, church, plume, fate, edge, book, boy, fan, day, piece, rope, spade, hero, dog, king, pew, stove, fire, lathe, hill.*

See if you can fit the nouns *leaf, life, wife, mouth, house* into the grouping.

---

[64] See George Hempl, "Grease and Greasy," *Dialect Notes*, I, ix, 438 ff.

(2) The nouns of this sort ended in ME in -ɪz or -əz. In which groups has the vowel of the ending been lost? In which group has the consonant of the ending also been changed, and why?

(3) See if the same grouping can be applied to the sound of s on nouns in the possessive case. To the ending of verbs in the third person singular present tense.

ʃ

193. (1) Repeat the organic description and the descriptive name of ʃ.

(2) Comment on the spelling and the sound of ʃ in *bishop, sure, champagne, machine, mission, nation, ocean, conscience, issue, anxious, luxury, dish-shaped.*

194. In the author's speech ʃ is formed with the tongue drawn slightly back from the position for s, so that the point and blade are more blunted than for s. The sides of the tongue touch the upper teeth only as far forward as the front bicuspids, leaving a considerably wider and deeper passage over the blade of the tongue than for s. The front of the tongue is at the same time raised higher toward the hard palate (see Fig. 6, p. 37).

195. (1) English ʃ has three principal sources historically. It first developed out of the OE combination sc in which c was at first a tongue-front palatal stop (IPA symbol c), no longer found in present English.[65] The combination sc gradually developed into the simple sound ʃ by loosening the stop contact and bringing the tongue front into the position for j. A comparison of Figures 5 and 6 (p. 37) will show the position for j and ʃ close to each other. Then the s was changed by the j position into ʃ, much as the words *miss you* mɪs ju now tend to

---

[65] This sound can be made approximately by holding the point of the tongue behind the lower teeth and trying to pronounce t.

become **mɪʃu** by assimilation. For a similar later change, see (3) below.

(2) A second source of ʃ is an Old French tʃ sound (spelt *ch*), which in later French lost its first (stop) element t, leaving the fricative part as a separate speech sound, as in Modern French words spelt *ch* (*charmant*, etc.). Some of these words were taken into Early Modern English with the ʃ sound, as in *chandelier* **ʃændəlɪr**, *Charlotte* **ʃɑrlət**. See also below, §§198 (1), 208 (2).

(3) The third source of ʃ is found in an Early Modern native sound change in words like *mission*. The sound of ʃ in these was originally **s**. To learn how it changed to ʃ we must first observe two phonetic tendencies.

(a) Observe what happens to the unaccented ɪ sound in the word *Indian*, first pronounced in three syllables, ˈ*In-di-an*, and then in two, ˈ*Ind-ian*. Show the difference by phonetic transcription. This same change took place in many words like *mission* about the time of Shakespeare. Thus *mission*, which had been pronounced in three syllables ˈmɪs-ɪ-ən came to be pronounced in two as ˈmɪs-jən with the same change of unaccented ɪ to **j** as in *Indian*.[66]

(b) The second phonetic tendency is seen at present in such a phrase as *miss you* or *this year*. In ordinary speech these are not **mɪs ju** and **ðɪs jɪr**, but **mɪʃu, ðɪʃ jɪr**. Now compare Figures 5 and 6 (p. 37) and observe the similarity of tongue position for **j** and ʃ. What light does this throw on the effect of the palatal sound **j** by place assimilation on a preceding **s**? So the change from ˈmɪs-ɪ-ən to ˈmɪs-jən continued further to ˈmɪʃən. The same change affected all words having the unaccented sounds **-sɪə(n)**, as *confession, discussion, impression, passion, session*.

---

[66] This change spread gradually, so that for a long time both pronunciations are found side by side. Thus in *Mids. Night's Dream*, 1. 23, *Hermia* was ˈhɛr-mɪ-ə and in l. 46 it was ˈhɛrm-jə.

(4) The change was exactly the same in words like *nation*, in which the -*tion* is merely a disguising spelling for the same sounds -sɪən (see §156). The same combination of sounds with other spelling is seen also in *ocean* ɔsɪən—ɔsjən—oʃən, *special* spɛsɪəl—spɛsjəl—spɛʃəl, *conscience, precious, complexion* kəmplɛksɪən—-plɛksjən—-plɛkʃən.

(5) The same change is also disguised by spelling in words like *issue*, in which the unaccented ɪ is present before **u,** but not spelt. The Early Modern sounds were ˈɪs-ɪu, the modern "long *u*" (as in *mute*) being ɪu in Early Modern. Here sɪ developed in the usual way to sj and ʃ, so that ˈɪsɪu became ˈɪsju and then ˈɪʃu. So with *sensual* sɛnsɪuəl—sɛnsjuəl—sɛnʃuəl; *luxury* lʊksɪurɪ—lʊksjurɪ—lʌkʃərɪ; *censure, fissure, pressure, tonsure,* etc.

196. English ʃ is a single sound, like s or f made with a single position of the speech organs, though commonly spelt with the digraph *sh*. This spelling comes from ME in which *ss, sch, ssh,* and *sh* were used to spell ʃ. *Sh* now spells no other sound (except in separate syllables, as in *sheepshead* ˈʃipsˌhɛd, cf. *sheepshed* ˈʃipˌʃɛd).

3

197. (1) Repeat the organic description and the descriptive name of ʒ.

(2) Comment on the sound and its spelling in *division, glazier, measure, usual, azure, luxurious, garage.*

(3) In what positions in the word (initial, medial, or final) may ʒ occur? Why is it not found doubled?

(4) State the relation of ʒ to ʃ.

198. (1) The sound ʒ was not a separate speech sound in English till modern times, and never had a spelling of its own. One source of ʒ is French, corresponding to the source of ʃ in *Charlotte* (§195 (2)). The Old French voiced sound correspond-

ing to voiceless **tʃ** (spelt *ch*) was **dʒ** (spelt *j* or *g+e, i*). This, like French **tʃ**, lost its stop element in later French and became **ʒ** as in present French *genre*. Some French words with this sound have come into Modern English with **ʒ** as *regime* re^lʒim. See below, §§208 (2), 211 (2).

(2) **ʒ** also developed in Early Modern English in a way exactly parallel to *ʃ* from **s** in *mission*. Remember that **z** is voiced **s**, and **ʒ** is voiced *ʃ*. As mɪsɪən first became mɪsjən, so vɪzɪən first became vɪzjən. Then just as modern *please you* pliz ju tends today to become pliʒu, so then vɪzjən became vɪʒən. The comparison of Figures 5 and 6 (p. 37) is equally applicable here, for the tongue positions for the change of zɪ—zj—ʒ are the same as for sɪ—sj—ʃ, with the addition of voice.

(3) When the ɪ sound was disguised by the spelling *-sure* as in *measure*, the sound change was the same: mɛzɪur became mɛzjur and then mɛʒur, mɛʒɚ. So with *azure, closure* kloʒɚ, *rasure, pleasure, seizure, leisure, treasure, usual* ɪuzɪuəl—juzjuəl —juʒuəl.[67]

h

199. (1) Repeat the organic description and the descriptive name of **h**.

(2) Comment on the sound and its spelling in *have, behind, who, whooping cough, exhaust, exhibit, John, ah, Sarah*.

(3) In what positions in the word can **h** occur? Why is it not doubled?

200. Pronounce the words *he, hat, high, hall, home, hoop*. Observe that the jaw, lips, and tongue tend to take shape for the different vowels **i, æ, u**, etc., at the very beginning of each word, without waiting for the **h** sound to be finished, so that so

---

[67] Some of these words originally did not have the ɪu sound, but had taken it on by analogy in time to undergo this Early Modern change.

far as **h** has any resonance quality, this varies according to what vowel follows.

To understand the nature of **h** it is necessary to observe the three ways of beginning a vowel sound. (**a**) If the vocal cords are firmly closed when breath pressure begins, and suddenly loosen to the position for voice (§28), we have a vowel beginning with a glottal stop (§48). (**b**) If the cords are placed in position for voice at the same time that breath pressure begins, we have the ordinary way of beginning an initial vowel in English, as in *I*, *old*. (**c**) If the cords are first wide open and then begin to close while breath is being emitted till they reach the position for voice, a slight fricative breath sound will precede the vowel. This breath fricative before voice begins may be stronger or weaker; but the speaker or the hearer is chiefly aware of the presence of the **h** sound by the manner in which the voice begins for the vowel with a certain momentum of breath from the previously open glottis, producing the effect of a stress pulse just when the breath "takes hold" of the vocal cords to set them into vibration, the breath being slowed by the vibration. Hence, even if the breath is expelled gently just before the **h** begins, the slight stress will be felt as the voice begins.

In English, this slight pulse invariably coincides with the beginning of a syllable. It follows that **h** occurs only before sounds that have unobstructed outflow of breath—the vowels, and the vowel-likes, the sonorants and glides, or semi-vowels. It actually occurs before **w** (**hwɛn**), **j** (**hjudʒ**). It could occur before **r** and **l**, as it did in OE **hrævɛn** "raven," **hlɑːf** "loaf"; though OE **h** and **r** were somewhat different from the present sounds. But since the articulation of **h** is entirely in the glottis, **h** can also be nasal before **m, n,** or **ŋ**. In certain nasal interjections, nasal **h** is a significant sound, as in **hm, hn,** which are very similar to **m̥m, n̥n** mentioned in §40, because of the **h**-like transition from the voiceless **m** or **n** to the voiced. The fact that the lips are closed for **hm** and the tongue closes the mouth passage for **hn,** does not prevent the sound from being **h,** for **h** takes the mouth articulation of *every* sound which it precedes.

Before voiced fricatives **v, ð, z, ʒ,** however, **h** is not so easily made, for the narrowing for the fricative articulation in the mouth prevents the free passage of breath and the resulting contrast with the beginning of voice.

201. Although from a physiological point of view, **h** might be regarded merely as a manner of initiating vowels or vowel-likes, it is yet a genuine distinctive speech sound in standard English, distinguishing many words, as *I, high; old, hold; all, hall,* etc. Certain other breath sounds often designated by the letter *h* are not speech sounds, as the aspiration of **p, t,** or **k,** often designated as **ph, th, kh.** Its presence or absence in English does not distinguish words.[68]

202. The **h** sound is sometimes voiced between vowels, as in *behind.* Here, without cessation of voice, the glottis opens sufficiently at **h** to give the contrasted freer movement of breath followed by the narrowed glottis again, which gives the impression of a **h** sound. Voiced **h** is not distinctive in English, and hence usually unobserved.

203. Transcribe your usual pronunciation of these words: (1) *heir, honor, honest, hour;* (2) *host, heretic, horrible, hospital, human, humane;* (3) *humble, herb, homage, humor, hostler, Humphrey.* In which group are you doubtful about any words?

These words and many others spelt with initial *h* were taken into English from Old French, chiefly during the 13th and 14th cc. The Latin originals of the French words had sounded the initial **h,** but in OF the sound had disappeared. In OF, however, and also after the words were adopted into English, the silent *h* was often written in imitation of the original Latin spelling. Therefore when initial **h** is now sounded on any of these words,

[68] For discussion of the view that **h** is a voiceless vowel, see *Webster* (1934), *Pron.* §44 (10).

it has been restored through the influence of the spelling. This influence has gradually brought the **h** to be pronounced again on most of these words after having been silent all through the OF period and much of their English history. E.g., such words as *hospital, hostler, heritage, humble,* and others, had no **h** sound as late as the 18th c., and often still lack it. This is true of the more of these words the farther back we trace them. Note Uriah Heep's pronunciation of *humble.* British and American usage differ in some of these words today. Look up *herb, hostler* in *Webster* and Jones.

The words *able, arbor,* and some others belong to the same group. They lost *h* in their spelling also, and so have never regained the **h** sound.

204. Present English shows a tendency in some words, no matter what their origin, to drop **h** in syllables having little stress; as in *annihilate* əˈnaɪəlet, *forehead* fɔrɪd (riming with *horrid*), *shepherd* ʃɛpɚd, *vehicle* ˈviːɪkl̩. This is common in names; as *Haverhill* hevərɪl, *Chatham* tʃætəm, *Durham* dʒɚm, *Fulham* fʊləm. Pronouns unstressed in the sentence regularly lose initial **h**. In ordinary cultivated speech *He thought he saw him* is hi θɔt i sɔ ɪm. It would sound affected to say, hi θɔt hi sɔ hɪm—indeed, it would be difficult. But when the pronoun is somewhat stressed, as at the beginning of a statement, or under some special emphasis, **h** is retained, as in the example.

205. In the pronoun *it,* which is nearly always unstressed, and in *'em,* which is always so, the **h** has been permanently lost, even when *it* is occasionally stressed. In earlier English, however, and in present dialect, *hit* hɪt is often found. Note Shakespeare's *Macbeth,* I, v, 50 ff.

> That no compunctious visitings of Nature
> Shake my fell purpose, nor keepe peace betweene
> Th'effect and hit.

Hit is common in southern American local dialect.

'Em is not, as commonly supposed, an abbreviated form of *them*, but of *hem*, a different word. *Hem* is a native English pronoun, while *them* was borrowed from Scandinavian. *Hem*, pronounced əm, has remained in cultivated use as a familiar colloquial form in unstressed position, but *them* has taken its place in stressed positions in familiar speech, and in both stressed and unstressed positions in formal speech and in literature. Compare "Did you take 'em?" with "I didn't take *them*, I took the others." The mistaken belief that *'em* is an abbreviation of *them* perhaps accounts for the use of the apostrophe in *'em*, while it is omitted in *it*.

206. The silent *h*'s thus far considered belong to cultivated British and American speech. Besides these, there is a tendency in the dialect speech of southern and central England either to drop or to add initial **h** where it is not done in cultivated speech. The facts are sometimes misunderstood, however. The mistaken idea that such speakers always drop **h** from words that should have it, and add it to those that should not, is no doubt due to the fact that the wrong pronunciations are noticed, while the right ones pass unobserved. The explanation is to be found in the fact that in those dialects **h** is no longer a speech sound, and the speakers of those dialects who have not learned to use **h** from standard English do not use it or hear it as a speech sound, since for them it is not distinctive. Though they frequently use **h**, it means no more to them than the aspiration of **p, t, k** does to the educated, who use it in certain positions, but pay no attention to it. So these dialect speakers use or omit **h** at haphazard, not knowing when they use it or not, or thinking they do when they do not, when speaking to the educated. They naturally often use **h** on strongly emphatic words beginning either with a vowel or with **h** in standard speech; but this use is not invariable.

The Affricates

tʃ

207. (1) Repeat the organic description and the descriptive name of **tʃ**.

(2) Comment on the sound and its spelling in *achieve, kitchen, righteous, question, creature, Dutch cheese.*

(3) The **tʃ** sound is one of the two English affricates that function as independent speech sounds (cf. §33). It is formed by a contact of the blade and a part of the front of the tongue at the border of the teethridge and hard palate, with consequent stoppage of the breath, followed by a slow explosive release that makes a fricative sound, with the tongue moving into the position for **ʃ**, the tongue front being nearly in the position for **j** (cf. Figures 5 and 6, p. 37). This fricative palatal release is an essential part of **tʃ** and cannot be omitted. The lips are sometimes protruded, but not usually in America.

(4) It has often been discussed whether **tʃ** and its voiced correlative **dʒ** are single sounds or two sounds each. Forchhammer[69] maintains that they are two. The matter is perhaps not of great importance for English, for in actual use they function as one speech sound. English **t** and **ʃ** do not combine in words to make **tʃ**, and neither element of **tʃ** can be omitted. Yet the double symbol conveniently suggests the double articulation (in fact there are many successive articulatory positions). Moreover, **tʃ** sounds have developed in English out of separate sounds (but not **t** and **ʃ**), as to be seen below (§208); and in French **tʃ** has become **ʃ** (§195 (2)).

208. (1) The **tʃ** sound in English has three sources. The oldest is from the OE palatal stop **c** (IPA symbol **c**; cf. §195 (1)). This developed a palatal fricative off-glide and produced the combination represented by IPA **tʃ**, in which the symbol

[69] *Grundlage*, p. 145.

t represents, not an alveolar **t**, but a tongue contact farther back toward the hard palate. This **tʃ** is found in native English words like *teach* **titʃ** (OE **tæːcɑn**), *child* **tʃaɪld** (OE **ciːld**).

(2) A **tʃ** sound came into ME from Old French. The OF **tʃ** sound mentioned above (§195 (2)) as having later lost its first element and become **ʃ** as in *Charlotte* and Modern French words (*charmant*, etc.) was taken into ME in a great number of words before it had changed from **tʃ** to **ʃ**, as in *Charles, chair, chain, charge, merchant*, pronounced in Chaucer and ever since with **tʃ**. Hence such pairs as *Charles—Charlotte* represent an earlier (ME) and a later (Early Modern) borrowing from French. See also **dʒ** and **ʒ** below, §211 (2). Other such pairs are *chair* **tʃær**— *chaise* **ʃez**; *chandler* **tʃændlɚ**—*chandelier* **ʃændəlɪr**. Sometimes the influence of modern French has changed to **ʃ** a **tʃ** in words borrowed earlier, as *chivalry* (Chaucer **ˈtʃɪvɑlˌriə**), now **ʃɪvəlrɪ** but sometimes **tʃɪvəlrɪ** as formerly in English (see *Webster* (1934)).

(3) The third **tʃ** developed in Early Modern as follows. When the ending *-tion, -tial*, etc., in Latin and later in French was preceded by **s**, as in *question*, the **t** did not change to a **s** sound as it did in *nation*, etc. But **-tɪə(n)** changed in Early Modern to **-tjən**, paralleling the change of **-sɪən** to **-sjən** (§195 (3)). We have now to note the tendency of **tj** to become **tʃ** seen in present-day *meet you* **mit ju**, *don't you* **dont ju**, which usually become **mitʃu, dontʃu**. Comparison of Figures 5 and 6 (p. 37) will show how alveolar **t** followed by palatal **j** might easily lead to a more palatal **t** followed by a fricative off-glide that might either be a very close **j** or **ʃ**. It eventually developed into **tʃ**, so that Early Modern **kwɛstɪən** first became **kwɛstjən** and then **kwɛstʃən**. So in *bestial* **bɛstʃəl**, *Christian* **krɪstʃən**. The same change occurred in the combination -tɪur, as in *nature* **næːtɪur**— **næːtjur**—**netʃɚ**. So in *adventure, creature, feature, future, literature*, etc. It affected words in *-teous*, as *righteous* **raɪtɪəs**— **raɪtjəs**—**raɪtʃəs**. The same occurred in *beauteous, bounteous, duteous, piteous, plenteous*, pronounced in the 18th c. **brutʃəs**,

dɪutʃəs, etc. But in these, spelling helped to restore the older
bɪutɪəs, etc.

This change of **tj** to **tʃ** (as in *righteous* raɪtʃəs) is mentioned
in 1764, and must therefore have occurred considerably earlier.
It affected all such words as *nature, fortune, courteous*, etc. The
mistaken effort to restore the 17th c. pronunciation has succeeded in most of the words in *-teous* (dɪutʃəs, bɪutʃəs, etc.,
are now substandard), but in the other words (*nature, fortune,*
Christian, etc.) **tʃ** is the normal cultivated pronunciation. Jespersen (*Gram.* I.12.41) says: "In some of the longer and more
literary words, -tjʊə may be comparatively natural besides -tʃə,
such as *literature, judicature*. But in all everyday words -tʃə is
the only natural pronunciation, in spite of the efforts of some
pedantic teachers who endeavor to reintroduce -tjʊə, often
with the funny result reported by Grandgent in the Mod. Language Notes, May, 1894, p. 272." The incident referred to is
thus reported by Professor Grandgent: "Once . . . a school-
mistress . . . turned suddenly upon her pupils—several of whom
had for some time been brandishing their arms and calling, in
a stage whisper, 'Teacher, teacher!'—and said to them: 'Now,
children, which do you think is the right pronunciation, *teacher*
or *teat-yure?*' And the class, with one voice, unhesitatingly re-
sponded, 'Teat-yure!' How could they answer otherwise? Had
they not been carefully taught to say *nate-yure, fort-yune,*
ed-yucate—clumsy combinations never heard from any human
being outside of the class-room?"

209. In America the **tʃ** sound is usually preserved in words
like *wrench* rɛntʃ, *inch* ɪntʃ, *gulch* gʌltʃ, which in England are
sometimes, but not invariably, pronounced rɛnʃ, ɪnʃ, gʌlʃ. The
word *Welsh* shows this variation in the spelling *Welch*—wɛlʃ
being in this case the original form and also usual in America.

dʒ

210. (1) Repeat the organic description and the descriptive
name of **dʒ**.

(2) Comment on the sound and its spelling in *joy, gentle, exaggerate, bridge, knowledge, soldier, verdure, George Jones.*

(3) State the relation of **dʒ** to **tʃ**. Observe that as a result of this relation, the tongue positions of the two sounds being the same, **dʒ** has the same history in the different particulars mentioned for **tʃ**.

211. (1) Thus like the OE voiceless palatal stop **c,** which became Modern **tʃ,** there was an OE voiced palatal stop (IPA symbol **ɟ**) which became modern **dʒ,** as in *edge, bridge.*

(2) As a **tʃ** sound came from Old French to ME in *chair, Charles,* etc., so an OF **dʒ** came to ME in words like *gentle, judge,* before OF **dʒ** lost its first element and became **ʒ** (as in Modern French *genre, gentilhomme*). Hence, as in the pair *Charles— Charlotte,* ME loan-words from OF have **dʒ** in *gentle, judge, regiment* **rɛdʒəmənt,** while modern loan-words have **ʒ** as in **reˈʒim, mɪˈraʒ, gəˈraʒ.**

(3) Again, paralleling the development of **tʃ** in Early Modern in *righteous, nature, fortune,* etc., a **dʒ** arose in words like *soldier, verdure, grandeur,* etc. Thus **soldɪər** became **soldjər,** and then **soldʒɚ; vɛrdɪur** became **vɛrdjur,** and then **vɝdʒɚ.**

(4) Another source of **dʒ** in English is from the voicing of **tʃ** by lack of stress (§140 f.) in unaccented syllables, as in *Harwich* **hærɪdʒ,** *Dulwich* **dʌlɪdʒ,** *Woolwich* **wulɪdʒ,** *cabbage* (ME *cabache*), *knowledge* (ME *knowleche*), *spinach* (OF *spinache, -age*). Look up the etymology of *partridge, sausage.*

The Sonorants
Nasals
m

212. (1) Repeat the organic description and the descriptive name of **m.**

(2) Comment on the spelling and the sound of **m** in *make, small* (§41), *amaze, common, dimmed, home-made, column,*

solemn, solemnity, autumn, autumnal, diaphragm, climb, limb (§154 (2)), *salmon, calm.*

(3) State the relations (identities and differences) of **m** to **p** and **b**. To **n** and **ŋ**. For syllabic **m̩** see §§88–91; for voiceless **m** see §§40 f.

(4) OE ˈæɪmɛtɛ became modern *emmet* ˈɛmɪt, and also, by loss of its middle vowel, became **ænt**. Explain the **n** from older **m**.

n

213. (1) Repeat the organic description and the descriptive name of **n**.

(2) Comment on the sound **n** and its spelling in *knife, gnaw, pneumonia, snail* (§41), *announce, sinner, unknown, penknife, mill* (earlier *miln*), *kiln, Milne* (**mɪl** or **mɪln**), *Milnes* (**mɪlz** or **mɪlnz**), *Milner* (**mɪlnɚ**). Compare *autumn—autumnal* with *Miln —Milner*.

(3) State the relations of **n** to **t, d, l** (see Figure 3, p. 36); to **m** and **ŋ**.

214. Many words were taken into ME from OF that had in French the palatal nasal (IPA ɲ) which may be approximated by planting the point of the tongue firmly behind the lower teeth and trying to pronounce **n**. As this was not a familiar sound to the English, it was replaced by them with **n**, but spelt *gn* as in French; as in *sign, benign, deign, impugn, reign*. What principle is here illustrated (see §177)? The words *foreign, sovereign* **sɑvrɪn, sʌvrɪn** never had this palatal ɲ sound. They were *foreine, sovereyn* in Chaucer, *forraine* in Shakespeare, and *sovran* in Milton. The spellings *foreign, sovereign* are imitations of *reign*, falsely based on a supposed connection.

(2) How do you account for the pronunciation of *signal* **sɪgnəl** (cf. *sign* **saɪn**), *assignation* ˌæsɪgˈneʃən (cf. *assign* əˈsaɪn)?

215. For syllabic **n̩** see §§88–91. Show by transcription whether you pronounce **n̩, ən,** or **ɪn** in the following words: *mitten, Britain, curtain, important, Latin, certain, mutton,* *mountain, sudden, pardon, garden, London, basin, mason, raisin, prison, pleasant, cushion, kitchen, pigeon, surgeon, soften.*

216. Note the following forms from Early Modern:

"Looke vpon **mine** affliction and **my** paine."—Ps. 25:18 (1611)

"Saue **thy** people, and blesse **thine** inheritance."—Ps. 28:9 (1611)

"It is **no** more of promise."—Gal. 3: 18 (1611)

"Make the promise of **none** effect."—Gal. 3:17 (1611)

"It is foule weather **in** vs all."—Shak. *Temp.* II.i.141 (1623)

"**I**' th'Commonwealth I would Execute all things."—*Ib.* 147. Discover some reason for the presence or loss of the **n** in *my—mine; thy—thine; no—none; i'—in.* Cf. also *none other* (still in use), *handicap* (hand in cap) and *o'—of, a—on* in §137 at *of* and *on.* In what modern word has this treatment of final **n** become invariable? Avoid the common erroneous view that *none* = *no* + *one.* It is merely one form of *no,* as *an* is one form of *a.*

ŋ

217. (1) Repeat the organic description and the descriptive name of **ŋ**.

(2) Comment on the sound **ŋ** and its spelling in *singer, finger, long, longer, England, anchor, instinct, conquer.* Compare the tongue positions for **ŋ** in *sing* and *song* (see **k, g**).

(3) Why is **ŋ** never doubled?

(4) Show by symbols just what sounds are spelt by the letters *ng* in *thing, linger, strength, cringing, engage.* What sounds do the letters *nk* represent in *ink, unkind, unknown?*

(5) When *running* is pronounced "runnin'," it is called "dropping the *g.*" Does this phrase exactly describe what happens? What does happen?

218. (1) Until Early Modern, the sound **ŋ** occurred only before **k** or **g** sounds. How does that explain why **ŋ** cannot begin words or syllables? How do you account for its presence in **æŋʃəs, æŋzaɪətɪ, lɛŋθ?** Explain **lɛnθ, strɛnθ.**

(2) Though commonly spelt with the two letters *ng* (*thing*),
ŋ is a **single sound,** formed by a **single position** of the speech
organs. State the relations of ŋ to k and g and to n (see Figures
4 and 3, p. 36). Before Early Modern, the letters *ng* always
spelt the two sounds ŋ+g, as still in *linger* lɪŋ-gɚ. In Early
Modern, final g began to be omitted in pronunciation from the
group -ŋg—earliest from unaccented syllables, as in ˈsi-ɪŋg—
ˈsi-ɪŋ, and later in all final positions, as θɪŋg—θɪŋ. The two
sounds ŋg are kept when not final, as in mɪŋ-gl̩, lɪŋ-gɚ, æŋ-gɚ,
hʌŋ-gɚ, lɪŋ-gwɪst, etc. Reconcile this statement with sɪŋɚ,
brɪŋɪŋ, kɪŋlɪ, sprɪŋɪ, lɔŋɪʃ. Why do we say lɔŋgɚ but lɔŋɪŋ?
strɔŋgɚ but strɔŋlɪ? jʌŋgɪst but jʌŋɪʃ?

(3) The foregoing pronunciations exemplify the fact that
when **analogy** interferes with **phonetic tendency,** neither completely wins. The phonetic law stated in (2) wins in lɪŋgɚ, sɪŋgl̩,
hʌŋgɚ, æŋgɚ, lɪŋgwɪst, lɔŋgɚ, lɔŋgɪst, strɔŋgɚ, strɔŋgɪst, jʌŋgɚ,
jʌŋgɪst; but analogy wins in sɪŋɚ, lɔŋɪŋ, kɪŋlɪ, strɔŋlɪ, jʌŋɪʃ.
Explain how this is true in each of the examples. If you wished
to say "This answer is wronger than the other," would you say
rɔŋɚ, or rɔŋgɚ?

219. The substitution of -ɪn for -ɪŋ in words ending in *-ing*,
as *coming, doing*, etc., was once more widespread than now. It
is now by no means unusual among the educated and higher
classes, as well as the illiterate and speakers of dialect. The tendency to be "correct" by pronouncing -ɪŋ in place of the once
general -ɪn is probably an instance of spelling-pronunciation.
According to Wyld, -ɪn is still common among the higher classes
in southern England.[70] In America it appears to be more com-

---

[70] *History of Modern Colloquial English*, p. 289. Authorities (Wyld, Wright)
cite early (14th c. on) spellings like *holdyn, walkyn, fardin, standyn*, etc. as
evidence of the pronunciation -ɪn for -ɪŋ. These could just as well be evidence
for the change from -ɪŋg to -ɪŋ. In fact, that would be the only natural way to
express -ɪŋ till after the complete loss of final -g from -ŋg. The same spelling

mon among the educated in the South than in the North and East. The spelling-pronunciation -ɪŋ for -*ing* is now so general that it is in excellent usage; but it must not be hastily concluded that the pronunciation -ɪn instead of -ɪŋ in *coming, going,* etc., is necessarily a mark of ignorance or lack of cultivation. It is still commoner than most people suppose. It is a good illustration of the ignorant "muddling through" by which forms and usages regularly become established in standard use. Hundreds of people have religiously practiced saying kʌmɪŋ instead of kʌmɪn without ever intelligently considering the facts, or whether the effort was worth while. What would now be thought of a teacher or critic who, acquainted with the earlier facts, should also insist on restoring the old stop g to the combination -ɪŋ, making it -ɪŋg as it is spelt? We condemn the speech of the dialect speaker who has preserved the complete ending -ɪŋg (with devoiced g) in "*somethink*," "*anythink*" (cf. lɛŋkθ, strɛŋkθ). We condemn as dialectal a statement like "wɔk raɪt əlɔŋgɪr (*along here*)," made to the author in Coventry, in which there is no "dropping of the *g*"! For syllabic ŋ see §§88–91.

The Lateral

l

220. (1) Repeat the organic description and the descriptive name of l.

(2) Comment on l and its spelling in *elect, Ella, elm, little, all, calm, almond, half, folk, yolk, solder.*

(3) Pronounce the word *haul,* continuing the l as long as possible. Observe that the point of the tongue is against the teethridge, and that the voiced breath passes out on one or both sides of the tongue. See whether your own l is bilateral or uni-

---

would continue after -ɪŋ became -ɪn. On the other hand, it is very likely that -ɪn began to be used by many almost immediately after -ŋg changed to -ŋ.

lateral. Pronounce *illness* and then state the exact difference
between **l** and **n**. Pronounce *salt* and *scald*, and state how **l**
differs from **t** and from **d**. What is common to the formation of
l, n, d, t? Compare *retain* and *battle* **bætl̩** to discover the difference in the manner of exploding the **t**. Do the same for the **d**
in *ready* and in *saddle* **sædl̩**.

221. Since **l** is a voiced oral continuant, there is a vowel-like
resonance in the sound. Though the tongue point remains in
contact with the teethridge during the continuance of the **l**
sound, the rest of the tongue is somewhat free to assume various
vowel positions. In fact, there are as many differently sounding
l's as there are different vowels. If **l** has the resonance of a front
vowel (see chart, p. 61), as in *leave*, it is often called 'clear' **l**;
if it has that of a back vowel, as in *feel*, it is called 'dark' **l**. In
south England 'clear' **l** is found before vowels in the same
syllable, as in *lily, low;* and 'dark' **l** before consonants, as in
field, elder; finally, as in *feel, full;* and when syllabic, as in *battle*
bætl̩, *rattling* **rætl̩ɪŋ,** *rattled* **rætl̩d.** The same is generally true in
America, but here many speakers use a slightly 'dark' **l** before
vowels, and a 'darker' one in the other positions; and others,
especially in the South, use 'clear' **l** in nearly all positions.

When 'dark' **l** is sounded, the hearer is apt to hear an **ʊ**
sound with it, and before some consonants may not hear at all
the **l** proper (i.e., the contact of the point of the tongue with the
teethridge). Thus in dialect speech, *calculate* **kælkjəlet** is often
pronounced **kaʊkəlet** because the 'dark' **l** before **k** was heard
and imitated as **ʊ**. So a child says **ɪtʊ** for **lɪtl̩** because he does not
distinguish the initial 'clear' **l** from the following front vowel **ɪ,**
and hears the final 'dark' **l** as **ʊ.**[70a] This change of 'dark' **l** to **ʊ**

[70a] One child whose family perhaps used initial 'dark' **l**'s, habitually said
ʊkʊ for **lɪtl̩**. Explain both **ʊ** sounds. Why was **k** sounded for **t**? Recall that **ʊ** is a
high-back vowel, and see §96.

Explain the frequent child's pronunciation **mɪʊk**.

was universal in Old French; so Vulgar Latin *palmu* became OF *paume* pɑʊmə, Modern French poɪm. Hence in ModFr only 'clear' l's are used, for all 'dark' l's have changed to ʊ. In Italian, on the other hand, 'clear' l turned into ɪ, j; so VL *platea* became Italian *piazza* pjɑttsa. In English, 'clear' l has remained l, while after certain vowels 'dark' l has developed an ʊ, as after ɑ; so ME ɑl, sɑlt became 15th c. ɑʊl, sɑʊlt, and then ɔl, sɔlt. Before some consonants, the tongue point ceased to touch the teeth-ridge; so ME tɑlkən became tɑʊk,[71] and then tɔk; before others, both ʊ and l were lost; so ME hɑlf became hɑʊlf, and then hɑf, hæf.

222. The change of ɑl to ɑʊ and then ɔ took place in these native English words from the 15th to the 18th cc. (The change from ɑʊ to ɔ was regular in all English words.) But in another group of words, as *altar, fault, vault*, borrowed from Old French, the change of ɑl to ɑʊ had already taken place before the words were taken into English, and afterwards in English ɑʊ became ɔ as in all other English words that had it. In the words *fault, vault*, etc., the l had become silent before the words became English, and continued silent till well into the 18th c., though very often written. Note the rime from Goldsmith:

> Yet he was kind, or if severe in aught (ɔt),
> The love he bore to learning was in fault (fɔt).

Finally, owing to the influence of the written *l* in these French loan-words, which was retained in imitation of the original Latin forms, the l sound was restored to most of them. So the l sound in fɔlt, vɔlt is a spelling-pronunciation. See §150. For syllabic ḷ, see §§88–92.

---

[71] The intermediate stage tɑʊk has been reported from present Southern American dialect.

The Glides

w

223. (1) Repeat the organic description and the descriptive name of **w**.

(2) Comment on the sound and its spelling in *water, swing* (§41), *dwell, persuade, quart, anguish, memoir, choir, one, once, toward, answer, sword, write, wrong, two, sorrow, snow, how.*

(3) In what position in the words does the **w** sound occur? Why is it not doubled? Account for the name and the form of the letter.

224. Pronounce before a mirror the words *wood, woe, wall, watch, way, we.* It will be observed that at the beginning of each word the lips contract into a small circle. On reaching the sound of **ʊ** in *wood*, the lips widen a little, then a little more for the **o** of *woe*, and successively more for the vowels **ɔ, ɑ, e, i**. See Figure 8, p. 57. A similar result may be got by pronouncing a very brief **u** before each of these vowels, with the accent on the second element, thus **u-ˈo, u-ˈɑ, u-ˈi**. If care is taken not to dwell on the **u,** but to make the transition quickly and continuously to the following vowel, the result will be practically a **w** followed by the vowel. Compare the two pronunciations of *bivouac,* **ˈbɪv-ʊ-æk** and **ˈbɪv-wæk.**

The experiment reveals several facts. (1) Strictly considered, **w** is not precisely even a brief **u** before another vowel, for that implies a *fixed position* of the lips and tongue for the duration of the vowel, as in **æ, i.** In describing **w** the symbol **u** merely indicates the position of the lips and tongue at the beginning of **w**. In forming **w** the lips and tongue begin at once to take the position for the following vowel. See §§327 ff. **w** is therefore not a consonant uniform during its whole utterance like **s, v, m,** but is a glide sound, made while the lips and tongue are in motion.

(2) In **w**, though the continuous movement begins in a similar position, it proceeds and ends entirely according to the nature of the vowel that follows. In reality, therefore, the symbol **w** stands for as many different sounds as there are different vowels. In fact, **w** passing continuously into the various vowels that follow it constitutes a whole group of diphthongs, differing from such a diphthong as **au** in having the stress on the second part instead of the first. Observe that the lips are more closely rounded for **w** than for the following vowel; hence **w** is most closely rounded before **u**, and less so before **o, ɑ, æ, i,** etc.

(3) The sound that the ear recognizes as **w** is not the friction of air on the lips, though a frequent description is that of a lip fricative, but is the quick and continuous modulation of the voice by the motion of the lips and tongue in passing from the **u** position to that of the following vowel.

(4) It follows that **w** can occur only before a vowel sound. It cannot be pronounced without this following vowel. An attempt to pronounce **w** alone results in **wɔ**.

225. There is a tendency for **w** to become silent in unaccented syllables, especially in names. Note the British pronunciation of *Warwick* **wɒrɪk,** *Greenwich* **grɪnɪdʒ,** *Norwich* **nɒrɪdʒ.** *Warrick Co., Indiana,* has kept the traditional pronunciation by spelling it accordingly. The village of *Brunswick, O.,* was always called **brʌnzɪk** by its early inhabitants. The family name *Woodward* is often pronounced **wudɚd.** *Awkward, backwards, forwards* in the 18th c. were regularly **ɔkɚd, bækɚdz, fɔr-ɚdz,** as now in dialect; and *towards* is regularly **tordz.** Sometimes the *w* has disappeared in spelling also, as in *Edinburgh,* Scotland, **ɛdṇbʌrə,** from older *Edwinesburch* ('Edwin's town'); in the family name *Gouldin* **goldɪn** from earlier *Goldwin; Aylard* **elɚd,** from *Æthelweard.* Spelling-pronunciation has restored many of these lost **w** sounds, as in *Cromwell, Sandwich,* etc. The student should watch for other examples. Note the two spelling-pronunciations in *Cromwell,* spelt *Crumwella* in the 12th c., and

in England still often pronounced **krʌmwəl**. Explain the sur-
name *Crummles* (*Nicholas Nickleby*), *Crummel*, the phonetically
normal form of *Cromwell*.

hw

226. For **hw** as the voiceless correlative of **w**, and for the
distinction between **hw** and voiceless **w** (IPA **ʍ**), see §38 and
Webster, Pron. §45. In the author's speech, and he believes in
America generally, when the sound is used at all it is **hw** rather
than voiceless **w**, with the usual conformation of the mouth for
h to that of the following sound.

227. The distinction between **hw** and **w** by which, e.g.,
whether is distinguished from *weather* is still standard usage in
America, though there are a great many speakers who do not
make the distinction. Reliable statistics are lacking as to
whether the substitution of **w** for **hw** is increasing here. It has
probably been frequent for many generations.

In the standard speech of south England the distinction is
no longer usual except as it is made by some individuals as a
spelling pronunciation, or from a desire to avoid homophones.[72]
Hence in Southern British the following are homophones:
whale—wail; wheel—weal; what—watt, and many more. But in
northern England, Scotland, and Ireland the distinction per-
sists as in America.

228. In the expletive and the interjection *why*, **w** is usually
heard, while in the interrogative *why?* **hw** is usual in America.
Thus the following would be usual: "**waɪ! hwaɪ dɪdʒu du ðæt?**"
"**waɪ, aɪ dont no.**"

j

229. (1) Repeat the organic description and the descriptive
name of **j**.

(2) Comment on the **j** sound and its spelling in *year, used,*

---

[72] The distinction is observed by Mr. F. G. Blandford in his excellent pronunciation of "Everyday Sentences in Spoken English" (Linguaphone Records).

ewe, Europe, unite, opinion, regulate, volume, particular, familiar, behavior, hallelujah.

(3) In what positions in the word does **j** occur? Can it be doubled? For the tongue position of **j**, see Figure 5, p. 37, and for its effect on **s**, §195 (3).

230. Pronounce the vowel **i** before the words *oak, ell, am,* allowing the voice to glide from **i** to the following word, and stressing the second part in each case. Observe that the more quickly you pass from **i** to the following vowel, the more these words sound like *yoke, yell, yam.* Thus it is seen that **j** is a glide sound made by the modulation of the voice as the tongue moves continuously from the position for **i** to that for another vowel. It is thus parallel to the glide **w**—the tongue, instead of the lips and tongue, forming the glide. As with **w** also, an actual **i**—a fixed vowel—is not made, but the tongue only starts with the position for **i** and immediately moves toward that for the following vowel. So too, **j** can occur only before vowels, and, as with **w**, **j** and its following vowel constitute various diphthongs with rising stress. One of them, **ju**, is the diphthong **ɪu** with the stress shifted.

231. In the author's dialect, **j**, like **w** and **r**, has no audible sound except the modulated voice. To the ear, the impression of a consonant, rather than a vowel, is given because of the rapidity of the voice modulation by the movement of the tongue. There is no audible friction of air between the tongue and the hard palate.

232. Some phoneticians describe **j** as a palatal fricative, and this may be true in some regions or with some speakers. This can be tested by attempting to produce with the breath a natural **j** sound without using either the speaking or the whispering voice. The fricative, when used, is made by pressing the tongue a little closer to the front palate than for **i**, and holding it there while the breath is forced over it. An approach to the fricative **j** is heard when the sound is followed by the vowel **i**

as in *ye*. Here the tongue is pressed for an instant a little closer
than for **i**, so that a slight lowering of the tongue is perceived in
passing to the **i** of *ye*, and a slight acoustic difference is heard
between **j** and **i** of **ji**. In this respect cf. the nature of **w** in **wu**.
Like **w**, **j** is closest (highest) and most resembles a fricative
sound before **i**, the vowel most like it, as **u** is most like **w**.

233. What sounds are spelt by the letter *y* in *day, boy, sky,
steady, aye* ("yes"), *myrtle, martyr, analysis, yet?* Is the letter *y*
used in any way not paralleled by *w?*

r

234. (1) Repeat the organic description and the descriptive
name of **r**.

(2) The consonant **r** is a glide sound. Just as **w** is made with
the lips and the tongue, or **j** with the tongue alone, starting in
the position for a vowel **u** or **i** and moving to the position for a
following vowel, so **r** starts with the tongue in the position for
a vowel and moves toward that of the following vowel, as in
rate **ret**. In the case of **r**, the vowel position from which (in the
author's speech) the tongue movement starts is that of the
vowel in *hurt* **hɜt**—a simple vowel with the tongue point turned
toward the hard palate, or retroflexed. Not all speakers of GA
have exactly the same tongue position for the vowel as for the
beginning of the consonant, but the formation is analogous.
The degree of retroflexion varies; in some cases the tongue for **r**
is merely raised toward the teethridge; in others it is merely
retracted and laterally contracted; but the acoustic effect is
strikingly similar. If the tongue be fixed in the starting position
for the **r** in *rate* and voice uttered, the vowel **ɜ** in *hurt* **hɜt** is
made. Hence, combinations of **r**+any vowel[73] form rising diphthongs exactly as do **w** and **j** in *we, woe, ye, you.*

[73] Consonant **r** occurs before the syllabic *r*-colored vowel **ɚ**, as in *deliverer*
dɪˈlɪvərɚ, dɪˈlɪvrɚ. It occurs rarely before **ɜ**, as in *chirurgeon* **kaɪˈrɜdʒɜn**, *sid-
erurgical* ˌsɪdəˈrɜdʒɪk|.

235. Just as there is no fricative sound in **w, j,** so in **r** the only sound conveyed to the ear is voice, modulated, as in **w, j,** by the movement of the tongue toward the position for the following vowel (see §63). When **r** follows **t** (*try*), **d** (*dry*), and to some extent when after ʃ (*shriek*), **z** (*misery* **mɪzrɪ**), it is fricative. But the friction is not significant or distinctive, being due to neighboring sounds, and so constitutes no exception to the general character of nonfricative **r.**

236. It has long been recognized that there is a marked difference between **r** before vowels and the sound spelt *r* after vowels, as in *far*.[74] The difference is so great that in large areas of the English-speaking world only prevocal **r** has survived. For GA, I have reached the conclusion also arrived at by Dr. Joos and others that the postvocalic sound written *r* is the non-syllabic vowel element of a falling diphthong (§328).[75] For further discussion, see ɜ, ɚ, and the *Diphthongs* under *Vowels in Detail*.

237. Other varieties of consonant **r** exist, as the tongue-point trill (vibrating against the teethridge), heard in Scottish, Anglo-Irish, Italian, Spanish, and sometimes German and French, including the "single-tap **r**" sometimes heard in English; the fricative **r,** still described as usual in Southern British, though Sweet described it as without fricative quality;[76] the "frictionless continuant" **r** of England; the uvular trill (vibrating against the soft palate) of Northumberland dialect, French, and German; and the uvular fricative, or uvular "scrape," found in French and German. Prevocalic (consonant) **r** occurs in all types of standard English wherever it is spelt in the written language.

[74] Cf. Ben Jonson, *English Grammar*, 1640: "It is sounded firme in the beginning of the words, and more liquid in the middle and ends: as in *rarer, riper*." Quoted by Grandgent, *Old and New*, p. 44.

[75] This, in principle, is the treatment of postvocalic *r* given by Mr. Martin in Palmer, Martin, and Blandford, *Dictionary of English Pronunciation with American Variants*.

[76] *Sounds of English*, §122. Jones, *Phonetics*, §§747, 796.

238. In Southern British, in eastern New England and most New England larger cities, in the speech of the natives of New York City and suburbs, and of the larger part of the South, *r* (either the consonant or an "*r*-colored" vowel) is pronounced only before a vowel in the same or a closely following word. More specifically, when no vowel follows, what is pronounced in GA as ʒ in *fur* fʒ appears in the regions mentioned as ɜ—fɜ; what appears in GA as ɚ in *better* bɛtɚ, appears there as ə—bɛtə. The diphthongs ir, ir, ɛr, ær, or, ur there appear as iə, ɪə, ɛə, æə, oə, uə. The GA diphthong ɑr there regularly loses its second element and becomes ɑ, and GA ɔr often does likewise: ɔ(ə). The following words show (before the dash) the GA and (after the dash) the British, Eastern, and Southern American corresponding forms **when no vowel follows:**

fur fʒ—fɜ	*sure* ʃur—ʃuə
firm fʒm—fɜm	*assured* əʃurd—əʃuəd
better bɛtɚ—bɛtə	*far* fɑr—fɑ
perceive pɚ'siv—pə'siv	*farm* fɑrm—fɑm
fear fir—fiə	*for* fɔr—fɔ(ə)
feared fird—fiəd	*form* fɔrm—fɔ(ə)m
fare fɛr—fɛə	*fire* fair—faiə
fared fɛrd—fɛəd	*fired* faird—faiəd
fare fær—fæə	*sour* saur—sauə
fared færd—fæəd	*soured* saurd—sauəd
four for—foə	*cure* kiur—kjuə
gourd gord—goəd	*cured* kiurd—kjuəd

In the East and the South, instead of accented ʒ, an "*r*-colored" vowel varying to ʒ is often heard. See §§305–11.

239. When a vowel follows in the same word, as in *flattery, weary, very, carry, starry, warring, story, surest,* in the "*r*-less" regions named the *r* sound is retained as in GA: **flætəri, wiri, vɛri, kæri, stɑri, wɔriŋ, stɔri, ʃurist.** For *furry* and *hurry* see §309.

240. Linking r. When a vowel follows without pause at the beginning of the next word, the **r** is likewise regularly retained. This is called **linking r,** since **r** that was formerly pronounced is here restored and makes an easy transition from the preceding word to the following initial vowel. Thus in the "*r*-less" territory we find such pairs:

fur fɜ—*the fur is wet* ðə fɜrɪz wɛt　　　*more* moə—*more attractive*
flatter flætə—*flatter us* flætərəs　　　　　morə ˈtræktɪv
hear hɪə—*hear us* hɪrəs　　　　　　　　*sure* ʃuə—*sure effect* ʃurəˈfɛkt
care kæə—*care at all* kærəˈtɔl　　　　　　*fire* faɪə—*fire is out* faɪrɪz aut
far fɑ—*far away* fɑrəˈwe　　　　　　　　*our* auə—*our idea* aurɑɪˈdiə
war wɔ—*war is over* wɔrɪz ovə　　　　　　*cure* kjuə—*cure it* kjurɪt

241. Intrusive r. In the examples of linking **r** shown above, it will be observed that in the "*r*-less" regions all words ending in a written *r* have two forms, one without an *r* sound, when no vowel follows (hɪə, kæə, ʃuə), and the other with linking **r,** when a vowel follows (hɪrɪˈtɪz, kærəˈtɔl, ʃurəzˈfet). Thus the speakers have become accustomed to such pairs as hɪə—hɪr, kæə—kær, ʃuə—ʃur, the second of each pair only before vowels. Hence it is also natural that such words as *idea* aɪˈdiə, *sofa* sofə, *America* əˈmɛrəkə, *Ada* edə, *Maria* məˈraɪə should seem to end exactly like words with final silent *r* (hɪə, etc.) and therefore natural to add the **r** in the same way when a vowel follows: *the idea of it* ðɪ aɪˈdiər ɒv ɪt, *the sofa is new* ðə sofər ɪz nju, *America and England* əˈmɛrəkər ənd ɪŋglənd, *Ada Ann* edər æn, *Maria Eads* məˈraɪər idz. This is called **intrusive r.** Observe that linking **r** is the use between words of an *r* that is spelt and was formerly pronounced (as now in GA); while intrusive **r** is the use, in the same way, of an *r* sound that is not spelt and was originally not sounded. It is a very common practice among cultivated speakers in England and eastern America (but apparently less in southern America). The evidence of its universality in these regions is so overwhelming that it is mere ignorance of the facts of cultivated usage to deny it.[78] Though one may choose to avoid it, there is hardly warrant for condemning it in others as "incorrect." See *PDAE*, §85.

242. Linking **r** is sometimes omitted in Southern British, and the omission appears to be increasing. It is perhaps in part due to reaction against the use of intrusive **r**.[80] In the South of America, though **r** is regularly preserved before a vowel in the same word, as in *starry* **stɑrɪ**, linking **r** is often omitted, as in *more ice* **moə aɪs**.[81]

243. In a few words an *r* sound has been lost (especially from an unaccented syllable) by dissimilation (see *PDAE*, §121). Examples are: *Canterbury* **ˈkæntə|bɛrɪ**, *caterpillar* **ˈkætə|pɪlə**, *elderberry* **ˈɛldə|bɛrɪ**, *February* **ˈfɛbju|ɛrɪ**, *governor* **ˈgʌvənɚ**, *northerner* **ˈnɔrðənɚ**, *reservoir* **ˈrɛzə|vɔr**, *St. Bernard* **sɛntbə|ˈnɑrd**, *southerner* **ˈsʌðənɚ**, *surprise* **sə|ˈpraɪz**, *thermometer* **θə|ˈmɑmətɚ**, *Waterbury* **ˈwɔtə|bɛrɪ**. It will be noted that each of these words contains at least one other *r* sound than the lost one. That this loss of an *r* sound is not the same as the regional "dropping of the *r*," may be seen by comparing some of the words with their pronunciation in the East and South; as **ˈkætə|pɪlə**, **ˈgʌvənə**, **ˈnɔðənə**, **ˈrɛzə|vɔə**, **sɛntbə|ˈnɑd**, **ˈsʌðənə**, **θə|ˈmɑmətə**.

For further matter on the *r* sounds see the *r* vowels ɝ, ɚ, ɜ (§§304–15), and the *R Diphthongs* (§§352 ff.).

Vowels in Detail

244. As it throws light on various aspects of the study of present English vowels, the changes of Middle English (ME)

---

[78] See Jespersen, *Gram.* I, 13.42 ff., where much evidence is given; Jones, *Phonetics*, §759; *Webster, Pron.* §213. Intrusive r is less common after ɑ (which is rarely final) and ɔ, as in *the law of the drama* **ðə lɔr əv ðə ˈdrɑmə**.

[80] See Jones, *Phonetics*, §758.

[81] Read, *Jour. Eng. and Germanic Philol.*, April, 1923, p. 222, says that the Southern practice does not differ essentially from Southern British. But it is my impression that in southern America linking r is much more often omitted than in England. Intrusive r seems to be rare in the South.

long vowels and their spelling to Modern English (MnE) corresponding vowels and their spelling are here shown in a condensed summary of the Great Vowel Shift (§10, p. 21). Length of MnE vowels is omitted as not significant. Only the most common ME spellings are given. EM = Early Modern, and LM, Late Modern. The arrowhead means 'became.'

ME iː, spelt *i, y,* > MnE aɪ—ME liːf *lif* > MnE laɪf *life*
ME eː, spelt *e, ee,* > MnE i—ME seːd *seed* > MnE sid *seed*
ME ɛː, spelt *e, ee, ea,* > EM eː > LM i—ME sɛː *sea* > LM si *sea*
ME aː, spelt *a, aa,* > MnE e—ME maːdə *made* > MnE med *made*
ME ɔː, spelt *o, oo,* > MnE o—ME hɔːm *hom* > MnE hom *home*
ME oː, spelt *o, oo,* > MnE u—ME doːm *doom* > MnE dum *doom*
ME uː, spelt *ou, ow* > MnE aʊ—ME huːs *hous* > MnE haʊs *house*

Observe that in each case the ME long vowel is raised to the next higher long vowel in MnE (see Fig. 9, p. 61), except that ME iː and uː, being already highest, are broken up into diphthongs in MnE. ME ɛː is raised to the next higher eː in Early Modern, and then within the Late Modern period is further raised to i. ME aː, the lowest, is both fronted and raised. After being fronted to æː, it was raised to ɛː in Early Modern, and then in Late Modern to e.

Note, too, that in each example at least one MnE spelling comes down from a ME spelling (except for an occasional silent final *e*) but with changed sound values of the vowel letters. Review carefully p. 21 of §10, and see *PDAE*, §124.10.

i

245. (1) Repeat the descriptive name of i.[82]
(2) Comment on the sound and its spelling in *be, see, these,*

---

[82] The student should from the first associate each vowel with the description of its tongue and lip position. When the lip position is not mentioned, it is assumed that the lips are not rounded. See §71 and Fig. 9, p. 61.

breeze, people, receive, believe, key, ravine, idea, suite, Caesar,
Phoebe, reiterate, atheist.

(3) What is the difference in sound between the first and
the second vowel in *deceive?* Between the sound of *de-* in *deceive*
and *deportation?* For the diphthongal quality of **i**, see §85.

246. What is the usual Irish dialect pronunciation of *tea,*
speak, repeat? What can you infer about cultivated 18th c. pronunciation from the following rimes in Dryden and Pope:
obey:sea; great:repeat; way:sea; awake:speak; great:seat; great:eat;
days:ease; away:tea? Other local dialects throughout England
and Scotland also have the same pronunciation of *tea, repeat,*
etc. Make an observation on the historical relation between
these pronunciations and standard English pronunciation of
the same words. Note that the words now sounded with **i** are
spelt with *ea.* What words so spelt have kept their 18th c. pronunciation? Can you give a reason for the pronunciation of *yea?*
Compare these further rimes from the same authors: *mien:seen;*
be:see; scene:spleen; yield:steeled. The *ea* in these words spelt
the Early Modern sound **eː**, and *ee* or *ie* spelt **iː** as now. Words
of the *ee*-class, such as *green, meet, see,* are pronounced in Irish
dialect in the same way as in standard English except as analogy
has operated; e.g., *speech* is sometimes pronounced **spetʃ** by
analogy of *speak* **spek**. Would it be accurate to represent an Irish-
man as saying, "**aɪl metʃu ɒn ðə gren**"?

Look up in the *Oxford,* Jones, *PDAE,* or *Webster,* the words
either, neither, Elizabethan, leisure, penal, penalize, penalty.

247. What is your customary pronunciation of *been, creek,*
sleek, breeches, breeching, steelyards?

The word *creek* in ME had two forms: *crike* pronounced
krɪkə, and *crek,* pronounced **kreːk,** which resulted from lengthening the **ɪ** in *crike* (see §75, note 31). The first, **krɪkə**, became
present English **krɪk**, which is still current throughout America,
and **kreːk** became **krik,** now spelt *creek.* The prejudice often

encountered against the pronunciation **krɪk** is due to ignorance of actual historical usage and to reverence for the spelling. The word *sleek* has the same history, now preserved in the two spellings *slick* and *sleek*, with meanings not yet entirely separated. See *creek* in the *PDAE.* On the other hand, just as *breeches*, *breeching*, *steelyards*, pronounced by people familiar with them, were shortened to **brɪtʃɪz, brɪtʃɪŋ, stɪljɚdz,** so the words *livelong* **ˈlɪvˌlɔŋ,** *nickname* (§93), *rick*, *riddle*, *sick*, *silly* all were once spelt *ee* and pronounced accordingly with the long vowel (ME **eː,** Modern Eng. **iː**), and later shortened to **ɪ.** As they are now also spelt with *i*, no one attempts to restore the early pronunciation, as is done in *breeching*, *steelyards* by those unfamiliar with the things themselves. Reflect on this process; it is typical.

248. Lack of stress usually shortens and slightly lowers a long vowel except a low one. E.g., *been* is often unstressed in the sentence. At a time when it was pronounced **beːn** if stressed, it was pronounced **bɛn** if unstressed. Later, after historical vowel shift had changed the stressed form **beːn** to **biːn** (see §244), then the unstressed form became **bɪn.** Now **bɪn** is the regular form, both stressed and unstressed, in America, and **bin** is the prevailing form in England, while **bɛn** is old-fashioned, but still widely current, especially when unstressed.

249. Note the second vowel in *studying*. It is a little higher than the **ɪ** of *-ing*, and is therefore represented as **i.** This very brief **i** occurs oftenest unaccented before **ɪ,** as in *atheist*, *pitying*, *happiest* **hæpiɪst,** *twentieth* **twɛntiɪθ.** When unaccented before other vowels than **ɪ,** the sound varies between **i** and **ɪ,** as in *chariot* **tʃærɪət,** *reality* **riælɪtɪ, rɪælɪtɪ,** *radiate* **rediet, redɪet.**

ɪ

250. (1) Repeat the descriptive name of **ɪ.**

(2) Comment on the sound and its spelling in *mill*, *hymn*, *England*, *sieve*, *busy*, *business*, *women*, *build*, *pretty*, *Greenwich.*

(3) *England, English, ink, link, linger, wing* all formerly had the same vowel sound ɛ. What has happened to sound and spelling? Is the pronunciation ɪndʒən for *engine* a mere "mispronunciation"? Comment.

(4) What vowel do you pronounce in the first syllable of *really, theater?* What is the difference of meaning in **bɪznɪs** and **bɪzɪnɪs**? What do these words and the words *slick, sleek* show about the way a word splits up into different words, finally becoming as distinct as *human* and *humane?*

(5) Which is the longer vowel, the "short *i*" of *sins* or the "long *e*" of *seat?*

251. The pronunciation **waɪnd** for the noun *wind*, heard in singing, and often found in verse riming with words like *find*, is regarded as exceptional. If compared with *behind, bind, find, grind, hind, kind, mind, rind*, which appears exceptional, **wɪnd** or **waɪnd**? In *windy, windmill, windfall* the *i* has always been ɪ. Does that throw any light on the pronunciation **wɪnd**?

252. In OE the letter *y* spelt a lower high-front-round vowel and *i* spelt the lower high-front unrounded vowel ɪ. Later the first vowel lost its lip rounding and became ɪ, but long continued to be spelt with *y*. What light does this throw on such modern spellings as *copy, copies, staid, stayed*, and the general interchange of *i* and *y?*

253. Unstressed ɪ. The unaccented final sound of words like *ready* varies considerably in different regions, with different speakers, and according to what sounds immediately follow in actual speech, as *Are you ready? I'm ready to go; I shall be ready in a moment; a ready answer*, etc. This unaccented sound varies from a higher sound suggesting, but not reaching, the **i** of ˈ*trochee* ˈ**troki** to a lower sound virtually identical with the accented ɪ. With the latter pronunciation the two vowels in *pity* are practically the same—ˈ**pɪtɪ**. Dictionaries continue to show the pronunciation ɪ for the final sound of words like *ruby* **rubɪ**, *valley* **vælɪ,** *collie* **kɑlɪ,** and for the corresponding vowel in their derivatives *rubies* **rubɪz,** *valleys* **vælɪz,** *collies* **kɑlɪz,** in which the sound is not final.

There appears to be a tendency in the younger generation of the North and West to use in all this class of words a higher vowel that may be transcribed with **i.** Such speakers usually distinguish in pronciation between such pairs as *candied* (from *candy*) **kændid** and *candid* **kændɪd** or **kændəd,** *posies* **poziz** and *poses* **pozɪz** or **pozəz,** *pitied* **pɪtid** and *pitted* **pɪtɪd** or **pɪtəd.** The **i** is especially noticeable when lengthened, as in the hymn "Holy, Holy, Holy" **holiː, holiː, holiː.** The **-i** is rarer in the South. The author has **-ɪ** in such words. See *PDAE* at the entry *-y.*

254. It would sometimes be useful for certain purposes (as in study of dialect; see §85) to use a special symbol for the un-stressed **ɪ** just as **ɜ** and **ɝ, ʌ** and **ə** are distinguished as stressed and unstressed; and this has sometimes been done. Yet it is customary with many phoneticians to use the one symbol **ɪ** for both, and in practical teaching the author has experienced no difficulty thereby. In this book, therefore, the variation of unstressed **ɪ** is indicated only when it reaches the stage **ə.** If teachers prefer to use a special unstressed symbol, the printed form of an italic *i* without the dot would serve.

255. Transcribe the following according to your easiest pro-nunciation, being careful not to be influenced by the spelling in the unaccented syllables: *benefit, roses, ended, hostess, goodness, endless, besides, scarlet, women, forfeit, money, message, senate, character, marriage, Wednesday, fountain, minute* (noun), *biscuit, greatest, knowledge, profit, prophet, loveth, declare, example, fur-nace, Mrs., mistress, resist, prepare, lettuce, foreign, coffee.*

256. At an earlier period of the language, the vowels in the unaccented syllables of these words were sounded much more distinctly than today, and corresponded more nearly to the stressed sound suggested by the spelling in each instance. Most of them were high-front or mid-front vowels, and when, in process of time, they came to be pronounced less distinctly, they came to resemble the ɪ of *bit*. Observe that in some of these words this unstressed ɪ can be changed by deliberate pronunciation to its original distinct vowel without too great artificiality; as in *prepare* **pripær**, *besides* **bisaɪdz**, *declare* **diklær**. But in most of the words the earlier sound cannot now be restored without an unnatural effect; as in *message, Wednesday, fountain*, which would sound affected if pronounced **mɛsedʒ, wɛnzde, faʊnten**.

257. In the first syllable of words like *employ, engage, essential, exact, expect*, etc., British usage differs slightly from American, which often has **ɛngedʒ, ɛkspɛkt, ɛgzækt**, etc., where British has **ɪngedʒ, ɪkspɛkt, ɪgzækt**, etc. In colloquial speech, however, the American sound in these words approaches ɪ.

258. *Effect* and *affect* are usually both pronounced **əfɛkt**. When they are distinguished, *effect* is **ɛfɛkt** or **ɪfɛkt**, and *affect* is **əfɛkt**. When *except* and *accept* are, as often, pronounced alike, they are either **ɪksɛpt** or **əksɛpt**, but are sometimes distinguished as **ɛksɛpt, ɪksɛpt** and **əksɛpt, æksɛpt**.

In words ending in *-ile*, such as *agile, docile, fertile, fragile, hostile, juvenile, servile, tactile, textile, virile*, American usage prefers ɪl while British prefers aɪl. See *Webster, Pron.* §155.

259. Unaccented ɪ before a vowel shows a tendency to become **j** (as in *Indian;* see §195 (3, a)). Transcribe and compare the following: *audience, behavior, bilious, colloquial, convenient, familiar, genius, glorious, industrious, Italian, junior, Northumbrian, pedestrian, radiance, serious, terrestrial*. In which is it difficult to pronounce **j**? Why? Cf. §348(3).

e

260. (1) Repeat the descriptive name of **e**.

(2) Comment on the sound and its spelling in *aim, age, base, bass, say, they, vein, break, gauge, gaol, chaotic, fatality, vacation*.

261. The sound **e** has become a diphthong in some dialects.

It is much more diphthongal in standard Southern British than elsewhere, a common form there being ɛɪ, though the simple vowel is not unknown there (see §85). But in America the second element of the diphthong eɪ is less marked, and the vowel is not infrequently simple e. When it is a diphthong the first element is usually e rather than ɛ. eɪ is more frequent when final (*day* deɪ) or before a voiced consonant (*dale* deɪl). The diphthong, however, is not uncommon in America, even before voiceless consonants (*date* deɪt). The more marked diphthongal quality when final or before voiced consonants is due to its greater length in those positions, and illustrates the greater tendency of English long vowels to break up into diphthongs. The same process has been completed in the two ME long vowels iː and uː, which have now become the full diphthongs aɪ and aʊ, while the ME short ɪ and ʊ have remained simple vowels ɪ and ʌ. The lengthening and diphthonging of several formerly short vowels is a marked tendency in present American English, especially Southern.

262. The same statements about the simple e and the diphthongs eɪ, ɛɪ apply to the o sound in America and England. o is diphthongized to oʊ (with variation of the first element) in America and England under the same conditions as e. The farther north we go in England, the less diphthongal e and o become.[84] In standard English of Scotland e and o are still not at all diphthongal, in this respect resembling continental e and o.

263. According to the phonemic principle it is not necessary in phonetic transcription to spell the diphthongs eɪ and oʊ with two symbols, as in *may*, *made*, for in both British and American

---

[84] This similarity of American and Northern British does not indicate that American was derived from Northern British, as is often assumed, but merely that both types of English represent older and more conservative forms of English, preserving what Southern British had been in the past. In the degree of diphthongization of e and o, American pronunciation is today about what Southern British was in 1800–50.

English the vowels **e, eɪ, eɪ, ɛɪ** all belong to the same phoneme. The substitution of any one of them for another will not change any English word to another word.[85] See §85.

264. In England and America *Monday* is **mʌndɪ**,[86] and so with the other days of the week. In America *holiday* is **ˈhɑləˌde** while in England both **hɒlɪdɪ** and **hɒlɪde** are found. **ɔlwɪz** is general in America and frequent in England, and **ɔlwez, ɔlwəz** are common in both countries.

265. Remembering that in southern England the vowel in *hate* is **ɛɪ**, note the result, in sounding the first element of this diphthong, of gradually lowering and retracting the tongue from **ɛ** to **æ, a, ɑ**, thus producing **æɪ, aɪ, ɑɪ**. In the vulgar dialect of London, or "Cockney" English, *day* is pronounced with **æɪ, aɪ, ɑɪ**, so as to sound to an American like *die*. The Cockney does not, however, confuse *day* with *die*, for he also retracts the tongue for the first element of **ɑɪ** in *die*, till it becomes **ɒɪ** or even **ɔɪ**.

266. When the sound **e** loses its accent, it is regularly reduced to **ɪ**, as in *daily* **ˈdelɪ**—*Monday* **ˈmʌndɪ** (see *Gradation*, under **e**, §130). Instances like **ˈstebļ**—**stəˈbɪlətɪ** represent an earlier reduction of the shortened vowel (see the remark on **mænlɪ**—**postmən** in §131). Note also that after **e** has become **ɪ**, as in *Saint sent*—*Sinclair* **sɪnˈklær**, it may be further obscured to **ə** or disappear, as in **sənˈklær, sn̩ˈklær**. See §§131 and 137 (*Saint*).

This reduction of **e** to **ɪ** is seen in such endings as *-ace* (*palace* **pælɪs**), *-age* (*message* **mesɪdʒ**), *-ate* (*senate* **senɪt**). Cf. also *orange* **ɔrɪndʒ**, *Highgate* (London) **haɪgɪt**. This accounts for the pronunciations **kærɪktɚ, ɑbstɪkļ, mɪrɪkļ, spɛktɪkļ, rɪˈsɛptɪkļ**, which

---

[85] It may be noted, however, that in Southern British **ɛ** and **ɛɪ** belong to separate phonemes, as in *met* **mɛt**, *mate* **mɛɪt**.

[86] As it has been for at least three hundred years. Walker recommends it in 1791 (*Webster, Pron.* §89) and Wyld records the spellings *Fridy*, 1642, and *Mundy*, 1647. See *English Journal*, 37.1, Jan. 1948, p. 26.

still have ɪ beside ə (kǽrəktɚ, etc.). Cf. Chaucer's forms mɪˈraːklə, ɒbˈstaːklə, etc., with long aː.

267. A large class of words with final ə in cultivated pronunciation, such as *soda, sofa, cholera, opera, America, Martha, Ella, Sarah, Utica,* and many other personal or place names ending in *-a* or *-ah,* are pronounced in the vulgar idiom with final ɪ, sodɪ, marθɪ, jutɪkɪ, etc. The cause of this is not quite certain. It seems most likely that ɪ goes back to an earlier pronunciation of *a* as **e,** which naturally becomes ɪ when unstressed. This is Jespersen's explanation of nonfinal ɪ in unstressed syllables spelt with *a,* as in *message* mɛsɪdʒ, *senate* sɛnɪt. But there is evidence that final *a* was sometimes so pronounced; e.g., Peele (16th c.) rimes *day:Ida;* the quarto of Shakespeare's *Much Ado* has *Ursley* for *Ursula* of the folios; Gill (1621) has *mopseys* for *Mopsas;* Pope rimes *conveys:operas;* and Professor Grandgent calls my attention to the current popular pronunciations *Nashua* nǽʃəwe, *Iowa* aɪəwe, *Mantua* mǽntəwe. See Jespersen, *Grammar,* I, §§9.14 ff.

A reverse result has come from such pronunciations as marθɪ for marθə, əˈmɛrɪkɪ for əˈmɛrɪkə, etc. Many people brought up on these pronunciations with ɪ who have later adopted the cultivated pronunciation with ə, have mistakenly applied the same correction to words like *Missouri, Cincinnati, prairie,* which properly end in ɪ, and so have made them məˈzurə, sɪnsəˈnætə, pəˈrɛrə.[87]

ε

268. (1) Repeat the descriptive name of ε.

(2) Comment on the sound and its spelling in *met, breath, breakfast, leopard, Leicester, friend, said, says, saith, any, many, Thames* (§§145, 157), *bury, again, Pall Mall.*

[87] See Allen W. Read, "Pronunciation of the Word 'Missouri'," *American Speech,* Dec., 1933, pp. 22–36, and R. J. Menner, *Am. Sp.,* Oct., 1937, p. 171.

269. (1) The spelling *ea* is found in many words now pronounced with ε, as in *bread, dead, death, dread, head, spread, thread, threat, tread*. In these and others the spelling *ea* indicates an Early Modern pronunciation with long eː, which became shortened to ε. In others the same vowel eː remained long and regularly changed (by the Great Vowel Shift, §10) to present-day i, as *bead, heat, knead, meat, seat, wheat*. For a time some words wavered in usage between the long and the short vowel. This is seen in the word *deaf* dεf, for which the pronunciation dif has only recently become substandard. Cf. also *to lead* and *lead* (metal). *Breakfast* now merely imitates the spelling of *break;* the vowel was already shortened to ε in ME (note the spelling *brekfast* in 1463 and *breckfast* in 1594). The past tense *read* rεd shows reverse spelling (§154 (2)); the ME form was *redde* rεd-də, and should now be spelt *red* (like *led*).

(2) The past tense of the verb *to eat* is pronounced et, εt, and it. The last, recognized by the *Oxford* (1897) and *Shorter Oxford* (1933), is generally regarded as dialectal in America. The pronunciation εt is now substandard in America, though very common in native dialect. εt is the prevailing form in Southern British, though et is also common.

Wyld (*Universal Dictionary*) lists the spelling *ate* with the pronunciation et, and the spelling *eat* with the pronunciation εt. Historically, he is of course right (cf. *threat*, etc., above). Under *ate* eɪt he says: "This form is obsolescent and rarely used, the normal past tense being *eat* εt." This is perhaps true of the word itself in Southern British, but hardly true of the spelling. It is one of many instances in English of a pronunciation that has got associated with a spelling that belongs to another pronunciation, as bɪzɪ has become associated with the spelling *busy*, which belongs to an obsolete pronunciation (see (4) below). There is little hope that usage will follow Wyld's spellings. The convenience of a written and printed form *ate* for the past tense different from the present *eat*, together with the widespread currency of the pronunciation **et**, will probably preserve the spelling *ate*. It should be noted that the pronunciation **et** is not a spelling-pronunciation, though the spelling *ate* may have helped to preserve this historical pronunciation.

(3) What is the difference of meaning in **klɛnlɪ** and **klinlɪ**? See §250 (4).

(4) The word **ɛnɪ** (ME *eni* ɛnɪ) has the spelling *any* of the obsolete form (ME *ani* ɑnɪ). Similarly **mɛnɪ** (of doubtful origin) is spelt *many* from the obsolete form **mɑnɪ** (ME *mani* mɑnɪ), which is preserved in *manifold* **mænəfold**. Cf. **bɪzɪ** above.

æ

270. (1) Repeat the descriptive name of **æ**.

The sound **æ**, commonly known as "short *a*," and also called "flat *a*," is the most frequent accented sound spelt with the letter *a* in both British and American standard speech,[88] as **ə** is its most frequent unaccented sound (sof*a*). **æ** is the regular descendant of ME short **ɑ** (spelt *a*), when not influenced by neighboring sounds. It appears in the common English words *back, cat, saddle, shallow, fan, man, hand, drank,* etc. For its sound in words like *carry, marry, tarry,* see **ær**, §360.

ɑ

271. (1) Repeat the descriptive name of **ɑ**.

(2) Comment on the sound and its spelling in *father, part, calm, stop, odd, pocket, wash, want, swallow, quality, was, drama, possibility.*

272. As seen in the foregoing examples, the sound **ɑ** in

---

[88] See *American Speech*, April, 1930, pp. 323 ff., and Charles H. Voelker, *Le Maître Phonétique*, Juil.–Sept., 1934, pp. 73 f. In Voelker's list the larger figure for **ɑ** than **æ** in America is due to the inclusion of words spelt with *o* ("short *o*").

America has three principal spellings: (1) *a* (*father*), (2) *o* (*stop*), and (3) *wa* (*watch*). A few spelt with *a* descend from ME *a* ɑ; those with *o* from ME *o* ɒ; and those with *wa* from ME *wa* wɑ.

In British English two groups are now distinct: (1) the *a* ɑ group (*father*), and (2) the *o* ɒ group (*stop*, *watch*), group (3) having shifted, under the influence of the lip-rounded w, from the ME ɑ group (1) to the ɒ group (2). In General American all the groups have fallen together into one with the sound ɑ; faˑðɚ, stɑp, wɑtʃ.[89] For greater simplicity, the ɑ words with the spelling *a* will be treated here, and the ɑ words with the spelling *o* and *wa* will be treated in §§286–291.[90]

273. To understand several related sounds now spelt *a*, it is necessary to consider a few historical facts.

(1) ME had a long ɑː sound and a short ɑ sound. The long ME ɑː (mɑːkə) became present English e (*make* mek), and will not concern us further here (§260).

(2) The **short ME ɑ** (man) is the source of all the different *a* sounds that will concern us here.

(3) This short ME **ɑ,** some time before 1600, by the advancing of the tongue became æ (see Figure 9, p. 61). It has remained æ in standard British and American English in the great majority of words with ME short ɑ (*cat*, *saddle*, *man*, *hand*, etc. See æ, §270). These are the "short *a*" words mentioned at æ (§270).

(4) As a consequence, Early Modern and Late Modern standard speech up to about 1775 had no ɑ sound in the words under consideration, including such words as *father*, *calm*, *hardly*, and such words as *ask*, *staff*, *bath*, *jaunt*, *aunt*, *half*, etc., which

---

[89] The principal variations from this in America will be further treated under ɒ, §288 and ɔ, §291. The change (chiefly unrounding) of ɒ to ɑ did not first take place in America, but in standard British in Early Modern times. British afterwards changed again to the ɒ sound in *stop*, *watch*, etc.

[90] For words like *Clark*, *sergeant*, see ɑr (§365).

now have ɑ in some types of English. Sheridan's pronouncing dictionary (London, 1780) shows no ɑ. Benjamin Franklin's phonetic transcriptions in 1768 have none. His pronunciation of *father, hardly* was **fæðr, hærdlɪ**.[91] Noah Webster in 1789 has **æː** in *aunt, jaunt, sauce*.[92] E. Hale in 1799 has **æ** in *aft, balm, carve, gaunt,* etc.[93]

The older sound æ where we now have ɑ is frequently shown in 17th and 18th c. rimes; as *prayer:afar* (**præɪr:ə˲fæɪr**—Johnson), *searches:arches* (**sæɪrtʃɪz:æɪrtʃɪz**—Swift), *was:brass* (**wæs: bræs**—Spenser), *was:glass* (**wæs:glæs**—Sackville), *was:ass* (**wæs :æs**—Shakespeare). It is also evidenced in present-day dialect pronunciations preserving an older stage of the language; as in **gænt** for *gaunt*, **gæntlɪt** for *gauntlet*, **fæðɚ** for *father*, **pæpɪ** for *papa*, **mæmɪ** for *mamma*, **pætrɪdʒ, kætrɪdʒ** for *partridge, cartridge* (with early loss of r), **sæm** for *psalm*, **kæm** for *calm*, **sæs, sæsɪ** for *sauce, saucy*, etc.

274. In certain groups of originally "short *a*" words that had æ in the 17th and 18th cc., the æ sound was retracted again to ɑ.[94] Three groups are concerned:

I. Words in which the *a* was followed by *r* final or+a consonant, as *bar, far, part, hardly*. In these GA now has the diphthong **ɑr** (**bɑr, pɑrt, hɑrdlɪ**) and Eastern and Southern American

---

[91] *Scheme for a New Alphabet and a Reformed Mode of Spelling.*

[92] *Dissertation on the English Language,* Boston. Webster's first dictionary was published in 1806.

[93] *A Spelling Book,* Northampton, Mass.—See C. H. Grandgent, "From Franklin to Lowell," *Pub. Mod. Lang. Assoc. of America,* XIV. 2. 207 ff. (1899).

[94] The length of the æ and ɑ is here disregarded to simplify the account, although it was an important factor in the change. Only the quality of the sound is here considered. The æ before *r, lm,* and the fricatives f, θ, s was first lengthened to æː in the 17th c. and afterwards retracted to ɑː. It is uncertain whether the varying length of æ in present GA in these words is an inheritance from 17th c. British, or is an independent development. The length is not now distinctive in America, but only quality.

and Southern British have ɑː, as bɑː, pɑːt, hɑːdlɪ. (But if *r* was followed by a vowel, æ remained: kærɪ, mærɪ.)

II. Words in which the *a* was followed by *lm* = m, as *balm*, *calm*, *psalm*, *almond*. These now have ɑ in both British and American: bɑːm, kɑːm, sɑːm, ɑmənd.

III. Words in which the *a* was followed by (1) a voiceless fricative (except ʃ) f (*staff*), θ (*path*), s (*ask*); by (2) m or n+ a consonant (*example*, *demand*, *chance*, *aunt*, *branch*). All these words will hereafter be referred to briefly as the "*ask*" words. The change from æ to ɑ in these words was, however, incomplete in two respects: (a) It has not occurred at all in General or Southern American (except the vicinity of Richmond), but only in British (chiefly Southern) and Eastern American (with Richmond). (b) With many speakers the sound has only reached the stage a, intermediate between æ and ɑ.

275. There are somewhat over 150 of these words, including derivatives from the main words (as *crafty* from *craft*). Following is a list of the most common words in Group III, in which Southern British regularly has ɑ and Eastern American ɑ or a.

(1) f—*aft, after, behalf, calf, chaff, craft, daft, draft, draught, graft, half, laugh, raft, rafter, shaft, staff, waft.*

(2) θ—*bath, lath, path, wrath* (Brit. rɔθ).

(3) s—*aghast, ask, asp, bask, basket, blast, brass, cask, casket, cast, caste, castle, caster, castor, clasp, class, disaster, fast, fasten, flask, gasp, ghastly, glass, grasp, grass, last, mask, mast, master, nasty, pass, past, pastime, pastor, plaster, rascal, rasp, raspberry, repast, task, vast.*

(4) m—*example, sample.*

(5) n—*advance, advantage, answer, aunt, blanch, Blanche, branch, can't, chance, chant, enchant; command, countermand, demand, remand, reprimand; dance, France, Frances, Francis, glance, grant, lance, plant, prance, shan't, slant, stanch, trance.*

To these must be added (1) derivatives from the main words

(*crafty* from *craft*, *dancer*, *dancing* from *dance*, etc.); and (2) a number of plural nouns and verbs such as *halves*, *to halve*, *paths* (-ðz), in which the fricative is voiced and would not normally cause the change from æ to ɑ. These words take ɑ by analogy of words like *half*, *path*, etc.

276. In these words toward the end of the 18th c. in south England the æ sound before **f, θ, s,** and nasals was retracted to **ɑ,** so that in Group III ɑ is now the prevailing sound. In GA, however, which was in the main derived from 17th c. standard British (see §5), this change did not take place. So all the words of Group III normally have æ in GA. The same is true of the South (with the exception of Richmond and vicinity), and of most of Canada. In eastern New England and New York City either **ɑ** or **a** is usual in the words (excepting, of course, the large portion of New York City population that derive their speech from Western or foreign sources).

277. The change of ɑ was not, however, so complete as thus far indicated. Many words with the same sounds following the *a* either waver between æ and ɑ or are pronounced with æ exclusively; in general, but not altogether, the less popular words, especially more recent foreign loan-words. A few examples among many are: *alabaster, ample, askance, asp, aspect, bass, cant, champion, classic, contrast, crass, expand, expanse, fancy, finance, franchise, grand, haft, hand, hasp, land, lass, mass, Mass, massive, mastiff, pant, passive, passage, passenger, pastern, plastic, rant, romance, sand, sang, sank, scant, stand, telegraph, trans-.*

278. No purely phonetic development will account for usage in all the words so far given and others similar to them. The element of fashion undoubtedly has played a part. Certain words have thus ranged themselves with these which are phonetically alien to the group. The word *father* is the most striking of these, with the ɑ sound now universal in all types of standard English. The reason for ɑ in *father* has never been explained with entire certainty.[95] *Rather* is in England now usually **raðə(r)**, but GA still has **ræðɚ**, **raðɚ** being a borrowing from British or Eastern. See *PDAE*. In England *lather* has started on the same road (*Oxford*, Baker, Wyld, æ, Jones ɑ, æ). Perhaps **gaðɚ** will come next.

279. In south England at the end of the 18th c. the ɑ sound in these words was looked upon as vulgar, possibly because the change from æ to ɑ first took place among the lower classes. Walker (c. 1800) objects to the ɑ sound in *last, past, chance*, etc., on the ground that it is used by the vulgar. He also objects to any intermediate sound as a compromise between æ and ɑ; apparently such a sound (a) was then heard, possibly from the Scottish and Northerners in London.[96]

280. In 1830 Worcester, the American lexicographer, recommends an intermediate sound (a) in words like *fast, last, glass, grass, dance*, etc., to avoid the affectation of æ and the vulgarism of ɑ.[97] Smart, the elegant British lexicographer and teacher of princes followed him with the same advice and for the same reason in 1838.[97a] Since then the same advice has been repeated

---

[95] See in particular, Kemp Malone, The *A* of *Father, Rather, Modern Philology*, May, 1918, pp. 11–22. Luick, *Gram.* I, 2, §§494, 537, 559, 1a, 560. Luick's view that ɑ is due to r in the following syllable (cf. Group I) hardly agrees with *gather, lather, Mather*, and the GA pronunciation of *rather* ræðɚ. Whatever the origin of ɑ in *father*, it seems likely that the Church service helped to make it universal.

[96] There was great diversity of usage in these words in London about this time, and probably much earlier. The situation was complicated by the large number of Scottish and Northerners in London for whom the change from æ to ɑ had not taken place, but whose æ sound in all "short *a*" words as well as these had probably reached (or preserved) the stage a which it has at present. If we may believe Walker, the ɑ sound had come into vogue before 1790 and given way again to the vogue of æ (to be replaced again by ɑ). Walker may merely have been calling ɑ old-fashioned to discredit it.

[97] Grandgent, *Pub. Mod. Lang. Assoc.*, 1899, p. 215.

[97a] Johan Storm, *Englische Philologie*, I, pp. 374 f.

for the opposite reason—to avoid the vulgar æ and the over-refined ɑ.

281. The present status of a in these words is indicated by the following: Daniel Jones: "In the South of England the use of a in these words is rare, and it seems that those who use it do so in a few words only. The pronunciation with a can hardly be considered as Received Pronunciation."[98] The *Oxford* recognizes for England as a whole the existence of various shades of vowel between æ and ɑ. "The vowel in *chant, past*, varies with different speakers from [æ] to [ɑ], with various intermediate sounds, . . . with intentional ambiguity indicated by ɑ."[99] In 1899 Grandgent says: "This compromise vowel, which was recommended also in England, does not seem to have been adopted, in actual speech, by any considerable number of Americans; it may be heard, however, on Cape Cod."[1] It is the author's opinion that this sound is somewhat more prevalent in parts of New England than Grandgent thought it to be at that time.

The Linguistic Atlas of New England and other observations show that in New England by no means all cultivated speakers pronounce a or ɑ in all the words (the "ask" words) in which we should expect it and in which native speakers of Southern British regularly pronounce ɑ. Though the shift from Early Modern æ to ɑ in the words in question appears to have been at first an unconscious dialect change, it later became a more or less conscious mark of class dialect, and, especially in America, of upper-class fashion, which has produced some rather ludicrous results when aped by those to whom it is not native from childhood. See §284.

282. Not as a consequence of the artificial attempts to es-

[98] *Phonetics*, 3d ed., 1932, p. 75.
[99] Vol. I, p. 1.
[1] *Loc. cit.*, p. 215.

tablish the intermediate **a,** but by normal dialectal development, the **a** sound (varying toward either **æ** or **ɑ**) not only in the *"ask"* words, but in all "short *a*" words, is regular in the cultivated English pronunciation of Northern Englishmen and Scotsmen, and also in the northern and various other local British dialects.[2] This sound in the same *"ask"* and "short *a*" words is also found locally in various parts of America, where it is usually attributable to Scotch influence (as in Alberta, Canada).

283. In General and Southern American the **a** sound has no general currency. In Richmond and vicinity **ɑ** is current in the *"ask"* words, while in the rest of the South, in General American, and in most of Canada **æ** is the universal sound in both groups of words. The **æ** is somewhat "flatter" (higher) in the South than in the rest of the country, in this respect resembling Southern British **æ.** It is usually longer than the British, and tends to be diphthongal.[3]

284. The pronunciation of *"ask"* words either with **a** or **ɑ** has been a favorite field for schoolmastering and elocutionary quackery. The practitioners seldom succeed in compassing more than a half-dozen words (*ask, half, aunt, laugh,* etc.). As a result of their efforts some individual speakers of GA now have an occasional pronunciation **ask, ɑnt, hɑf, rɑðɚ.**

A more serious result is the tendency among many aspirants to the "broad *a*" to apply it to words which are not pronounced **a** or **ɑ** in any type of standard English except Northern British and Scottish (where the practice is consistent and unaffected).

[2] Lloyd, *Northern English,* §90; Grant, *The Pronunciation of English in Scotland,* §143.

[3] In this condensed statement, no account has been taken of the historical difference between words like *ask, path, staff,* and words like *half, laugh, aunt.* For these are now identical in Southern British (with **ɑ**), and also in General and Southern American (with **æ**). In New England they are often identified (with **a**) and always by those who use **ɑ** instead of **a** in *"ask"* words. But in Northern British and in Scotland a distinction is often made (**staf** but **lɑf,** etc.).

Thus they favor us with **man, hapɪ, fɑnsɪ, roˈmɑns, pasɪdʒ, trafɪk, ˌmaθəˈmatɪks, gaðɚ, ampl, frantʃaɪz, pɑnt,** etc.[3a]

285. Those who maintain that the ɑ sound is intrinsically more beautiful than æ, not only forget that this argument exactly reverses that of the early objectors to æ, but that Southern British, which they usually hold up as a model because of its ɑ sounds, has far more æ sounds than ɑ sounds.[4] Moreover, GA has more ɑ sounds than Southern British, owing to the prevalence in GA of the ɑ sound in words that have "short *o*" in British.[5] To such theorists, however, an ɑ sound spelt *o* is not so beautiful, even if long, as one spelt *a*. They also seem to forget that many generations of our ancestors managed fairly well with æ in the words in question,

> "and yet thei spake hem so,
> And spedde as wel in love as men now do."[6]

ɒ

286. (1) Repeat the descriptive name of ɒ.

(2) Comment on the vowel you use in *doll, holiday, hot, pod, pond, on, was, swap, from, watch, what, wander, want, wash, wasp, quality, swallow.*

287. As pointed out in §272, n. 89, the ME short *o* ɒ sound changed in 17th c. British to an ɑ sound. It is likely that this is the chief source of the ɑ sound that is spelt *o* in America today. Its length varies greatly, and depends chiefly on sense-stress, emphasis, and neighboring sounds; hence, as usual, its length is not distinctive. In England this 17th c. ɑ again became ɒ.

[3a] All recorded from radio.   [4] See footnote 88, p. 176.

[5] The author's findings in this matter are fully confirmed by Voelker's independent investigation, by which he found for formal spoken American 27,457 (4.15%) ɑ sounds as against 20,417 (3.09%) æ sounds. Cf. *Le Maître Phonétique,* Juil.–Sept. 1934, p. 74.

[6] I acknowledge the kind permission of the G. and C. Merriam Co. to include in §§274–84, 291 a few details not in the fifth edition of this book, which were contributed to *Webster's New International Dictionary, Second Edition.*

288. The status of ɒ in America is hard to describe, for it is not fully known. The ɒ sound is regularly and naturally used by many New Englanders and some Southerners, who make consistent distinction between the vowels of *father* and *fodder*. Some New Englanders make the distinction by using ɑ for "short *o*," while using for *father*, etc., an advanced ɑ which is nearly or quite a. Thus the distance between the two vowels is preserved. The ɒ sound, or at any rate a sound intermediate between ɑ and ɔ, is used sporadically by many individuals in GA territory, especially in words with w (*want*) and with r (*sorry*). But it cannot be considered a stable and well-recognized phoneme in GA.

Organically and acoustically American ɑ and ɔ are closer together than present Southern British ɑ and ɔ, British ɑ being a trifle nearer to a and ɔ nearer to ɔː.[7] Hence in America ɒ is less distinct from either ɑ or ɔ than in England. Whether the change took place on British or American soil, the ɒ sound in America has in a part of the words spelt *o* fallen together with ɑ (*top*) and in other words with ɔ (*song*). These variations will be more fully illustrated under ɔ below.

The chief factor in the change of ɒ to ɑ is unrounding of the lips, the tongue positions of the two sounds (both low-back) being near together. Americans who do not naturally pronounce ɒ are often able to acquire an acceptable ɒ by rounding the lips and aiming at ɑ. See further under ɔ, §291.

ɔ

289. (1) Repeat the descriptive name of ɔ.

(2) Comment on the sound and its spelling in *awful, cloth, broad* (cf. *road*), *ought, aught, nought, taught, talk, quart, wall, war, augment, inauspicious, Utah, Washita, Wichita, Omaha, water*.

(3) Many American speakers pronounce in place of ɔ an

---

[7] In London local dialect it has reached ɔː.

unrounded vowel that resembles ɑ or ɒ. This can usually be corrected by being careful to round the lips decidedly in pronouncing words like *law, all* (see Figure 8, p. 57).

(4) British speakers often change ɔ to ɒ before l or s+a consonant (*always* ɒlwɪz, *also, fault, although* ɒlˈðo, *alter, Austen* ˈɒstɪn, *Austria, Aus*ˈ*tralia, au*ˈ*spicious*).

(5) Southern British ɔ is decidedly more o-like than American.

290. Two common ways of spelling ɔ, *au* (*aw*) as in *caught* (*saw*), and *ou* as in *bought*, are due to the fact that formerly *au* (*aw*) and *ou* were pronounced ɑu and ɒu in accord with the spelling. These two diphthongs afterwards changed to the simple sound ɔ, but the old digraph spelling was kept. The same sound-change is disguised in *talk, all*, in which ɑl had produced a diphthong ɑu, formerly sometimes spelt *au*, but now usually *al*. This diphthong changed to ɔ in the same way as other ɑu sounds did. See "dark" l, §§221 f.

291. In certain groups of words cultivated American usage varies among the sounds ɑ, ɒ, ɔ. It should be noted that in all the groups the words spelt *wa* are treated like those spelt with "short *o.*" See §272.

(1) Words like *foreign, horrid, laurel, tomorrow, orange, origin, sorrow, sorry; warrant, warrior, Warren, quarrel, quarry, quarantine.* In these words the vowel is followed by an *r* sound, spelt *r, rr*, and another vowel. In GA the main vowel and the *r* sound form an r diphthong, which is treated here for comparison of its first element with the other ɑ, ɒ, ɔ sounds (see §352). In these words the prevailing GA natural pronunciation is with ɔr; fɔrɪn, hɔrɪd, lɔrəl, təˈmɔro, ɔrɪndʒ, ɔrɪdʒɪn (ɔrədʒɪn), sɔro, sɔrɪ; wɔrənt, wɔrɪɚ, wɔrɪn, kwɔrəl, kwɔrɪ, kwɔrəntɪn. In all these, British has ɒr. The American ɔ sound is not so near to o as British ɔ is, which would sound dialectal in these words. Moreover, many Americans whose ɔ in *all, law* is but slightly rounded pronounce a sound in *sorry, orange*, etc.,

which is acoustically not far from ɒ. Many speakers of GA use
ʊ in these words, the *r* sound having assisted to preserve the
rounding of the preceding vowel in America.[8] The sound ɑ is
also often heard in this class of words (**sɑrɪ, hɑrɚ**), but this
is perhaps, in part at least, due to a reaction against the use of
ɔ and the advice of teachers to use a "short *o*" to those who
have no ɒ in their speech. This pronunciation is less common,
I believe, than ɔr.

This group must be distinguished from the words in which
the *r* sound is final or followed by a consonant, as in *for* **fɔr,**
form **fɔrm,** *war* **wɔr,** *warm* **wɔrm,** *quart* **kwɔrt.** These words
have the ɔ sound (GA ɔr, British ɔ) in all types of standard
English. See ɔr, §366.

(2) Words in which the vowel is followed by a voiceless
fricative (except ʃ) (a) **f:** *coffee, coffin, cough, doff, loft, off, offer,
office, often, scoff, soft;* (b) **θ:** *broth, cloth, froth, moth, troth, swath;*
(c) **s:** *boss, Boston, cost, cross, frost, gloss, loss, lost, moss, Ross.*
It will be noted that in these the vowel is followed by the same
voiceless fricatives as in the "*ask*" words. A parallel historical
fact lies behind them. As æ was changed before these fricatives
in south England and parts of New England to ɑ, so an earlier
ɒ was changed to ɔ. The geographical distribution is, however,
different. Northern British still has the ɒ sound in these words.
Southern British still has ɔ in many of them but the tendency
in south England is now toward ɒ (for details, see *Webster,
Pron.* §185). In GA ɔ still prevails except in some of the plurisyllables (*possible, profit, Gothic,* etc.). But some of these have
ɔ in GA, as *office, offer, officer, Boston, coffee.* The efforts to
change **bɔstn̩** and **kɔfɪ** to **bɑstn̩** and **kɑfɪ** have produced little
result in America as a whole. See *PDAE.* A number of persons

---

[8] The frequent rounding of ɜ in *hurt* and the rounding of r itself is recognized
both by Grandgent (*loc. cit.*, p. 221), and by William A. Read (*Jour. Eng. and
Germanic Philol.*, April, 1923, p. 235), who mentions its influence in preserving
ɒ from becoming ɑ in this class of words.

with phonetic training have begun to use ɒ in most of these words, and as in Group (1) many speakers with unrounded ɔ in *law*, pronounce a vowel that resembles ɒ in these words.

(3) Words like *splosh, squash, swash, wash*, with ʃ after the vowel. There are not many of these. These regularly have ɑ except as they contain **w**. This frequently has the effect of rounding the vowel to ɒ or ɔ. This is especially common in *wash*, and is found also in British cultivated speech. See below (9).

(4) Words with the affricates after the vowel, as *botch, blotch, crotch, notch, Scotch, splotch, watch; dodge, Hodge, hodge-podge, lodge, stodgy*. These all have ɑ except as ɒ or ɔ occasionally occurs in *watch* (see (9) below).

(5) Words with **l** after the vowel, as *doll, loll, Poll, folly, golly, holly, jolly, Molly, volley, follow, hollow, swallow, wallet*. These have ɑ except for the usual variation in the **w** words.

(6) Words with ŋ after the vowel, as *gong, long, prong, song, strong, thong, throng, tongs, wrong*. In these GA regularly has ɔ, differing definitely from British, which has ɒ. As an acquired pronunciation ɒ occurs occasionally, and also with those who have ɒ regularly in other words. But the preponderance is clear for ɔ. Grandgent believed that ɔ prevailed in New England in 1899.[9]

(7) *Gone* is irregular in its history (it would normally rime with *stone*). In GA it is generally **gɔn** (so New England in 1899[10]). In England it varies between ɒ and ɔ (Jones ɒ, ɔ; Wyld ɔ, ɒ; Baker ɔ, ɒ; *Oxford* both without choice). *Shone* is regularly ʃɒn in GA, the British ʃɔn, ʃɒn not being current here. But other words with nasals regularly have ɑ, as *from, Tom, non-, prompt, swan, swamp, wander, want*, except as usual the **w** words and occasionally *on*, with ɒ or ɔ. On the Western Reserve, **swɔmp** is common, and **wɔnt** is widespread beside **wɒnt** and **wɑnt** (**wɔnt** is also heard in England—Baker).

---

[9] *Loc. cit.*, p. 220.
[10] *Loc. cit.*, p. 220.

(8) Words with stops after the vowel. These are numerous: *bob, cob, cobble, fob, gob, gobble, hob, hobble, job, knob, mob, rob, robber, sob, snob, squab, swab, throb, wobble.*

chop, cop, crop, drop, flop, fop, hop, lop, mop, pop, prop, shop, slop, sop, stop, strop, swap, top.

clod, cod, fodder, God, hod, nod, plod, pod, prod, quad, rod, shod, sod, squad, tod, trod, wad, waddle.

blot, bot, clot, cot, dot, got, grot, hot, jot, knot, lot, not, plot, pot, rot, Scot, shot, slot, sot, spot, squat, swat, tot, trot, watt, what.

bog, clog, cog, dog, fog, frog, goggles, grog, hog, jog, log, nog, tog.

block, clock, cock, crock, dock, flock, frock, hock, Jock, knock, lock, mock, mockingbird, rock, shock, smock, sock, stock.

These words and many derivatives from them, or pluri-syllables with the same vowel, regularly have ɑ in GA, with the usual New England variant ɒ. There is, however, a good deal of variation between ɑ and ɔ in the -g words. *Dog* is universally dɔg in natural pronunciation (including New England[11]). The spelling *dawg*, used to ridicule a supposed mispronunciation, has led some timid speakers to use dɑg occasionally, but it is not general. lɔg is also usual within the author's observation. fɔg, frɔg, hɔg are frequent variants of fɑg, frɑg, hɑg. mɔk, and especially mɔkɪŋbɜd, are not infrequent. gɔd is looked upon either as dialectal or overpious, but gɒd is not uncommon.

(9) Owing to the influence of the rounded w, the w words are especially variable. In the GA territory, where the ɒ sound is not regular or stable, the usual variation is between ɑ and ɔ. But not a few speakers have a slightly rounded ɑ or ɒ in the w words that is acoustically distinct from ɑ and ɔ. Not only in words with final *r* or *r*+consonant after the vowel, as *war, warm*, but in words with intervocal *r*, as *warrant, quarrel*, and in such words as *want, wash, wasp, wander, wanton*, which would normally have ɑ or ɒ, ɔ is often used, both in America and

---

[11] Grandgent, *loc. cit.*, p. 220.

England (Baker has: wɔːn, wɔːnd, wɔːndər, wɔːnt, wɔːʃ, wɔːsp). *Warren*, Ohio, is regularly wɒrɪn.

The word *water* has had double forms since ME times. That with long vowel is now wɔtɚ, and with short vowel watɚ, wɒtɚ. In GA territory watɚ is very common. The pronunciation with intermediate vowel is frequent in GA territory. Convenient test phrases are *hot water, waterpot, falling water, waterfall.*

(10) Words like *daunt, gaunt, gauntlet, haunch, haunt, jaunt, laundry, saunter, vaunt,* in which *au* is followed by n+a consonant, vary in cultivated speech between ɔ and ɑ. The pronunciation with ɑ is especially frequent in New England. In England and the rest of America ɔ predominates. The 18th c. pronunciation dænt, hænt, gænt, dʒænt may still be heard in dialect.

o

292. (1) Repeat the descriptive name of **o.**

(2) Comment on the sound and its spelling in *go, rope, boat, old, folk, toll, won't, yeoman, shoulder, mould, soul, bowl, hoe, slow, though, beau, impost, obey, proceed, shadow.*

293. In south England, and often in America, this vowel is a diphthong, having a more or less distinct ʊ as its final element. The diphthong oʊ occurs in America under the same conditions as eɪ (see e, §261). As with British ɛɪ, the first element of the diphthong oʊ in England is somewhat different from the simple vowel o; it is sometimes lowered toward ɔ, but more usually advanced toward the central position, the symbols əʊ or ɜʊ fairly well representing the sound heard in Southern British. As we go northward in England we encounter the more o-like sound (mid-back-round), till in northern England and Scotland the pure o is found.

In both the diphthongs eɪ and oʊ the tongue often does not fully reach the position indicated by the second symbol of the diphthongs.

294. The word *brooch*, in origin the same as *broach*, is pronounced **brotʃ,** though the spelling-pronunciation **brutʃ** is not uncommon. The pronunciation **nolɪdʒ** for *knowledge,* often used by 18th and 19th c. British clergymen and literary men, which Tennyson also insisted upon, was merely the result of reasoning that it ought to be pronounced like *know,* in ignorance of the ordinary laws of historical sound-change. The *o* in *knowledge* was regularly shortened, as in *husband* (cf. *house*), *linen* (cf. *line*), etc. In the nouns *process* and *progress,* America favors **ˈprasɛs, ˈpragrɛs,** while England prefers **ˈprosɛs, ˈprogrɛs,** but the former are also used in England (with **ɒ**). Here two analogies interfere: that of verbs like **proˈgrɛs, proˈsid,** and on the other hand words that change their first vowel when the accent is shifted, as **proˈklem—ˌpraklǝˈmeʃǝn, proˈfen—ˌprafǝˈneʃǝn, proˈpoz—ˌprapǝˈzɪʃǝn, proˈdɪus—ˈpradɪus.**

295. The words *sew* **so,** *shew* **ʃo,** *strew* **strɪu, stru** and *shrew* **ʃrɪu, ʃru** illustrate a development often exemplified in English spelling and pronunciation. In Early Modern, each of these words was current in two pronunciations with a corresponding spelling for each: *sew* **sɪu**—*sow* **so;** *shew* **ʃɪu**—*show* **ʃo;** *strew* **strɪu**—*strow* **stro;** *shrew* **ʃrɪu**—*shrow* **ʃro.** Note the following rimes: *sew:new* (1600); *sow:show:know* (Dryden, c. 1700); *shew: hew, show:snow* (Wither, 1622); *shrew:pursue* (c. 1500); *shrow: woe* (Shakespeare, c. 1596); *strew:you* (Herrick, 1648); *road: strow'd* (Swift, 1727).

Of the pair *shrew, shrow* are now preserved only the pronunciation **ʃrɪu** or **ʃru,** and the spelling *shrew,* the pronunciation **ʃro** and the spelling *shrow* now being obsolete (except for an occasional pronunciation of *Shrewsbury,*[11a] especially in **ʃrozbǝrɪ skul**). Of *strew, strow* both pronunciations and both spellings are preserved, *strow* **stro** being, however, archaic or dialectal. Of *shew, show* only one pronunciation **ʃo** is preserved but (in England) both spellings are still used. Of *sew, sow* only one

---

[11a] Though of different origin, this conformed to *shrew.*

pronunciation, **so,** is preserved, and one spelling *sew,* which belongs to the obsolete pronunciation. How do you pronounce *ewe?* See *Webster.*

296. In New England a variety of *o* sound is heard in some words, which is thus described by Professor Grandgent: "In a great many words oː is shortened and slightly advanced, in rustic New England speech, becoming **ò.** This vowel is used by educated New England speakers in about fifty common words and their derivatives, and it certainly prevails in the cultivated usage of this region in *Polk, polka, whole,* and probably in *both, folks, Holmes, most, only,* and some others."[12] Professor Grandgent also describes this sound as a rounded ʌ.[13] In the rustic speech of Connecticut this **ò** is often unrounded, making a word like *home,* **hʌm.** Several words with this "New England short *o*" have found their way into the Middle West with New England emigrants, either in the unrounded pronunciation, or at least what sounds to unaccustomed ears like ʌ. The author's grandfather (a New England settler on the Western Reserve) pronounced what is now recalled as **kʌt, hʌl, stʌn,** but may have been **kòt, hòl, stòn,** for *coat, whole, stone.* Ellis[14] mentions the ʌ sound in England for words like *stone.* The author remembers a native of England who said **tʌm** for *at home* (or *to home*).

297. The unaccented vowel spelt *-ow* in words like *follow sparrow, swallow* has several times in its history been reduced normally to ə, and then artificially restored again to **o,** mainly from the spelling. This is now the conventionally "correct" pronunciation. But in GA these words are often pronounced in normal cultivated speech **falö, spærö, swalö,** in which **ö** represents a sound close to **o,** but with the tongue farther forward toward the central position (see Figure 9, p. 61). In ordinary transcription (as elsewhere in this book) this **ö** is represented

---

[12] *Loc. cit.,* p. 217. In the *PDAE* **ò** is represented by 5.

[13] *German and English Sounds,* p. 16.

[14] Alexander J. Ellis, *Early English Pronunciation,* London, 1869, I, 95.

by **o**—**fɑlo,** etc. This vowel is very like final unaccented **ʊ,** which might also be used to transcribe *follow,* etc. (**fɑlʊ, nærʊ,** etc.). See footnote 31 to §75. If the lip-rounding is lost, these words become **fɑlə, spærə, swɑlə,** etc., as they have repeatedly been in the past, and still are in the familiar speech of a great many Americans.

In the words *bellows, gallows* the older pronunciations **bɛləs, gæləs** are still sometimes used by the cultivated (Luick, *Oxford, Webster*). Note also the double plurals **bɛləsɪz, gæləsɪz,** with the special development of meaning in the latter. See §250 (4).

ʊ

298. (1) Repeat the descriptive name of **ʊ.**

(2) Comment on the sound and spelling in *pull, full, put, sugar, wolf, woman, worsted, good, wood, wool, would, should, could.* Chaucer's forms of the last three words were *wolde* **woːldə,** *sholde* **ʃoːldə,** *koude* **kuːdə.** How can you account for the spelling of *could?* How has it affected the pronunciation?

The name *Boleyn* **ˈbʊlɪn** is merely another spelling of *Bullen. Bolingbroke* is pronounced **ˈbʊlɪŋˌbrʊk,** except as spelling-pronunciation has altered it. See §325.

For the variation in standard pronunciation between **u** and **ʊ** in words like *root,* see **u,** below, §303.

u

299. (1) Repeat the descriptive name of **u.**

(2) Comment on the sound and its spelling in *loose, lose, school, move, who, shoe, you, group, route, wound, rude, true, threw, glue, flew, Hindu, whoever.*

For the diphthongal quality of **u,** see §85.

300. The name *Brougham,* and the derived noun *brougham,* are pronounced **brum, bruəm, broəm.** The name *Cowper* **kupɚ,** sometimes by spelling-pronunciation **kaupɚ,** is the same word as *Cooper, cooper* (see §303). The usual cultivated pronunciation of *route* **rut** is exceptional. In other words with the same original vowel (ME **uː**, spelt *ou*) the present pronunciation is **au** (*house, cow, bound*). The normal historical pronunciation is preserved in the popular pronunciation **raut**. The pronunciation **rut** is perhaps due to Modern French, and especially the phrase *en route*, partly Anglicized to **ɑn rut**.

301. The word *wound* **wund** has preserved its **u** sound owing to the influence of the rounded **w** before the vowel. But the pronunciation **waund** has also been in good use, and is not entirely disused. See *Webster*. Can you think of any reason why the past tense of *wind* **waind** is not also pronounced **wund**?

302. The spelling *oo* for the sound **u** results from the fact that this sound in ME was a long **oː** and was usually spelt *oo* to show its length (not its quality). By Early Modern, this sound had changed to **u**, but the spelling, as usual, did not change.

303. For various reasons this Early Modern **u** was often shortened and lowered to **ʊ**. In some cases it also changed from **ʊ** to **ʌ**; hence we have such words as *blood* **blʌd**, *flood* **flʌd**, *glove* **glʌv**, *done* **dʌn**, *gums* **gʌmz**. But in many words it remained in the intermediate stage **ʊ**, as in *good* **gʊd**, *foot* **fʊt**, *hood* **hʊd**, *stood* **stʊd**, *book* **bʊk**, *took* **tʊk**, *look* **lʊk**, etc. As a result of these different developments, many words in present English vary in pronunciation between **u** and **ʊ**.

Transcribe the following words in the pronunciation you can first remember: *broom, coop, Cooper, gloom, hoof, hoop, moon, nook, noon, proof, roof, rook, room, roost, rooster, root, soon, soot, spook, spoon, stoop, woof.*

The variation in cultivated usage between **u** and **ʊ** in these words is shown by Professor Grandgent[15] by statistics giving the pronunciation of a group of about 160 educated people so distributed as to give a fair estimate of the practice of cultivated

---

[15] *Mod. Lang. Notes*, VI, 458 ff. (1891).

speakers in the whole country. The whole report should be studied. Only illustrative statements are here quoted.

The report shows the whole country nearly unanimous for **u** in *gloom*, *moon*, *noon*, *roost*, *stoop*, and showing a strong preference for **u** in *proof*, *rooster*, *spook*, *woof*, and for **ʊ** in *butcher*, *rook*. For *broom*, the South is evenly divided between **ʊ** and **u**. For *Cooper*, the South prefers **ʊ**, while the North decidedly prefers **u**. For *hoof*, the South, Penn., and N. J. are about evenly divided between **ʊ** and **u**; New England, N. Y., and the West show strong preference for **ʊ**. For *roof*, the South is nearly unanimous for **u**, while the North shows only a slight preference for **u**. For *room*, the South is evenly divided between **ʊ** and **u**; Penn. and N. J. are nearly unanimous for **u**; New England shows 40% for **rum** and 60% for **rʊm**; N. Y. and the West, 60% for **rum** and 40% for **rʊm**. For *root*, the South, Penn., and N. J. show only **rut**; New England, 62% for **rut**; N. Y. and the West, 38% for **rut**. **rʊt** is particularly common in N. Y. and northern Ohio. For *soon*, the South, Penn., and N. J. are nearly unanimous for **sun**; New England shows a slight preference for **sʊn**; N. Y. and the West a slight preference for **sun**. For *soot*, New England, Penn., and N. J. are evenly divided between **sʊt** and **sut**; elsewhere there is a strong preference for **sʊt**. For *spoon*, the pronunciation **spʊn** is almost confined to New England, which shows 30% for **ʊ**.

For *broom* Jones gives **brʊm, brum**; for *room*, **rʊm, rum**; regularly **rʊm** in compounds like *bedroom* **bɛdrʊm**; for *soon*, "rarely **sʊn**." Wyld calls **rum** provincial, but prefers **rumɪ, rumɪlɪ, rumɪnɪs**; Blandford (see footnote 72, §227) pronounces **rum**. For the variation in this whole class of words, see *Webster, Pron.* §200.

Give an enlightened answer to the question, "Which is correct, **ruf** or **rʊf**? Would you give the same answer to the same question about **fud, fʊd, mun, mʊn**? What would be a more intelligent question than "Which is correct?" See §5, pp. 14, 15.

3

304. (1) Repeat the descriptive name of ɜ.

(2) Comment on the spelling and the sound in *fir, first, fur, turn, term, were, purse, myrtle, pearl, word, world, journey, colonel, stirring, conferring, purring, blackbird*.

305. This is the vowel in *hurt, stir, her, stirring*, of those speakers who do not "drop their *r*'s." In the author's speech its sound is identical with the whole word *err*. The point of the tongue is raised from the front of the mouth and curled more or less backward toward the roof of the mouth, without actual contact of the point. During the utterance of the vowel ɜ the tongue is held fixed in the same position that it takes momentarily in the beginning of the consonant **r** in *rate*. This produces the "inverted," or "retroflex" vowel. Other types occur in GA, in which the retroflexion is slight, or replaced by raising and retraction of the tongue, but in which the vowel is still "*r*-colored," giving the impression of an *r* sound. The symbol for this sound is the IPA symbol ɜ (as used in British *bird* **bɜd**) with the addition of the IPA hook indicating retroflexion. The symbol ɝ is used in syllables of perceptible stress. The corresponding sound in unstressed syllables is ɚ, formed from ə in the same way. The ordinary spelling of words like *hurt, stir*, etc., suggests a vowel followed by **r,** but in this case the *r* sound is itself the vowel. Hence the symbol ɝ alone is used in *hurt*.

306. In the author's speech, and in that of his region so far as he has observed, ɝ and ɚ are the only retroflex vowels in general use. With other vowels, as in *here, there, are, for, door*, etc., there is an *r* diphthong, in which the first element shows the quality of a separate vowel before the tongue takes the retroflex position. Other observers confirm this for GA.[16] Other retroflex vowels occur here and there, of course; but they are not characteristic

[16] W. A. Read, *Jour. Eng. and Germanic Philol.*, April, 1923; Martin Joos, *Le Maître Phonétique*, Jan.–Mars, 1934, pp. 5–6; Oct.–Dec., 1934, pp. 93 ff.

of GA in the same sense that they are said to be of certain British dialects.

3

307. This is the central vowel pronounced by those who "drop their *r*'s" in words like *stir, stirred, term, deter, fur, hurt*, particularly residents of southern England, parts of New England, of New York City and vicinity, and parts of the South. Those who are not accustomed to make this vowel may approximate it by first sounding their natural vowel in *fur*, and then repeating it with the point of the tongue thrown forward and lower. Another method is first to sound the word *bud* bʌd with a lengthened ʌɪ, and then repeat it with the jaw raised a trifle higher and the tongue slightly advanced. In both America and England the central part of the tongue is higher than the back and the point, and the tongue as a whole is in central position.[17] Like ɜ, ɜ is used only in stressed positions, the corresponding unstressed vowel being ə.

308. Observe that words spelt *ir* (*stir*) or *ir*+a consonant (*third*), those spelt *er* (*re*ˈ*fer*) or *er*+cons. (*term*), and those spelt *ur* (*fur*) or *ur*+cons. (*hurt*) are now all sounded alike— ɜ in GA (stɜ, θɜd, rɪˈfɜ, tɜm, fɜ, hɜt) and ɜ in southern England, eastern New England, New York City, and parts of the South (stɜ, θɜd, rɪˈfɜ, tɜm, fɜ, hɜt). In ME these three different vowel sounds were pronounced as spelt, like modern ɪ in *spirit*, ɛ in *very*, and ʊ in *sure* (stɪr, tɛrm, hʊrt, etc.). As the *r* sound after a vowel ceased to be trilled (as it still is in Scottish), there developed between the vowel and r a glide vowel ə (stɪər, tɛərm, hʊərt, etc.). Then in Early Modern the high-front ɪ, the mid-front ɛ, and the high-back ʊ were assimilated to this central glide vowel ə, and so became alike one central vowel of the quality ɜ.[18] The *r* sound following then "colored" this preceding

[17] Grandgent, *German and English Sounds*, p. 33; Jones, *Phonetics*, §§342 ff.

[18] The ɪ sound was first changed to an intermediate stage ɛ. This stage is preserved in an older pronunciation of *Miriam* as mɛrɪəm (the same name as

vowel to the sound ɜ, a vowel of more or less retroflexed tongue
like that of the *r* sound, which now disappeared as a separate *r*
sound. In south England, and parts of eastern and southern
America, the "*r* color" itself disappeared, leaving the sound ɜ.
The GA ɜ represents, as usual, an earlier standard British stage
(18th c.) and the British and Eastern and Southern American,
a later stage of development, in which the only trace of an
originally trilled r is now the centralized vowel ɜ without "*r*
color," in place of the original high-front ɪ, mid-front ɛ, and
high-back ʊ.

309. When the r was between vowels, as in *spirit*, *very*,
hurry, the same change also originally took place.[19] But parallel
and later developments (spelling influence and foreign loan-
words, etc.) tended to preserve or to restore the ɪ, ɛ, and ʊ
sounds. Thus the original ɪ and ɛ became re-established before
intervocalic r both in America and England, so that we now
pronounce spɪrɪt, vɛrɪ, etc. The ʊ sound, however, in GA was
not restored, but remains ɜ. Hence in words like *hurry*, *current*,
furrow, *courage*, *worry*, *thorough*, etc., GA still has hɜrɪ, kɜənt,
fɜo, kɜɪdʒ, wɜrɪ. But in British speech, and to some extent, but
not entirely, in eastern and southern America, the Early
Modern ʊ is now ʌ (as in other "short *u*" words), and these
words are now in England hʌrɪ, kʌrənt, wʌrɪ, etc., and to some
extent in America.[20] Intermediate sounds between ɜ and ʌ also
occur, but GA generally has ɜ in such words. Moreover, in

_____

Merriam), of *Tyrwhitt* as tɛrɪt (now tɪrɪt), of *miracle* as mɛrɪkl. Walker (1791)
says of *spirit:* "The general sound of the first *i* in this word and all its compounds, was, till lately, the sound of *e* in *merit;* but a very laudable attention to
propriety [i.e., to spelling] has nearly restored the *i* to its true sound; and now
spirit, sounded as if written *sperit*, begins to grow vulgar."

[19] Luick, §§552 ff.

[20] But when words like *fur* fɜ, *stir* stɜ, *refer* rɪˈfɜ are followed by vowels in
derivatives as in *furry*, *stirring*, *referring*, the ɜ does not become ʌ, but remains
ɜ after the analogy of the main word: fɜrɪ, stɜrɪŋ, rɪˈfɜrɪŋ, etc.

GA several words spelt *i* have also preserved their earlier ʒ sound, and the prevailing GA pronunciation of *squirrel, stirrup* is **skwʒəl, stʒəp**. *Sirup* is pronounced naturally in much of the GA territory **sʒəp**, especially in the maple sugar districts. For fuller information on *sirup* see *PDAE*.

The application of the same older pronunciation to ɛ words (*very, America*) though sometimes made by the illiterate, is everywhere substandard.[21]

310. A local dialect pronunciation in New York City of words like *bird* is popularly represented by the spelling *boid*. This is not, however, the diphthong **ɔɪ**, but rather **ʒɪ**, in which the latter part of an *r* diphthong is changed from **r** to **ɪ**. This change is also made independently of New York in parts of the South. It is reported in New Orleans, I have heard it from educated natives of Georgia, and it is reported sporadically elsewhere in the South.

311. In many parts of the South an *r*-colored vowel, with more or less simultaneous elevation of the tongue is found in stressed syllables, which strikes the ear as much more like ʒ than ʒ. It is especially frequent in the more northern parts of the South. But the same speakers usually have ə instead of ɚ in unstressed syllables. Thus they pronounce further **fʒðə**, and say **tʃʒtʃ**, but **bɛtə**. See *PDAE*, §99.

ɚ

312. This is the GA unstressed retroflex or *r*-colored vowel, represented by the letters *er* in *better* **bɛtɚ**, *perceive* **pɚˈsiv**. It corresponds to the stressed retroflex vowel ʒ, having similar tongue position, but shorter and laxer. Both vowels are shown

---

[21] The view that the pronunciation **hʒɪ, kʒənt**, etc., is substandard or dialectal only, was shown to be wrong by Grandgent (*Mod. Lang. Notes*, VI, 1891, p. 85), who found that ʌ was in the majority only in eastern Massachusetts, New York City, and perhaps Pennsylvania. It is probably even less frequent now.

in ˈfʒðɚ, pɚˈvʒs. Just as the stressed ʒ of GA is replaced by ɜ in the speech of those who "drop their r's" (southern England, eastern and southern America), so the unstressed ɚ of GA is replaced by the British, Eastern, and Southern unstressed ə. Thus GA fʒðɚ is replaced by British fʒðə, and GA pɚˈvʒs by British pəˈvʒs. The symbol consists of the IPA ə with the IPA modifier attached that indicates retroflexion, parallel to the symbol ʒ.

313. Just as ə is the unaccented sound corresponding to almost all the accented vowels (mæn—postmən, ɪmˈpoz—ˌɪmpəˈzɪʃən, see *Gradation*, §130), so ɚ is the unaccented *r*-colored vowel corresponding not only to stressed ʒ, but to other accented vowels that form parts of *r* diphthongs; as grəˈmærɪən —græmɚ, gɑrd—blægɚd, rɪˈkɔrd—rɛkɚd, bord—kʌbɚd. See also §21, last paragraph.[22]

314. In a large number of words final ɚ or ə is represented by various spellings; as -ar, -er, -ir, -or, -our, -ur. These endings come from various sources: from Old English -ere, Old French -ier, -aire, -our, -eur, and Latin -or. After these endings had come to be pronounced all alike (at least as early as the middle of the 18th c. and probably earlier), the spellings became much confused. Some speakers, unaware of the history of the ending ɚ, ə, attempt to distinguish the pronunciation of the endings -er and -or. Not only is such a distinction contrary to universal usage for at least 200 years, but its absurdity becomes apparent when one knows that, e.g., *bachelor* was formerly spelt *bacheler*,

---

[22] In the ordinary spelling of colloquial speech the letters *er* often represent a separate word, an expletive indicating hesitation or embarrassment, as in "I—er—really, I don't know." Here *er* represents the sound ə, more or less prolonged. This spelling doubtless arose from the fact that in southern England and eastern America the letters *er* commonly represent the sound ə in such words as *better* bɛtə, *uppermost* ʌpəmost, *permit* pəˈmɪt. Readers who do not "drop their r's" often misread this expletive *er* as ɚ or ʒ, though when not reading they use ə naturally enough in the pauses of their own speech.

-ier, -ere, -ar; that *tailor* was spelt *tailour, -ur, -ere, -er, -ear, -eor,*
-eour, -eur, -ior; that *sailor, chancellor, ancestor,* and many other
words now spelt with *-or* were formerly spelt with *-er.* It is ab-
surd to suppose that there was a different pronunciation for each
spelling; so today the final syllables of such words as *baker, liar,*
sailor, augur are exactly alike in cultivated speech, being either
ɚ or ə. A widespread popular notion that one is pronouncing
more correctly by saying ˈselɔr than by saying ˈselɚ is based on
the false idea that the present-day spelling-form of a word is the
word itself, to which the pronunciation ought to conform;
whereas, in fact, the present spelling-form is only one of many
spellings, which happens to survive, and the word itself has
lived for generations quite independently of the changing and
imperfect signs used to suggest it in writing. See *PDAE,* §124.10.

315. In the foregoing §§312–14 ɚ is a syllabic vowel, the
center of an unaccented syllable, either alone, as in *better* bɛt-ɚ,
or with one or more consonants, as in *perceive* pɚˈsiv, *papers*
pe-pɚz. For the nonsyllabic *r* vowel occurring as the latter element of *r* diphthongs see §236. Syllabic ɚ and ɜ, and the nonsyllabic *r* vowel, developed in the past two or three centuries out
of consonantal **r,** either trilled, as still in Scotland in words like
fear fiɪr, or fricative, as still in *try* tɹaɪ, or a glide consonant
(§§234 ff.), as in *rate* ret.

ə

316. (1) Repeat the descriptive name of ə.
(2) The symbol ə, as used in this book, represents a central
unstressed vowel of somewhat varying quality. It varies in
quality between the limits of unstressed ɪ, as in *added* ædɪd,
and stressed ʌ, as in *button* ˈbʌtn̩ (see Figure 9, p. 61). Its
quality is much affected by surrounding sounds. It may
roughly be described as an obscure neutral sound, made with
the tongue in a resting position, different in quality from any

stressed vowel, but most like ʌ. It is not, however, merely the unstressed form of ʌ. See §21, last paragraph. ə is often called *schwa* ʃwɑ.

317. Transcribe the following in your usual conversational pronunciation: *idea, several, indignant, distance, garland, William, Christmas, breakfast, gentleman, alone, awake, account, notable, quiet, science, judgment, telephone, effect, decent, elephant, specimen, gentlemen, quality, principle, ability, difficult, April, gallop, kingdom, welcome, purpose, connect, compel, obtain, nation, suppose.*

318. The ə sound in unstressed syllables of natural speech may be represented in the current spelling by almost any letter or digraph. This results from an important development of the language. In OE the vowels of these unstressed syllables were much more distinctly pronounced, and were different sounds in accord with the different spellings. The leveling of these different sounds to the one sound ə, with the old spelling retained, was a very gradual process, which is still going on. Compare the careful pronunciation of **progræm** with the more popular **progrəm.** By careful pronunciation, such as might be used in a public reading, some of these unstressed vowels may be restored to something like their full sound; as in **proˈdɪus** for **prəˈdɪus** of ordinary speech; **ɑbˈten** for colloquial **əbˈten; kɔˈrɛkt** for colloquial **kəˈrɛkt; æˈtɛnʃən** for **əˈtɛnʃən,** etc. It is, however, as the student can test for himself from any page of prose, **a very small proportion of words to which the full vowel sound of the unaccented syllables can be restored without making the pronunciation wholly unnatural and even unintelligible.** E.g., it will not do, even in formal address, to say **dɪstæns** for **dɪstəns, brɛkfæst,** for **brɛkfəst, dʒɛntɪlmæn** for **dʒɛntl̩mən, pɜpos** for **pɜpəs, rɪtɛn** for **rɪtn̩, ɑbʌv** for **əbʌv, prɪnsɪpæl** for **prɪnsɪpl̩, ɪgnoræant** for **ɪgnərənt, ði mæn** for **ðə mæn,** e

græˈmæriæn for ə grəˈmæriən, æn ɔrnemɛnt for ən ɔrnəmənt.[25]
Many words in ordinary speech would be unintelligible with the
unstressed vowels fully sounded.

319. The same law of obscuration of vowels in unstressed
syllables applies to words—chiefly monosyllables—that have
the full vowel when pronounced by themselves or when they
have sense-stress. See §§130–137 ff.

320. Schoolteachers and teachers of public speaking are in
danger of giving their pupils lasting false impressions by failing
to recognize this important law of the English language. In
their effort to inculcate habits of clear articulation—most com-
mendable in itself—they often give pupils the idea that distinct
pronunciation means giving equal prominence to the vowels of
all syllables. But disturbing the relation existing in natural
speech between the clear stressed and partly stressed vowels
and the obscurer unstressed vowels cannot make the result
either clearer or more beautiful. The artificial pronunciation
kɑnˈtɛntmɛnt is neither clearer nor more beautiful than the
normal kənˈtɛntmənt. Nor is there any reason why the latter
cannot be just as clearly enunciated as the former. Clear enunciation of the consonants and vowels as they are, with due attention to time-length and sonority, and with that naturalness
which is gained only by observing the normal relation between
stressed and unstressed syllables, distinct and obscure vowels,
will produce a clearness which is both beautiful and natural.

The late Professor Sweet, of Oxford University—a pioneer
authority on phonetics—expresses the views of competent
scholarship on this point when he says, "The general result [of

---

[25] The speech of many American public speakers is marred, for those accustomed to hear good English, and robbed of sincerity, by the frequent occurrence of the stressed forms e and æn for the correct unstressed ə and ən
See *American Speech*, June, 1931, p. 368, and *PDAE* at *a, indef. art.*

ignoring the relation between distinct and obscure vowels] is that the pupil is forced to acquire an artificial elocutionary language distinct from that of everyday life. His elocution suffers from this in many ways. The constant effort to avoid falling back into natural habits of speech robs his delivery of all freshness and freedom, the very muscles of his throat partake of the general rigidity, and the purity of his tone is impaired. Even when the artificial habits by long practice become a second nature, the result is always unpleasing, because it is artificial and unnatural. . . . It has often been argued that by giving an artificial distinctness to weak sounds, as in the orthographic pronunciation of our dictionaries, we make the words more distinct. It is of course true that in themselves such forms as **ænd, tu, fɔə** are more sonorous, and in so far more distinct, than **ņ, tə, fə,** but it does not necessarily follow that the context is made more intelligible by substituting an unexpected strong form for the natural weak one. In fact the contrary is so much the case that misunderstanding may arise from such substitutions. . . . The truth is, that we cannot make words more distinct by disguising them."[26]

A great American scholar, the late Professor William D. Whitney, in the Preface to the *Century Dictionary* (1889) says aptly, "To write (as systems of re-spelling for pronunciation, and even systems of phonetic spelling, generally do) the vowels of unaccented syllables as if they were accented, is a distortion, and to pronounce them as so written would be a caricature of English speech."

One of the most unfortunate results of such artificial emphasis by a speaker is the fact that his pronunciation calls attention to itself, since it differs from unconscious cultivated pronunciation, and thus distracts the attention from the thought

[26] See *The English Journal*, Vol. xxxvii, 1, Jan. 1948, pp. 25–27.

and feeling. The best pronunciation is that which is unnoticed by the hearer.

The student should rid himself of a common misconception; namely, that the obscuring of certain consonants and vowels owing to lack of stress on syllables or words is the result of a corruption of good English. On the contrary, it is the result of a perfectly normal linguistic development of English according to ancient laws well understood by linguistic scholars. It is the artificial departure from this characteristic of English that is a corruption of the actual pronunciation of the cultivated people who are carrying on the world's affairs.

321. In the unstressed syllables of many words good usage varies between ə or ļ, m̦, n̦ and ɪ. Transcribe the following words showing your own habit in this respect: *character, purchase, pigeon, cushion, curtain, evil, level, barrel, travel, squirrel, vowel, Caleb.* With many cultivated people the first five of these are pronounced kærɪktɚ, pɜtʃɪs, pɪdʒɪn, kuʃɪn, kɜtɪn. The pronunciations ivɪl, lɛvɪl, bærɪl, trævɪl, skwɜɪl, momɪnt have only recently become unusual, and vauɪl is still heard.

With some speakers the unstressed ɪ of words like *message* mɛsɪdʒ, *goodness* gudnɪs, *greatest* gretɪst, tends to become lowered and retracted to ə. This results in such pronunciations as ɛndəd, rozəz, gudnəs, gretəst, ɑnəst, aɪ no ət, etc. Professor Grandgent's investigations in 1895[27] indicated that this was then commonest in New York City, Philadelphia, and parts of the West and South, and that it was regarded as vulgar in other parts of the country. Krapp[28] believed the last statement no longer true. It is true that to the ears of many accustomed to say gudnɪs, aɪ no ɪt, the pronunciation gudnəs, aɪ no ət is unpleasant. But apparently ə for ɪ in such cases is on the increase.

Speakers who habitually substitute ə for ɪ in such unstressed

[27] *Die Neueren Sprachen*, II, 449.
[28] *Standard English in America*, §173.

syllables and monosyllabic words pronounce alike *I met 'em* and
I met him aɪ mɛt əm; *He wouldn't do at all* and *He wouldn't do
it all* hi wʊdṇt du ət ɔl. The substitution of ə for ɪ is especially
common in the endings *-ed* of verbs (*stated, needed*), *-es* of verbs
(*passes, loses*) and of plural nouns (*places, noses*), and possessive
-'s of nouns ending in sibilants (*Keats's, Jones's*). Observe your
own practice in this regard.[29] Do you pronounce alike *Louisa's*
and *Louise's? Georgia's* dʒɔrdʒəz and *George's? Rosa's* and *roses,
Rose's?* See if you can find other pairs differing (if at all) only in
the sound of the last vowel.

ʌ

322. (1) Repeat the descriptive name of ʌ.

(2) Comment on the sound and its spelling in *sun, son,
shove, done, does,*[30] *doth, among, mongrel, cover, plover, ton, front,
compass, constable, flood, double, enough, income, undo, misunderstand.*

323. This is the so-called "short *u*" sound in *run, come.* In
tongue position it varies somewhat in different regions. The
author's ʌ is somewhat higher and farther forward than that
described by Jones for Southern British,[31] being definitely a
central vowel, but low and retracted. It lacks the slight a or ɑ
coloring which the American often detects in the British ʌ.

324. Modern ʌ developed from Early Modern ʊ, probably
through the stages of ʊ, advanced o, ɜ, ʌ with successive de-

---

[29] The native speech of the Western Reserve in Ohio shows ɪ in these words,
but recent college classes gathered from Ohio and neighboring states show many
instances of ə. Grandgent was perhaps wrong about its frequency in the South.

[30] Cf. William Dwight Whitney: "I myself, with many others, grew up (in
Northampton, Mass.) to pronounce *does* naturally with the real short *ŭ* of *full*,
the true and natural abbreviation of the long *ū* of *do*—like *says* (sĕz) from *say*
(sē)." *Oriental and Linguistic Studies*, New York, 1874, p. 224.

[31] *Phonetics*, §§334 ff.

crease of lip-rounding. The stages o+ and ɔ may be heard in Southern American pronunciation. In England the ʊ sound (or near it) is preserved in the Northern dialects, but in Scotland it has become ʌ as in standard British.

325. In many common words such as *come, love, some, honey,* the ʌ sound is spelt with *o*. In OE the corresponding sound (then ʊ as in *full*) was spelt with *u: cuman, lufu, sum, hunig*. But somewhat before Chaucer, when French scribes in England were making many manuscripts, they were in the habit of spelling with *o* words that had the ʊ sound, because French had an ʊ sound derived from an older o and still written with *o*. So these scribes spelt with *o* English words that had the ʊ sound, whether they were native English or borrowed from French, especially if *u* was next to *n, m, u, v, w,* with similar strokes, writing English *come, love, some, honey,* as well as French derivatives *cover, front;* and we have followed their custom ever since. The common words we continue to pronounce ʌ regardless of the spelling, because they are all familiar before we learn to spell. But less familiar ones, which we learn from print or see in print oftener than we speak them, such as *bombast, dromedary, combat,* we are apt to pronounce with ɒ or ɑ because they are spelt with *o*. Such words therefore frequently have two pronunciations, one a traditional, and the other a spelling-pronunciation. Sometimes only the latter prevails. See §§142 ff., *Spelling-pronunciation.*

A different group of words, such as native English *other, mother, brother, flood, blood,* etc., with ʌ are spelt with *o, oo,* because they were formerly pronounced with o, which later changed to ʌ. See §303.

Frontier is variously pronounced. See *Webster, Pron.* §277, for the different pronunciations. The prevailing one in America is frʌn'tɪr. The word *wont* "custom," is historically wʌnt, having developed regularly from Early Modern wʊnt. But the

word being now somewhat rare tends to the spelling-pronunciation **wont**. The verb *won't* contains the same vowel, from ME
wol not ˈwʊl nət, wʊnt, wʌnt. The influence of the spelling,
backed by the schoolteacher, and possibly the analogy of the
word *don't* **dont**, has made general the pronunciation **wont**.
But wʌnt is still used by many cultivated speakers.

326. The word *hiccup* is pronounced hɪkʌp or hɪkəp. The
spelling *hiccough* is a result of the imaginary notion that the
word had something to do with *cough*. The correct spelling is
hiccup, given first place in the *Oxford*, *Webster*, *New Century*,
Standard; and *hiccough* "ought to be abandoned as a mere
error" (*Oxford*). If it is not abandoned, we may look forward to
the spelling-pronunciation hɪkɔf, which is actually cropping up
in college classes. Organically, a hiccup is precisely the opposite
of a cough. Explain.

Diphthongs

327. Though the term *diphthong* means "two sounds,"[32]
strictly a diphthong consists of one continuous gliding vowel
sound within one syllable. For example, the diphthong aʊ in
house consists not merely of a + ʊ, but of one continuously
changing sound beginning with the tongue and lips in the position for a without remaining thus long enough for a distinct a,
changing through a series of positions intermediate between a
and ʊ, and coming at the end to or near the position for ʊ. The
same is true of aɪ and ɪu.

The foregoing diphthongs do not give the impression of two
syllables, because the force of utterance is strongest at the first
and decreases through the whole diphthong, whereas if the
diphthong be made into two separate sounds, as in *awe-inspiring*
ɔ ɪn-, the sonority nearly ceases at the end of the first element,
and then increases again in the second element.

---

[32] As distinguished from *digraph*, "two letters for one sound," as in *beat*.

Though true diphthongs are continuous glide sounds, for convenience we speak of the first and second elements. In saying that the first element of **aɪ** is **a**, we mean that the diphthong begins with the position for **a**. The stressed part of a diphthong is called the **syllabic vowel** of the diphthong, and the unstressed part the **nonsyllabic vowel**. But it must be remembered that they are not separate vowels, being only parts of a continuously gliding vocalic sound.

328. Diphthongs which receive the main stress on the first element, as **aɪ, aʊ, ɪu, ɔɪ**, are known as **falling diphthongs**. There are also **rising diphthongs**, receiving greater stress at the end. The combination **wɪ** in *win* is a rising diphthong that is the opposite of the falling diphthong **ɪu**. Strictly, therefore, the symbol **w** does not stand for a uniform sound, but for the first element of as many rising diphthongs as there are different vowels to follow **w: wɪ, wi, we, wo**, etc. So the symbol **j** represents the first element of an equal number of rising diphthongs **ji, je, jə**, etc.—for neither **w** nor **j** can occur without their following vowel. Cf. §§224 (2), 230, 234 (2).

When **w** or **j** is followed by a falling diphthong, as in **waɪ, jaʊ**, we have a rising-falling triphthong, for it still remains one syllable, with stress first increasing and then decreasing. But falling-rising triphthongs do not occur, for though such falling-rising combinations as **aɪwɑ, aʊjɑ** might occur, they are always resolved into two syllables.

329. Besides the so-called full diphthongs **aɪ, aʊ, ɪu, ɔɪ**, there are the partial or imperfect diphthongs often heard in America, as in final vowels: **sno(ʊ), de(ɪ)**; and regularly in southern England, as in **snoʊ, deɪ**. In such partial diphthongs the glide movement does not begin till a distinct vowel is first heard, and then there follows a more or less distinct "finish" or "vanish." See §§261–3. The significant difference between the full diphthongs **aɪ, aʊ, ɪu, ɔɪ** and the "imperfect" diphthongs **eɪ,**

ou is that a and aɪ, ɑ and ɑɪ, ɔ and ɔɪ, etc., are mutually distinctive, while e and eɪ, o and ou do not distinguish different words.

aɪ

330. (1) This diphthong is commonly called "long *i*," and often mistaken for a simple vowel because of its spelling with one letter, as in *ride*. That it is not a simple sound, but a gliding sound, can easily be seen by trying to prolong it, or by continuously repeating it without break in the voice. The spelling *i* for the diphthong aɪ comes from ME, when the sound was a simple iː. This gradually became a diphthong, through the probable stages ɪi, eɪ, ɜɪ, ʌɪ to present-day aɪ. (Trace the change of the first element on Figure 9, p. 61.) But the ME spelling *i* for iː has been kept for aɪ.

(2) Comment on the sound and its spelling in *aisle, height, rite, right, write, wright, buy, sky, lie, lye, fire, liar, choir, eye, aye, I, idea, biology, diameter.*

331. The quality of the aɪ sound varies in different regions, or among different speakers in the same region, chiefly in its first element. The author's sound has its first element intermediate between a and the central ʌ or ɜ. The GA aɪ is not essentially different from the standard Southern British diphthong. Both are approximately represented by the symbols aɪ. As with eɪ and ou, the tongue usually does not quite reach the position of ɪ for the second element. See §293, end. An American variety has its first element nearer ɑ.

332. In eastern Virginia (and probably other places in the South) and in Toronto, Canada (possibly in other parts of eastern Canada), a difference is made in the aɪ diphthong according as it occurs (1) before voiceless consonants or (2) before voiced sounds or finally. Thus *advice, bite, life, rice*, are there pronounced əd'vʌɪs, bʌɪt, lʌɪf, rʌɪs, while *advise, abide, lives, rise,* *bias, high, fly* are əd‖vaɪz, ə‖baɪd, laɪvz, raɪz, baɪəs, haɪ, flaɪ.[34]

A similar distinction, found in Virginia, the Carolinas, and probably in other places in the South, but with different vowels, is the use of aɪ or ʌɪ before voiceless consonants (*wife* waɪf or wʌɪf) but simple a or aː before voiced or finally (*wives* wavz, waːvz). A phonograph record of a distinguished Virginian has mʌɪtɪ taːd (*mighty tired*). The simple aː, less frequently ɑː, is fairly common in many parts of the South. In words like *knife, life, wife*, in which such difference is made according to following sounds, the singular has a different vowel from the plural: *knife* nʌɪf—*knives* naɪvz or naːvz; *life* lʌɪf—*lives* laɪvz or laːvz; *wife* wʌɪf—*wives* waɪvz or waːvz. But analogy tends to break down the difference between singular and plural: wʌɪf—wʌɪvz or waɪf—waɪvz.

A similar distinction exists in Scottish dialect and standard Scottish English, though the diphthongs differ somewhat from the American. Thus *rice* is rɜɪs, but *rise* is raɪz; *sight* is sɜɪt, but *sigh* is saɪ; though here, owing to the law of Scottish "stopped vowels," the ɜɪ form is used not only before voiceless consonants, but also before voiced stops (*tide* is tɜɪd, but *tied* is taɪd by analogy of *tie* taɪ). The Southern and Canadian pronunciation is perhaps connected historically with the Scottish.[35]

aʊ

333. (1) Comment on the aʊ sound and its spelling in *loud*,

[34] See E. F. Shewmake, *Mod. Lang. Notes*, December, 1925, p. 491, and *American Speech*, February, 1943, pp. 33–38. For information about the Canadian pronunciation, I am indebted to Professor Gordon C. Patterson, University of Toronto.

[35] See *Webster, Pron.* §199, third paragraph; Heinrich Mutschmann, *A Phonology of the North-Eastern Scotch Dialect*, Bonn, 1909, pp. 14 ff.; James A. H. Murray, *Dialect of the Southern Counties of Scotland*, Trans. Philol. Soc., London, 1873; Grant, p. 63; and Eugen Dieth, *A Grammar of the Buchan Dialect (Aberdeenshire)*, Cambridge, 1932, §65.

hour (§353), *plow* (British *plough*), *slough, sauerkraut, flower*
(§353), *flour, doubt, accompt, MacLeod, bough, bought, through,
though, borough, hough, tough, cough.*

334. The sound aʊ is more easily recognized as a diphthong
because of its frequent spelling with *ou* or *ow*. It developed,
however, from a simple vowel in ME just as did aɪ. As aɪ developed from the long high-front iː, so aʊ developed from the
long high-back-rounded ME uː through the probable stages ʊu,
oʊ, ɜʊ, ʌʊ, aʊ. The fact that uː was spelt *ou* in ME gives us the
same spelling today. If it were not that French scribes introduced into ME the digraph spelling *ou* for the then simple
sound uː, we should probably today be spelling the diphthong
aʊ with the letter *u*, just as we spell the diphthong aɪ with the
letter *i*. So it is a kind of accident of language that we now have
an appropriate two-letter spelling for the diphthong aʊ.

335. The quality of the aʊ sound varies somewhat as does
that of aɪ. The most general American and British form is aʊ,
but many Americans use the form ɑʊ. The *Oxford Dictionary*
writes ɑu without defining the first element. A form with the
first element approaching or reaching æ is widespread in both
British and American dialects. æʊ is a frequent form heard in
British local dialect, and it has been one of the conventional
marks of "Yankee" dialect. Either æʊ or ɛʊ is probably what
Lowell meant in the *Biglow Papers* by the spelling *neow* for
now. A sound æʊ, or a diphthong with first element so much
nearer æ than a that it is noticeable to those who use aʊ, is a
characteristic of much Southern American cultivated speech
and is often heard from educated British speakers.

As with eɪ, oʊ, and aɪ, the tongue usually does not reach
the full position for ʊ in the diphthong aʊ. See §293, end.

336. There is a distinction in the aʊ diphthong before voiceless consonants and before voiced consonants and finally that
corresponds to that of aɪ (§332). In parts of eastern Virginia, of

the Carolinas, and of Canada, there is a difference in the au
diphthong before voiceless consonants from that before voiced
consonants or finally that is similar to that of aı. For example, in
Virginia east of the Blue Ridge the diphthong is usually æu before voiced consonants and finally, as in *ground* **græund,** *bowed*
bæud, *how* **hæu.** Before voiceless consonants the sound is ʌu
(varying to ɜu or ou), as in *house* **hʌus,** *bout* **bʌut,** *mouth* **mʌuθ.**
So there is a difference between the diphthong in the singular
house **hʌus** and the plural *houses* **hæuzız,** or in the noun *mouth*
mʌuθ and the verb *mouth* **mæuð.** In Toronto, and probably elsewhere in eastern Canada singular **hous** and plural **hauzız** are
heard. But as with the diphthong **aı,** analogy is apt to make the
diphthongs alike in singular and plural.

337. The behavior of **aı** and **au** before voiceless and voiced
consonants and finally is an illustration of the tendency of
English long vowels to become diphthongs (see §261). Before
voiceless consonants ME **iː** and **uː** were shorter than before
voiced and finally (see rules of *Quantity*, §76). In the regions
referred to the ME **iː** and **uː** before voiced consonants and
finally, being longer, were diphthongized more rapidly and
reached the stage reached in standard speech, **aı** and **au.** Before
voiceless consonants, where they were shorter, as also in Scottsh
before voiced stops, they did not diphthongize so rapidly, and
have only reached the Early Modern stage ʌı (for **aı**) and ou, or
ʌu (for **au**). See §§330, 334. Though the sound in standard speech
is approximately **aı** or **au** in all positions, if the student will
listen sharply, he will often be able to detect a slight difference
in either diphthong according as it is before a voiceless sound or
before a voiced or final one.

ɔı

338. The first element of ɔı in America is generally ɔ, sometimes ɒ. In British cultivated speech there appear to be two types of the diphthong. One is similar to the American sound, with the first element between ɔ and ɒ, as described by Jones (*Phonetics*, §437); the other is described by Sweet (*Sounds of English*, p. 74) and Jespersen (*Gram.* I, §15, 93) as having the first element similar to the lax o in *obey*.

Under what conditions are the different spellings for ɔɪ used?

339. Note the following rimes from Dryden and Pope: *design : join; find : joined; lie : joy; wild : spoild; smiles : toils; mind : purloined;* and the lines from Gray:

> Let not Ambition mock their useful *toil*,
>
> . . . .
>
> Nor Grandeur hear with a disdainful *smile*.

The rimes show identity or similarity of the vowels in *toil, smile*, but they do not show what the vowel was. Both differed from the present sound, but not greatly. By Dryden's time the diphthong in one group of words that was ʊɪ in ME, spelt with *oi*[37] (*toil*) had become ɔɪ. In another group in which it was ɔɪ in ME, spelt with *oi* (*voice*) it had become ɑɪ. But in a third group, words with ME iː (*smile* smiːlə), it had also become ɔɪ (see §330), though still spelt with *i*. So the three groups of words (with ɔɪ, ɑɪ, ɔɪ) all had diphthongs enough alike to make passable rimes in Dryden's and somewhat later times. The result in actual speech of this similarity was much confusion of the three groups of words (like *toil, voice, smile*). We even find *smile* spelt *smoile* in Early Modern, which only shows the confusion, not the pronunciation (reverse spelling, §154.2). A result of this confusion was that many speakers pronounced in any of these words a diphthong that became Late Modern ɑɪ and is still heard in illiterate speech in **paɪnt** for *point* (cf. "*pime blank*," §102), **dʒaɪn** for *join*, **aɪl** for *oil*, **klaɪd** for *cloyed*, **maɪst** for *moist*, **vaɪs**

[37] Since in ME *o* was often used to spell ʊ, as in *love* lʊvə, now lʌv, *oi* was likewise used to spell ʊɪ.

for *voice*, etc. But since two groups of these words were spelt with *oi*, and the third with *i*, the corresponding pronunciations finally prevailed in educated speech, largely by spelling-pronunciation, though words in the second group (like *voice*) could develop phonetically from ME ɔɪ through EM ɑɪ to LM ɔɪ again (Luick §545).

340. In a few words, however, the Early Modern confusion among these three groups of words effected a transfer in educated speech from the "long *i*" words to the *oi* words: *joist*, *hoist*, *boil* 'ulcer,' *groin* originally belonged to the "long *i*" words (ME iː), and in ME were spelt *gyste*, *hyce*, *bile*, *grine*, all now spelt with *oi* and pronounced with ɔɪ. But the phonetically normal pronunciation is still preserved in dialectal **dʒaɪst, haɪst, baɪl, graɪn,** which are etymologically correct. Shakespeare texts have only *byle* for *boil* 'ulcer,' and the 1611 Bible has both; Job ii (heading): "He smiteth him with sore *boiles*," and (verse 7) "Satan . . . smote Iob with sore *biles*.'

ɪu, ju

341. These diphthongs are found in American pronunciation in such words as *beauty*, *feud*, *view*, *tune*, *cure*, *suit*, *mule*, *new*, etc. The Early Modern sound in such words was a diphthong that may be represented by **ɪu.** It had many slight variations, as the corresponding sound still has. Only the main lines of development can here be given. This Early Modern **ɪu** was at first a falling diphthong ˈɪu, accented on the first element ɪ. In one important type of pronunciation the stress soon shifted to the second element, making a rising diphthong that may be represented by **jˈu.** This, with some varieties, including simple **u** derived from jˈu, is regarded as prevalent in standard British and in parts of America. Another variety kept the falling diphthong with initial accent (ˈɪu), often with the second element longer (as observed by Grandgent), and a third distributed the accent evenly over the two elements. The last two varieties are still current in America.

342. Murray, in the *Oxford*, evidently recognized varieties of the sound. He represented it by the symbol iu (with diacritics for variations), but distinguished, e.g., the **ju** sound in *misused*, which he marked misyūzd, from the sound in *abused*, marked abiūzd (*Webster, Pron.* §241). It is certain that the **j** element is more obvious when **ju** begins a syllable, as in *misused* **mɪs-juzd,** *statue* **stæt-ju,** than when after a consonant in the same syllable, as in *abused* **əˈbɪuzd, əˈbjuzd.** Compare *Jacob used it* **dʒekəb juzd ɪt** witb *Jake abused it* **dʒek əbɪuzd ɪt.** Even if the last is pronounced **dʒek əbjuzd ɪt,** the **j** is not so clearly consonantal as in *used* **juzd.**

343. The author's pronunciation **ɪu** is usually given in this book, together with the other main type (**ju** or **u**), minor variations being in the main disregarded. The two types have long been recognized (Ellis, Whitney, Jespersen, Grandgent). But the usual conventional representation of the type "with the *y* sound" (i.e., **ju**) as the only "correct" one, obscured the facts in American pronunciation till Grandgent demonstrated the existence of both types in cultivated American speech.[39]

344. In the author's pronunciation the vowel sound in words like *few, new, mute, duty, cure, suit, stew* is a diphthong **ɪu** with retracted **ɪ** and advanced **u** (see Figure 9, p. 61). In some cases the two elements are still closer together, so that the sound might be represented by **uu+,** there being only a slight glide from the first to the second element, both of which are advanced toward the central position. The **uu+** type is more apt to occur after **r,** as in *rude, true*. In the **ɪu** type either the stress is on the **ɪ** with a longer **u,** or it is about even on both. The stress is never wholly on the second element of **ɪu** or **uu+.**[40] In the present

---

[39] *Mod. Lang. Notes*, VI, pp. 466 ff. (1891).

[40] See Martin Joos's interesting comments on the various American types

(10th) edition of this book the symbols ɪʊ and ʊ are replaced by ɪu and u for greater simplicity in written work. But it is to be understood that in this diphthong the ɪ is retracted (ɪ̈) and the u advanced (ʉ). The difference is not phonemic.

345. In the other type (the ju-u type) the u is also advanced owing to the fronting influence of the j, so that jʉ fairly well represents it. Even in cases in which the j is not sounded (as in *rule, true, lute*) the effect of a former ɪ or j sound is usually heard in the advanced character of the u; so they could be written rʉl, trʉ, lʉt. In so transcribing these pronunciations, it is to be understood that the amount of fronting of the u varies.[41]

346. The retraction of the ɪ, and the advancing of the u, the indistinct border line between the vowel ɪ and the consonant j, the varying stress on this diphthong, and the mixture of speech habits of different regions, all combine to make the observation of this sound difficult, and also contribute to variation in current usage. Certain tendencies, however, can be observed in the different groups of words containing this sound. Since in the ju type ju is often replaced by u after certain consonants, usage varies among the three sounds ɪu, ju, u.

347. The noteworthy fact about the ɪu type is that it varies only slightly according to the consonant that precedes it. It or a near variety (still diphthongal) is used (except initially) not only in the words in which the ju type occurs, as *beauty, mute,*

---

of this diphthong in *Le Maître Phonétique,* Jan.–Mars, 1934, pp. 3–6, noting his remark, "many other things also happen, too numerous to mention." Joos's statement that the ɪ̈ü variety (which I take to be my ɪʊ) is principally found in Ohio and a strip from the Ohio River east to New Jersey, and settlements therefrom, seems a little surprising in view of the fact that my Western Reserve speech shows in other respects all the features that characterized the line of "Yankee" migration across New York State to northern Ohio and Indiana, and differs markedly from the speech of central Ohio, Pennsylvania, and New Jersey.

[41] *Webster, Pron.* §§241 ff.

feud, etc., but also in words in which the **ju** is replaced by **u**, as *rule* **rɪul**, or **ruul**, *true* **trɪu**, or **truu**, *lute* **lɪut**, *blue* **blɪu**, as contrasted with the other type **rul, tru, lut, blu**.

348. The following classes of words are to be considered.

(1) Words in which the diphthong is initial; as *yew, you, youth, yule, ewe, union, use, Europe, unite*. In the initial position **ɪu** is not found; such words always begin with the **j** sound whether it is spelt (*yew*) or not (*use*): **ju, juθ, jul, ju, junjən, juz, jurəp, ju'naɪt**. In these words, however, in addition to the usual fronting of the **u**, there is often also an **ɪ** glide after the palatal **j**; so that pronunciations like **jɪuz, jɪunjən** are not uncommon.

The same law holds when the diphthong is initial in the syllable, though not in the word; as in *deluge* **'dɛl-judʒ**, *value* **'væl-ju**, *statue* **'stæt-ju** (or **'stætʃu**), *continue* **kən'tɪn-ju** (cf. **ˌkɑntɪ'nɪuətɪ**), *regular* **rɛg-julɚ**, *salutation* **ˌsæl-ju'teʃən** (cf. **sə'lɪut**), *cherubim* **tʃɛr-jubɪm**, *reputation* **ˌrɛp-ju'teʃən** (cf. *repute* **rɪ'pɪut**), etc.

(2) Words in which the diphthong follows consonants that do not use the forward part of the tongue in their formation (**p, b, k, g, f, v, m, h, hw**). In these words the current pronunciation is either **ɪu** or **ju**: — **p**: *dispute* **dɪspɪut, dɪspjut**; *pew* **pɪu, pju**; so *pewter, pugilist, puny, pupil, pure, repudiate, repute, spew;* **b**: *abuse* **əbɪuz, əbjuz**, *beauty, bugle, bureau, imbue;* **k**: *accumulate* **ə'kɪumjəlet, əkjumjəlet**, *accuse, acute, cube, cue, culinary, Cupid, cure, curious, obscure, pecuniary;* **g**: *gules* **gɪulz, gjulz**, *gubernatorial, legume, lugubrious;* **f**: *feud* **fɪud, fjud**, *feudal, few, fugue, fume, funeral, fury, fuse, fusion, future, re'fuse, refute;* **v**: *view* **vɪu, vju**; **m**: *amuse* **əmɪuz, əmjuz**, *demure, immune, mew, mucus, mule, mural, music, mute, mutilate, mutual;* **h**: *hew* **hɪu, hju**, *Hubert, hue, huge, Hugh, human, Hume, humor* **hɪumɚ, hjumɚ, hçɪumɚ, hçumɚ, jɪumɚ, jumɚ**. (Do you note any different meanings in the different pronunciations of *humor?* Cf. §250 (4)); **hw**: *whew* **hwɪu, hwçu** (with voiceless **w** and **u**).

In these words **u** is rarely if ever used. So there is no confusion between *beauty* and *booty* **butɪ**, *cue* and *coo*, *feud* and *food*, *hue* and *who*, *mute* and *moot*, *pew* and *pooh*, *pure* and *poor*.

(3) Words in which the diphthong follows consonants that use the forward part of the tongue, which is used also in forming **j**, and in which there is more or less hindrance to forming the **j** sound (least in **t, d, θ, n,** and most in **l, r**). These consonants are: **t, d, θ, n, s, z, ʃ, ʒ, tʃ, dʒ, l, r.**

(a) The **ɪu** speakers regularly use some variety of **ɪu** distinct from **ju** or **u** in these words: *tune* **tɪun**, *duke* **dɪuk**, *enthusiast* **ɛnˈθɪuziæst**, *suit* **sɪut**, *resume* **rɪˈzɪum**, *issue* **ˈɪʃɪu**, *luxurious* **lʌgˈʒɪurɪəs**, *chew* **tʃɪu**, *juice* **dʒɪus**, *new* **nɪu**, *lute* **lɪut**, *blue* **blɪu**, *rule* **rɪul, ruul**, *true* **trɪu, truu.** These speakers regularly distinguish in sound between *brewed* **brɪud**—*brood* **brud**, *chews*— *choose*, *due*—*do*, *duly*—*Dooley*, *lute*—*loot*, *rheum*—*room*, *rumor* —*roomer*, *suit*—*soot*, *sue*—*Sioux*, *tutor*—*tooter*, etc.[42]

(b) i. Among the **ju-u** speakers, after **t** (*tune*), **d** (*duke*), **s** (*suit*), **z** (*presume*), the earlier **ju** sound tended to become palatalized (see §§195 (3), 198 (2), 208 (3), 211 (3)). Thus **t** became **tʃ, d** became **dʒ, s** became **ʃ,** and **z** became **ʒ,** giving the pronunciations "*chune*" **tʃun**, "*juke*" **dʒuk**, "*shute*" **ʃut**, "*pre-zhoom*" **prɪˈʒum,** which are occasionally now heard in British dialect. The reaction from these pronunciations by a part of the **ju-u** speakers was to **tun, duk, sut, prɪˈzum.** The pronunciations **tjun, djuk, nju,** and so in other words with initial **t, d, n,** are still regular in England, but in America the **ju-u** speakers are increasingly saying **tun, duk, nu,** etc., and both in England and America the **u** is heard after **s, z,** and **θ** (**sut, prɪˈzum, ɛnˈθuzɪˌæzəm**).

ii. After **l,** usage of the **ju-u** speakers is divided. In words like *lute,* in which **l** is not preceded by a consonant in the same syllable, the more usual pronunciation is with **u** (**lut**), but

[42] *Webster, Pron.* §242.

ju (**ljut**) is sometimes heard. It is somewhat difficult to pronounce a full consonantal **j** after **l** in the same syllable, though it is easy when **l** is in the preceding syllable, as in *resolute* **ˈrɛzl̩-ˌjut**, and **ju** is thus initial in the syllable (see (1) above.) When a consonant precedes **l** in the same syllable, as in *blue*, the **j** sound has generally been abandoned, if, indeed, Early Modern **ɪu** in this latter position ever changed into **ju**. These speakers therefore say **blu**.

iii. After **r** the **ju-u** speakers omit the **j**, as in *rude* **rud**, *rheum* **rum**. But here also if **r** is in a preceding syllable, and the **ju** therefore initial in the syllable, the **ju** is used both by **ɪu** and **ju** speakers; as in *virulent* **vɪr-jʊlənt**, *garrulous* **gær-jʊləs**. But after **r** there is a tendency to drop even initial **j** (**vɪrʊlənt**, **gærʊləs**, **gærələs**). For further examples, see *Webster, Pron.* §249.

iv. After **tʃ** and **dʒ** sounds (*chew, juice*) the **j** is usually absorbed in the preceding palatal and hence the **ju-u** speakers pronounce **tʃu, dʒus**, though here also (see (1), above) the palatal glide **ɪ** is not uncommon (**tʃɪu, dʒɪus**).

v. After **n** the usage of the **ju-u** speakers is divided, some using the pronunciations **nju, njuz, njumərəs**, and others **nu, nuz, numərəs**. The forms without **j** appear to be increasing in America.

349. Following are some of the words to which the statements in **3**, **(a)**, **(b)** apply: **t:** *constitution, contusion, mature, stew, steward, student, stupid, Teuton, tube, Tuesday, tulip, tumor, tune, tutor;* **d:** *adieu, credulity, deuce, dew, dubious, dude, duly, dupe, duty, endure;* **θ:** *enthusiast, Malthusian, thews, Thucydides, Thule;* **s:** *assume, pseudonym, sewer, sue, suet, suicide, suit, super-, Susan;* **z:** *presume, resume, Zeus, Zurich* **zɪurɪk, zjurɪk;** **ʃ:** *chute, issue, Shunammite;* **ʒ:** *luxurious;* **tʃ:** *chew, fitchew, virtue;* **dʒ:** *abjure, Jew, jewel, Julia, July, June, jury;* **n:** *knew, neurotic, neuter, new, newt, Newton, nude, nuisance,* *numerous;* l: *absolute, absolution, allude, blew, blue, clew, con-clude, glue, lewd, lieu, Lucian, lucid, Lucy, luminous, lunatic, lure, lurid, lute, revolution, salute, slew, sluice, solution;* r: *brew, bruise, bruit, brute, crew, crucify, crude, cruel, cruise, drew, fruit, garrulity, intrude, peruse, rheum, ruby, rude, rudiment, rue, ruin, rule, rumor, rural, screw, scrutiny, shrew, threw, truce, true, truth.*

350. It is generally true, as Joos has pointed out,[43] that intelligent speakers who have inherited historical distinctions in sound between similar words, as between *chews—choose, due—do, tutor—tooter,* feel a natural desire to maintain it against what seems to them unwarranted carelessness and confusion of pro-nunciation. Lowell in the *Biglow Papers* brought against this tendency the force of his humorous sarcasm regarding such pro-nunciations as *"dooty"* for *duty, "loot"* for *lute,* etc. The same statement applies to the distinction between words like *hoarse—horse, worn—warn, mourning—morning,* etc., still maintained in America and England against an increasing tendency to con-fuse them.[44]

351. In certain local dialects, in America, particularly in New England, the ɪu sound has been extended to words that originally had only **u**, as *two* **tɪu,** *do* **dɪu,** *smooth* **smɪuð,** etc. (Certain Scottish dialects have made a similar change in the **u** sound, as in *moor* **mjur,** *book* **bjuk,** etc.) This has become some-what general in the word *shoe* **ʃɪu,** perhaps owing to the palatal **ʃ;** see *shoe* in the *PDAE.* In the word *choose* a historical pronuncia-tion (probably also due to the palatal **tʃ**) goes back to a 16th c. form **tʃɪuz,** and was commonly spelt *chuse* till the end of the 18th c. (as in Jane Austen).

---

[43] *Le Maître Phonétique,* Jan.–Mars, 1934, p. 6.
[44] On the general principle, see Robert Bridges, *Tract on the Present State of English Pronunciation,* Oxford, 1913, and *English Homophones, Soc. for Pure English, Tract* No. 2, Oxford, 1919.

352. R Diphthongs: General American has a series of *r* diphthongs analogous to the British centering diphthongs, as Palmer has called them.[45] As the British and the Eastern and Southern American centering diphthongs end in the central vowel ə (*fear* fɪə, *there* ðæə, ðɛə, *for* fɔ(ə), *gourd* gɔəd, *poor* pʊə), so the GA *r* diphthongs end in the central *r*-colored nonsyllabic vowel r. Thus we have the diphthongs ir (*we're* wir), ɪr (*weir* wɪr), ɛr (*there* ðɛr), ær (*there* ðær), ɑr (*far* fɑr), ɔr (*for* fɔr), or (*gourd* gord), ʊr (*poor* pʊr). These will be more fully illustrated below, §§356 ff.

353. There are also *r* **triphthongs:** as in *fire* faɪr, *flour* flaʊr, *pure* pɪur, pjur. Triphthongs, however, very easily break up into diphthong+syllabic vowel. Thus words like *fire, flour* are often actually pronounced in two syllables, however much they look like one syllable in spelling: faɪ-ɚ, flaʊ-ɚ. So, too, words like *fewer, newer*, though conventionally regarded as dissyllabic, are in actual speech often perfect rimes to monosyllables: *fewer* fɪur, fjur : *pure* pɪur, pjur; *newer* nɪur, njur : *cure* kɪur, kjur, etc. This wavering between monosyllable and dissyllable has been freely made use of by poets, as shown by both rimes and the verse rhythm. Note the rimes: *briar : fire* (B. Jonson); *higher : fire; tower : hour* (Shelley); *power : hour* (Shakespeare). Note the difference in the rhythm of the word *power* in the following from Milton:

(Dissyllabic) Whose ˈpow-er ˈhath a ˈtrue conˈsent—*Il penseroso*, 95.

(Monosyllabic) His ˈutmost ˈpower with ˈadverse ˈpower opˈposed—*Par. Lost*, I, 103.[46]

354. The same wavering is indicated by present-day monosyllables formerly also spelt and treated as dissyllables; as *fire*, formerly *fier, feyer; pure*, formerly *puer; lure*, formerly *lewer;*

---

[45] Jones, *Phonetics*, p. 95.
[46] Robert Bridges, *Milton's Prosody*, 1921, pp. 20 f.

fowl, formerly *fowel;* and vice versa by dissyllables formerly also spelt as monosyllables; as *bower*, formerly *bour; shower*, formerly *shour; tower*, formerly *tour. Flower* and *flour* are usually pronounced alike. Though now regarded as different words, they are in origin one word (ME *flour* **fluːr**). See §250 (4).

This difference is shown, for example, by the rhythm and corresponding spelling in the First Folio (1623) of Shakespeare. In *The Merchant of Venice*, II. ix. 63, we find:

> The |fier |seauen |times tried |this

in which the rhythm requires two syllables in *fier*. But in *The Tempest*, V. i. 45, the spelling indicates one syllable as needed for the rhythm:

> Haue I |giuen |fire, and |rifted |Ioues stowt |Oke.[a]

355. Some other triple combinations such as **aɪə** in words like *trial* **traɪəl**, *quiet* **kwaɪət**, or **auə** in words like *towel* **tauəl**, *vowel* **vauəl**, though conventionally regarded as dissyllabic, are in fact often so pronounced as to rime with monosyllables; as *trial* **traɪ(ə)l** : *file* **faɪl**; *vial* **vaɪəl**, **vaɪl** : *vile* **vaɪl**; or *towel* **tau(ə)l** : *foul* **faul**, in which 'dark' **l** (§§221 f.) is acoustically very like **əl**.

ir

356. This diphthong is rare in American English. Yet in GA it is a separate phoneme from **ɪr**, being acoustically distinct in *we're here* **wir hɪr**, in which the difference is not due to phonetic surroundings, and is therefore phonemic. It is distinctive in *we're* **wir** as compared to *weir* **wɪr**. It is also often distinctive in phrases like *see her*, frequently pronounced as one syllable **sir**, as compared with *seer* **sɪr** or *sere* **sɪr**; *fee her* **fir**, compared with *fear* **fɪr**. But **ir** tends to become **ɪr**, the **i** being lowered by the central vowel **r**. Only recently have dictionaries shown such

---

[a] For the early spellings see §§8–9.

words as *here, fear* with a different vowel from *he, fee*. But the sound has long been lowered in English. On the other hand, in Scottish the **i** is still heard in *fear* **fiːr**, with trilled **r**.

ɪr

357. This is the very common diphthong heard where formerly an **i** was followed by consonant **r**, with later diphthongization and lowering to **ɪr**. This is heard in *beer, bier* **bɪr**, *near* **nɪr**, *peer, pier* **pɪr**, *queer* **kwɪr**, etc. This diphthong may result from either a former **ir** or an **ɪr**; hence *spear it* and *spirit* are exact homophones (**spɪrɪt**).

er

358. This diphthong is not frequent in GA. It is found in a few words like *they're*, and is distinctive in *they're there* **ðer ðær**, **ðer**. Many Americans pronounce *their* **ðer**, owing, perhaps, in part to Northern British and Scottish pronunciation, and in part to the analogy of *they*. In this pronunciation, **er** is distinctive in *their(s)* **ðer(z)** and *there('s)* **ðær(z)**. When *mayor* is pronounced **mer**, in one syllable, as frequently, it is distinct from *mare* **mær**. But the tendency of **er** is to break into two syllables, as *mayor* **me-ɚ**, *payer* **pe-ɚ**, *slayer* **sle-ɚ**, or to become lowered to **ɛr**, **ær**. In one pronunciation of *vary, Mary, Carey, Sarah, barbarian*, heard in the South[47] and occasionally elsewhere, in which a vowel follows the diphthong, the **r** is apt to become consonantal **ve-rɪ**, **me-rɪ**, **se-rə**, **bɑrˈbe-rɪən**. Some speakers who do not use all these pronunciations distinguish *very* **vɛr-ɪ** from *vary* **ve-rɪ**. See **ɛr**.

ɛr

359. We may distinguish **ɛr(1)** and **ɛr(2)**. **ɛr(1)** represents the sound in GA in words like *very* **vɛrɪ**, *merry* **mɛrɪ**, *ferry* **fɛrɪ**, *Perry* **pɛrɪ**, *necessary* **ˈnɛsəˌsɛrɪ**, *cemetery* **ˈsɛməˌtɛrɪ** (and all words

---

[47] Read, *Jour. Eng. and Germanic Philol.*, April, 1923, pp. 217–44.

in -*ary*, -*ery*), *querulous* **kwɛrjʊləs.** This diphthong arose either from an originally short ɛ before **r,** or from a long **eɪ** shortened by reduced accent (ˈ*neces*ˌ*sary*).

ɛr(2), as in *there, care, air*, etc., often has the ɛ somewhat lower than in **ɛr**(1) (*very*). This arose from an Early Modern long **eɪ** before **r.** With some American speakers **ɛr**(1) and **ɛr**(2) have fallen together in a part or all of the words concerned now that vowel length has ceased to be distinctive.

ær

360. Here also we may distinguish **ær**(1) and **ær**(2). **ær**(1) occurs in words with ME short **ɑ+rr+**vowel, which became Early Modern **æ,** as now in *carry* **kærɪ,** *marry* **mærɪ,** *Harry* **hærɪ,** *narrow* **næro,** *sparrow* **spæro.** These words are marked in dictionaries without exception with the equivalent of "short *ă*," *cărry, nărrow*, etc. See §274, I, and §362(a).

361. **ær**(2) arose, like **ɛr**(2), from an Early Modern long **eɪ** before **r.**[48] It is an alternative pronunciation to **ɛr**(2) in words like *there, care, air*, etc. Its **æ** is slightly higher than the **æ** of *man* or of *carry* **kærɪ.** The variation between the use of **ɛr**(2) and **ær**(2) or their equivalents is widespread both in England and America.[49] **ær** was once general in New England[50] and is

---

[48] It is possible that **ær**(2) arose from an Early Modern variant of ME **ɑ:** and **ɛ:** before r which did not reach the Early Modern stage **eɪr.** The testimony of early American writers to the prevalence of **ær**(2) in New England in words like *care* (ME **ɑ:**) and *bear* (ME **ɛ:**), and its decreasing use in later times suggests that it may have reached America from a 17th c. **æɪr** sound. Its great frequency in southern America and in England also indicates its age. The later influence of post-vocalic **r** sounds tends to raise low vowels, which would account for the present general tendency toward **ɛr**(2) or **ɛr**(1). Origin in a 17th c. **æɪr** seems more likely than in **eɪr** later lowered to **ɛɪr,** then **ær,** and then back again toward **ɛr.** See Wright, *New English Grammar*, §§119, 122; Luick, *Gram.* §493.

[49] Jones, *Dictionary*, 1924, p. xxii; *Phonetics*, 1932, §449.

[50] Grandgent, *Pub. Mod. Lang. Assoc.*, 1899, pp. 217 f.

still so in the South. In the author's speech the vowel in *there*, *fare*, etc., is nearer to ær than to ɛr, and is accordingly here written: ðær, fær, with the alternative ɛr often added. It is the author's opinion that ɛr(2) is on the whole now more frequent in GA. Convenient test phrases are *elsewhere, hair-net, spare that, a flat spare, we'll get there yet, that square mat*.

362. There is much vacillation and dialect mixture in the American pronunciation of such words as *there, fare, vary, carry, narrow*. (**a**) Many speakers of the younger generation have no ær sound in any words, not even in *carry, marry*, etc. These latter they pronounce kɛrɪ, mɛrɪ, etc. Thus with them *merry, Mary, marry* are all alike mɛrɪ. (**b**) Others keep the ær in the "short ǎ" words *carry, marry*, etc., but divide the other words into two groups, with ɛr and ær, with no difference between ɛr(1) and ɛr(2) or between ær(1) and ær(2). For example, the following are the author's pronunciations:[51] *very* vɛrɪ, *vary* vɛrɪ, *various* vɛrɪəs, *variation* ˌvɛrɪˈeʃən, *variegate* vɛrɪget, *merry* mɛrɪ, *Mary* mɛrɪ, *marry* mærɪ (and all similar "short ǎ" words), *Marian* mɛrɪən, *Marion* mærɪən, personal name, but mɛrɪən, Ohio, *ferry* fɛrɪ, *fairy* færɪ, *fair* fær (and all -*air* words), *ere, e'er* ɛr, *chary* tʃærɪ, *wary* wærɪ, *beware* bɪˈwær, *care* kær (and all -*are* words), *pear* pær (and all such -*ear* words), *Sarah* sɛrə, *Harold* hærəld, *barbarian* barˈbɛrɪən, *Hungarian* hʌŋˈgɛrɪən, *librarian* laɪˈbrɛrɪən, *precarious* prɪˈkærɪəs, *hilarious* haɪˈlærɪəs, *there* ðær, *where* hwær (and all such -*ere* words except *ere*, a book-word), *prayer* prær, *prairie* prɛrɪ. (**c**) Others, who have no ær, divide the words into ɛr(1) *very* vɛrɪ and ɛr(2) *there* ðɛr, with ɛr(2) clearly lower than ɛr(1). (**d**) Others are fairly consistent in pronouncing ɛr(1) in *very*, ɛr(2) in *there*, and ær(1) in *carry*.

---

[51] I do not attempt to explain the inconsistencies. Some are almost certainly due to analogy or to spelling. How far they are merely individual, the reader must judge.

363. A noteworthy feature of Scottish standard English and dialect is the preservation of Early Modern eɪ before r in the whole group of words (*there* ðeɪr, *care* keɪr, *air* eɪr, etc.), except, of course, words like *carry*, which had Early Modern æ. The same pronunciation eɪr was insisted on for English by most dictionaries till the middle of the 19th c. See *Webster, Pron.* §79, fifth paragraph.

ar

364. This diphthong is found in the three types of words *star* (final *r*) stɑr, *starry* (intervocal *r*) stɑrɪ, and *farm* (*r*+cons.) fɑrm. It usually remains the same, except for length, when final before a vowel, as in *far away* fɑr əˈwe.

365. In *sergeant* sɑrdʒənt the sound ar is represented by the spelling *er*. Note also the British pronunciation of *clerk* klɑɪk, and the name *Clark*, which is the same word spelt as it sounds. A large number of words in Middle English spelt with *er*, such as *clerk, sergeant, smert, sterve*, and at first pronounced klɛrk (with ɛ as in *very*, not as in *person*), sɛrdʒɑnt, smɛrt, stɛrvə, gradually lowered the ɛ to æ and then retracted it to ɑ, so that these words are now klɑrk (the name), sɑrdʒənt, smɑrt, stɑrv. Other examples in ME are *ferre, herte, herth, kerve, sterre*, all spelt with *er* and pronounced with ɛr, since changed to ar: fɑr, hɑrt, hɑrθ, kɑrv, stɑr. Nearly all this group of words have also changed their spelling to *ar*, though a few older spellings remain in *sergeant, heart, hearth*. Some of them, however, changed the sound ɛr to ɜ instead of ar and kept the spelling *er* (*ear*), as *sermon* sɜmən, *certain* sɜtɪn, *learn* lɜn. In 16th–18th c. English, however, many of these latter had ær: note the rimes from Dryden and Pope: *art : desert; guard : heard; starve : reserve; remarks : Barks* (= *Berkshire*). Many of these words have now also changed to ɜ, owing, perhaps, to the influence of the spelling and to some other causes, such as the varying length of the vowel in many words. Observe that both sounds ɜ and ɑr are different from the original ɛr sound, as in *very* (not as in *her*). But because many of these words also changed their spelling to *ar* (*star, smart,* etc.), the spelling *er* came to be associated with those that changed in sound to ɜ. Hence *er* exerted an influence by spelling-pronunciation, and many words varied in pronunciation between the sound of *star* and that of *her*, as some still do. But the older pronunciation may still be heard in dialect and in names; as *"sartin"* for *certain, "sarmon"* for *sermon, "sarvant"* for *servant, "varmint"* for *vermin, "varsity"* for *university, "tarnal"* for *eternal;* the name *Kerr* (often pronounced kɑr), which is the same as *Carr; Carnahan,* the same name as *Kernohan; Barkly, Barclay,* the same as *Berkley; Clark,* the same as *clerk,*[52] *Larned = learned; Marcy = mercy.* The word *parson* is merely another pronunciation of *person.*[53] Americans often criticize the English for pronouncing *clerk* klɑːk or *Derby* dɑːbɪ. "What reason," they say, "can there be for pronouncing *e* as ɑ?" The answer is, exactly the same reason as for pronouncing *star* stɑr, *heart* hɑrt, or *starve* stɑrv; namely, they have been so pronounced for generations by large numbers of cultivated people, regardless of the spelling. The accident that the spelling has been changed to suit the pronunciation in *star* and not in *Derby* is of no consequence. *Starve* is not pronounced **stɑrv** because it is spelt with *ar,* for **the new pronunciation was established long before the spelling was changed from** *er* **to** *ar.* In point of fact, the sound ɑr for the spelling *er* is no less reasonable than is the sound ɜ, for both are normal phonetic developments from the sound ɛr which the spelling *er* formerly represented.

[52] In the town records of colonial New England the word *clerk* is often spelt *clark, clarke,* showing its early American pronunciation.

[53] In *person, parson,* however, the two pronunciations and meanings appear considerably earlier than in most words. Cf. also *darn* dɑrn, dɜn.

ɔr

366. This diphthong is found in words like *border* bɔrdɚ, *born* bɔrn, *morning* mɔrnɪŋ, *horse* hɔrs, *for* fɔr, etc. It originated in a ME short *o* ɒ before r final, or r+a consonant. In Early Modern it changed from ME ɒr, through the stage ɑɪr, to ɔr. For the interchange with **or**, see **or**. For the sound ɔr followed by a vowel in words like *sorry* sɔrɪ, etc., see above at ɔ, §291 (1).

or

367. This diphthong is found in words like *boarder* bordɚ, *borne* born, *mourning* mornɪŋ, *hoarse* hors, *four* for, etc. It originated in a ME long ɔː before r final (*boor* boːr), r+a consonant (*hoors* hoːrs "hoarse"), or r+a vowel (*boren* boːrən); also from ME uːr+a consonant (*mournen* muːrnən), and from ME oːr (*floor* floːr). In the last two groups modern pronunciation fluctuates somewhat between the sounds **or** and **ur**, as in *Moore* mor, mur, the same word as *moor*, also spelt *More*. Cf. also the frequent "*of course*" əv kurs, for əv kors, and *poor*, GA pur beside Southern puə, poə (dial. po) and British puə, poə, pɔ(ə).

368. A large group of words in which an *o* sound is followed by r show a variation in cultivated usage between ɔr and or. In the first group, derived from ME short *o* ɒ+r, usage is fairly uniform in both England and America with ɔr or ɔ(ə).

I. (1) *Accord, border, chord, cord, lord, order, re'cord;* (2) *dormer, form, normal, storm;* (3) *adorn, born, corn, horn, morn, scorn;* (4) *cork, fork, stork, York;* (5) *exhort, fortify, fortune, forty, important, mortar, resort, short, snort, sort;* (6) *corse, gorse, horse, remorse;* (8) *corpse, for, forfeit, forward, nor, north, or, torch, George, gorge.*

But in the words of the following group, derived from the ME long vowel (ɔː, oː, or uː)+r, usage varies:

II. (1) *Afford, board, boarder, ford, gourd, hoard, horde, sword, toward;* (2) *court, courtier, fort, fourteen, port, deport, import* (etc.), *sport;* (3) *forth, fourth;* (4) *coarse, course, divorce, force, hoarse, resource, source;* (5) *borne, mourn, shorn, sworn, torn, worn;* (6) *pork, porch;* (7) *adore, before, boar, bore, chore, core, door, floor, fore, four, glory, gore, hoary, ignore, implore, more, oar, ore, pore, pour, porous, restore, roar, score, shore, snore, soar, sore, spore, store, story, swore, tore, wore, yore.*

In the cultivated speech of south England, and by some speakers in eastern New England and New York City and vicinity, these words are pronounced with the ɔ sound of the word *all.* But by the majority of Americans elsewhere, by most Canadians, and also by the cultivated classes in Midland and northern England and in Scotland, the words in Group II are pronounced with **or, oə.** Hence by these speakers the following pairs of words are not confused in pronunciation: *border* **bɔrdɚ**—*boarder* **bordɚ;** *born* **bɔrn**—*borne* **born;** *cord* **kɔrd**—*cored* **kord;** *corse* **kɔrs**—*coarse, course* **kors;** *for* **fɔr**—*four* **for;** *horse* **hɔrs**—*hoarse* **hors;** *Laura* **lɔrə**—*Lora* **lorə;** *morn* **mɔrn**—*mourn* **morn;** *morning* **mɔrnɪŋ**—*mourning* **mornɪŋ;** *or* **ɔr**—*oar, ore* **or;** *rawer* **rɔr**—*roar* **ror;** *sawer, saw her* **sɔr**—*sore* **sor;** *therefor* **ðærˈfɔr**—*therefore* **ˈðærfor;** *war* **wɔr**—*wore* **wor;** *warn* **wɔrn**—*worn* **worn.**

The following phrases may be used as tests: *forestall, foregone, warworn, before dawn, before long, short sport, all four, all the more, hall door, north door, tall story, forty-four, four-forty, more horses, restore order, short oar, hall dormer, small horse, all normal, fall storm, corn-law.*

369. I have no hesitation in designating the distinction of vowel between *mourning* and *morning* as prevailing American pronunciation. It is true, of course, that the quality of the **o** in **or** is not identical with that in *note* **not,** *know* **no(ʊ).** The **o** is somewhat lowered by the **r** and in narrower transcription may be expressed by the symbols **ǫr.** This transcription is not necessary as a rule, however, for **or** and **ǫr** belong to the same phoneme, different from ɔr in *morning*.[54]

370. Another treatment of these two groups of words is becoming increasingly noticeable. With many speakers of the younger generation the two groups of words have fallen together in sound, but both sorts of words are pronounced with a diphthong that is neither **or** nor ɔr, but may be indicated by **ǫr** as an intermediate sound. Their sound is clearly not the sound **or** heard from the speakers who still maintain the old distinction; but it is equally clear that it is not ɔr with the sound of ɔ as in *all*.

Regions where the two groups of words (*mourning* and *morning*, etc.) are pronounced alike, but mostly with a vowel between **o** and ɔ (a lowered **o** or a raised ɔ) are found in southern New Jersey, northern Delaware, most of Maryland west of Chesapeake Bay, and probably also Philadelphia and vicinity. The author has often noticed scattered instances in the pronunciation of students from York State, Pennsylvania, and Ohio.[b]

[54] See G. W. Gray, *Le Maître Phonétique*, Avril–Juin, 1934, p. 49; Grandgent, *Pub. Mod. Lang. Assoc.*, 1899, p. 218; *Mod. Lang. Notes*, 1891, p. 462; *Die Neueren Sprachen*, II, pp. 449 ff.; and W. A. Read, *Jour. Eng. and Gc. Philol.*, April, 1923, pp. 217–244. If, in the broad transcription of C. K. Thomas (*Le Maître Phonétique*, Avril–Juin, 1933, p. 35), the symbol ɔ represents the same sound in *board* bɔrd as in *all* ɔl, the loss of the distinction between or and ɔr has extended to Central New York State. Perhaps the intermediate sound ǫr is intended (see §370). O. F. Emerson in 1891 said that in words like *mourn*, *hoarse*, etc., "the London English ɔə" (i.e., American ɔr) was "never heard in the Ithaca Dialect" (*Dialect Notes*, Vol. I, Part 3). There is little reason to suppose that cultivated speech in Central New York then differed in this particular from the local dialect Emerson was investigating.

The consciousness of making a distinction between *mourning* and *morning*, etc., is not a condition of making it. I have repeatedly found individuals who declared they made no distinction, when in fact they did so.

[b] See Hans Kurath, *"Mourning and Morning"* in *Studies for William A. Read*, University, La., 1940, pp. 166–72.

It was mentioned above that the diphthong **or** contains a lowered **ǫ,** but that in distinguishing *mourning* from *morning,* the symbols **or** and **ɔr** are correct on phonemic principles. Where the two groups of words are identified, **ǫr** is a proper and convenient symbol, provided the sound is not **ɔr.**

371. The tendency to identify the two groups of words is recent both in England and America. The distinction is found in virtually all British local dialects, both north and south. The two British dictionaries that give other standard pronunciations than Southern British (the *Oxford* and Baker) maintain the distinction. How rapidly the loss of the distinction is proceeding in America we shall know better when the *Linguistic Atlas* is farther along.[55]

Those speakers who have inherited the historical distinction between **or** and **ɔr** may well feel that it is important to maintain it. Since the loss of the distinction impairs the difference between a great many words otherwise pronounced alike, thus creating new homophones, it is a defect in English; but since the distinction was an unconscious development from long ago, the loss of it is likewise unconscious, and little can be done to prevent it.

372. Some words waver between the two groups not by recent confusion but because they represent alternative earlier forms with long and short vowel. Thus, among speakers who still maintain the distinction, the word *forge* is both **fordʒ** and **fɔrdʒ;** *shorn* is **ʃorn** or **ʃɔrn;** *worn* is **worn** or **wɔrn.** *Born* (Group I) and *borne* (Group II) were at first such a pair with wavering pronunciation, which later developed a distinction of meaning that fixed them in the two groups. *Born* **bɔrn** is from ME *borne*

---

[55] In a list of some sixty words with an *o* sound+*r* given by Grant, *Pronunciation of English in Scotland,* §§163 ff., with the sound **or,** all but *forge* agree with my pronunciation. This is one of the words with double pronunciation, both **fordʒ** and **fɔrdʒ** being common in America. See §372.

bɒrnə, with short vowel, becoming regularly present **bɔrn**. The other ME form of the past participle was *boren* **bɔːrən**, with long vowel, regularly becoming *bore* **bor**. Cf. Sterne (1769): "to have bore the expence." *Borne* finally replaced the older *bore*, taking the same vowel: **born**. The spelling *borne*, which in ME represented the short form (now *born* **bɔrn**) was later used to spell the long-vowel form (**born**), the final -*e* being then looked upon as the sign of the "long *o*."[56]

ur

373. This diphthong occurs in words like *sure* ʃur, *your* jur, *you're* jur, *poor* pur. It arose chiefly from a former **u** before **r**, as in *moor* mur, *tour* tur, or from **iu** before **r** as in *sure* ʃur, *Europe* jurəp; not infrequently from a recent **iu+r**, as in *endure* inˈdur, very often heard both in America and England, in place of inˈdiur, inˈdjur. The sound of the **u** in **ur** is often a trifle higher than **ʊ** in *full*, *good* gʊd, being marked by the *Oxford* as a sound intermediate in length, and probably in quality, between that of *full* and that of *two* tuː.

374. The lowering effect of **r** on a preceding **u** appears to be complete, so that the occasional diphthong **ur** is not distinctive from **ʊr**, as **ir** is distinctive from **ɪr**; see §356. The diphthongs are alike in *you're sure* jur ʃur. When *two or* tu-ɚ becomes one syllable, as in *two or three*, it is pronounced tʊr θri. *Doer*, du-ɚ, *bluer* blu-ɚ, *truer* tru-ɚ are usually dissyllabic; when they are monosyllabic, they are **dur**, **blur**, **trur**. The last part of **iu** is also lowered before **r**; *cure* kiur, *pure* piur, *bluer* bliuɚ, bluɚ, *truer* triuɚ, truɚ, but this need not always be indicated.

375. In British and occasionally in Eastern American a further lowering before ə reaches the stage oə, and even ɔ(ə); as *poor* poə, pɔ(ə), *pure* pjoə, pjɔ(ə), *your* joə, jɔ(ə), *sure* ʃoə,

---

[56] The development was complicated. See *Oxford*, s.v. *bear*, v., and Jespersen, *Gram*. I, 13.353.

ʃɔ(ə); but not in *doer*, *bluer*, *truer*, owing to the analogy of *do*, *blue*, *true*. Some are lowered only to oə, as *boor* buə, boə (thus one British pronunciation of *boor* boə is like one American pronunciation of *bore* boə, while *bore* in Southern British is bɔ(ə)). With the lowering of u+r is to be compared that of ir to ɪr, er to ɛr, and or to ɔr; see these sounds.[57] In southern America uə is often lowered to oə in *poor* poə, *sure* ʃoə, and the like. In substandard Southern they often become poɪ, ʃoɪ.

376. As a result of these changes, together with the loss of the *r* sound, the following words and phrases are homophones in Southern British, and to some extent in Eastern American. The GA pronunciations are also given for comparison: GA *cored* kord, *cord* kɔrd, *cawed* kɔd—Brit. kɔd; GA *floor* flor, *flaw* flɔ—Brit. flɔ; GA *gored* gord, *gaud* gɔd—Brit. gɔd; GA *lore* lor, *law* lɔ—Brit. lɔ; GA *mourn* morn, *morn* mɔrn, *Maughan* mɔn—Brit. mɔn; GA *oar* or, *or* ɔr, *awe* ɔ—Brit. ɔ; GA *orphan* ɔrfən, *often* ɔfən—Brit. ɔfən; GA *shore* ʃor, *sure* ʃur, *Shaw* ʃɔ—Brit. ʃɔ; GA *wore* wor, *war* wɔr, *Waugh* wɔ—Brit. wɔ; GA *yore* jor, *your* jur, *yaw* jɔ—Brit. jɔ; GA *bored and sawed* bord ṇ sɔd, *Borden soared* bɔrdṇ sord, *board and sword* bord ṇ sord—Brit. bɔdṇ sɔd; GA *roared and pawed* rord ṇ pɔd, *Rawdon poured* rɔdṇ pord, *roared and poured* rord ṇ pord, *Rawdon pawed* rɔdṇ pɔd—Brit. rɔdṇ pɔd. Yet the possibility of these and many other such homophones creates no real difficulty among those who so pronounce. See §84, n. 41.

[57] See *Webster*, *Pron.* §199; Jones, *Phonetics*, §§459, 466.

INDEX

Index of speech sounds and phonetic symbols

As in the body of the book, phonetic symbols are printed in **boldface** type, words and letters of ordinary spelling in *italics*, and authors and subjects in roman.

Numbers refer to sections, except as noted.

a 12, 71
  in *"ask"* words: present status 281
  in Scotland and northern England 18, 282
  southern variety of **aɪ** 332
aɪ 12, 85, in detail 330 ff
  before voiceless sounds, voiced sounds, and finally 332
  for **ɛɪ** in Cockney 265
  from ME **iː** 330
  in eastern Virginia 332
  positional and local varieties 332
  Scottish varieties 332
  southern varieties 332
  spelt *i* 330
  varieties of, 331 f
aʊ 85, 333 ff
  before voiceless sounds, voiced sounds, and finally 336
  from ME **uː** 334
  in eastern Virginia 336
  positional and local varieties 335 f
  southern varieties 336
  spelt *ou, ow* 334
  varieties of, 335
ɑ 12, 71, in detail 271 ff
  closer to **ɔ** in America than in England 288

  esthetic value of, 285
  in *past, chance,* etc. once thought vulgar 279 f
  spelt *a, o, (w)a* 272
  spelt *o*, origin of American 287
  ɑ, ɒ, or **ɔ**? 291
ɑɪ variety of **aɪ** 331
ɑr 364 f
  from **ɛr** 365
ɑʊ variety of **aʊ** 335
ɒ "short o" 12, 19, 71, 272, in detail 286 ff
  ɒ, ɑ, or **ɔ**? 291
  status in America 288
æ 12, 71, 270, 291.10
  æ, a, or **ɑ**? 274 ff
  for later **ɑ** in early rimes 273
  ædəl for *addle* substandard 86
ær 360 ff
  ær or **ɛr**? 17, 361 f
æʊ variety of **aʊ** 335 f

b 12, 29, 30 f, in detail 153 ff
  dropped or excrescent 154
  bætəl for *battle* substandard 86
  labiodental 179.5

c 25, 195.1, 208.1

y 25, 69

z 12, 29 f, 32, in detail 190 ff
    not distinctive in OE 80[88]
    from unstressed **s** 140

ȝ 12, 29 f, 32, in detail 197 f
    sources 198

ʔ glottal stop 28 f, 31, 48
    not distinctive 48

Index of words, letters, subjects, and authors

a in *ask* 274.III
    in *balm, calm* 274.II
    in *bar* 274.I
    in *carry, marry* 274.I, 360, 362
    in *make* 273.1
-a final sounded **ɪ** 267
a article 137
a man—some men 137 (*some*)
a- 'on' 137 (*on*)
ability 130.2
ablaut 136
able 130.2, 203
-able, -ible, -uble 121
abstract 111
abuse 22, 348.2
accent 13, 104
    British and American 115
    even 117
    foreign 111
    free 114
    history of loss of secondary 118
    in compounds 108
    light 122
    loss of secondary shortens words 116
    marks 13
    of loan-words 109
    of nouns, adjectives, and verbs 110
    pitch, force, and time 105
    primary 106
    of words in *-ary, -ery, -ory* 115

    recessive 114
    rhythmical 112
    secondary 108, 111
    shift in British 117
    shifting 123
accent (n.) 111
accumulative 120
-ace **-ɪs** 266
ache 168
ach, German 25
acknowledge 172
-acle 266
across, acrost 159
act 49
-acy 121
"Adam's apple" 28
adaptation 122, 131[66]
adept 130.1
administrative 120
adventure 208.3
advice—advise 332
adz 79
affect and *effect* 258
affricate 29, 31, 33, 207 ff
    doubled 56
against 159
-age **-ɪdȝ** 266
Aggborough 102
air 17, 359, 361
    eːr in Scottish 363